V. A.

CW00693980

# LEGAL PROBLEMS IN NURSING PRACTICE

## Second edition

# LEGAL PROBLEMS IN NURSING PRACTICE
## Second edition

Ann P. Young, BA, RGN, RNT
Senior Tutor
Thomas Guy and Lewisham School of Nursing
Guy's Hospital
London

**Harper & Row, Publishers**
London

Philadelphia  San Francisco
New York London
St. Louis Singapore
Sydney Tokyo

Copyright © 1989 Ann P. Young

All rights reserved.

Harper & Row Ltd.
Middlesex House
34–42 Cleveland Street
London
W1P 5FB

No part of this book may be reproduced in any manner whatsoever without written permission except in the case of brief extracts embodied in critical articles and reviews.

British Library Cataloguing in Publication Data

Young, Ann P.
  Legal problems in nursing practice. – 2nd
  ed.
  1. U.K. Law. For nursing
  I. Title
  344.204'414

ISBN 0–06–318434–6

Typeset by J&L Composition Ltd, Filey, North Yorkshire
Printed and bound by The Alden Press, Oxford

# Contents

# The Author

After undertaking her general training, Ann Young specialised in geriatric nursing in which she worked for a number of years, with a spell in a hospice caring for the terminally ill. As a ward sister, Ann's experience in a surgical unit included gynaecology. Her teaching career has involved her in a wide variety of clinical situations. Now as senior nurse (education/management) for general training, Ann's present role includes regular liaison with colleagues and students from the psychiatric, paediatric, community and postbasic departments.

An interest over the years has been in the assessment of learners and she took a major part in implementing one of the first continuous practical assessment schemes in the country. She has had many years involvement with the Diploma in Nursing, both as chairperson and external assessor. Her expertise in law and nursing dates from the early 1970s and she lectures regularly on the subject to audiences ranging from students to nurse managers. Ann's degree is in sociology and education. Her other publications include articles on law and continuous assessment in the nursing journals, and a legal input into the Distance Learning Centre's Diploma in Nursing.

# Preface

Most nurses feel diffident on law, in spite of the fact that their work brings them into contact with so many legal situations. They hear mention of crime, compensation and coroners' courts, and become anxious about accidents, negligence and conditions of work. The very complexity of law is scarely encouraging to further learning, after all, the study of law can be a lifetime occupation for those specially trained in it, and nurses have many other concerns.

However, as this book will illustrate, nurses are often closely involved with the law, perhaps without realising it. For this reason, it is essential that all nurses have a working knowledge of the law and its application to their work. Although normally the nurse should be able to call on senior officers for help, the problem is that initially the nurse must be able to recognise where there are likely to be legal problems, and also where she could lay herself open to criminal, civil or disciplinary action. In many instances this occurs when small, seemingly unimportant details have been overlooked. In addition, even the most junior nurse can help to prevent legal problems arising in the first place if she has some knowledge of why certain procedures must be so strictly adhered to.

This book therefore aims to outline the UK legal system, and to relate the relevant parts of the law to the nurse's work in the hospital and the community. In addition, it is felt that the law is sometimes poorly defined in many controversial areas that the nurse may meet, and an attempt is made to link the role of ethics in nursing to the legal aspects of the nurse's job.

At the start of each chapter, a list of relevant Acts and cases are given for the reader who wishes to follow up the legal basis of the text. In addition, references are given at the end of each chapter and these should assist the reader who has an interest in a particular legal situation to explore this in much more depth than is possible in this book. Frequently, situations will be presented to help the reader to focus her attention, and at the end of most sections there are questions which the reader may work through to check her understanding of the text.

The author wishes to point out that the guidelines given and comments made are based on personal experience and for the readers' practical consideration. They in no way replace the professional advice of health service administrators and solicitors who should be consulted when necessary.

The nurse throughout this book for convenience will be designated 'she' but this includes male nurses. For clarity, other professionals will be designated 'he' but this includes female doctors, solicitors, etc.

Many examples are used to illustrate the relevant legal and moral problems discussed. While some of these are based on actual situations, certain details have been altered in order to respect confidentiality and aid clarity.

# Acknowledgements

My sincere thanks to my husband Robert for his patience and support, to Theresa Latuskie, my secretary, for managing to decipher my notes, and to the representatives of the legal profession who have read my work and whose comments have been so helpful and encouraging.

# Part I
# An Outline of Law in the United Kingdom

# 1. The Growth and Structure of Law

Relevant Acts:

NHS Act (1946)
NHS (Amendment) Act (1986)
Legal Aid Act (1974)
Legal Aid Act (1979)
Police and Criminal Evidence Act (1984)
Prosecution of Offences Act (1985)

## 1.1 SETTING THE SCENE

A nurse is helping a patient to walk to the toilet. Suddenly, the patient stumbles and falls. What should the nurse do? If the patient has been badly injured, will she be blamed?

A patient is being given an injection of a painkilling drug. On signing that the drug has been administered, the nurses realise that the injection has been given to the wrong patient. Have they committed a crime or may they be sued in a civil court? What disciplinary action may be taken against them?

A ward sister is writing a report on a junior nurse. She feels that the nurse is unsatisfactory in many respects. But if she writes this down, will the nurse sue her for compensation?

A patient is refusing treatment that could be lifesaving. What if the nurse or doctor cannot persuade him to change his mind? Is there any way that they can help him if he refuses his consent, while still keeping within the law?

These are problems that arise frequently and involve a number of different areas of the legal system. The legal systems of the United Kingdom have evolved over many hundreds of years and the brief description that follows should help to clarify its structure and development.

## A brief history of UK law

The United Kingdom is one state made up of four countries, and its legal systems originally developed separately.

England and Wales are the most closely linked and historically have identical legal systems. The law in Northern Ireland has also developed along very similar lines since the twelfth century. However, a few differences still exist, and whereas any legislation now passed always links England and Wales together, separate orders may still have to be made for Northern Ireland and some Acts are different. For example, there is no Abortion Act in Northern Ireland and its Mental Health Act awaits updating in line with that of England and Wales.

The roots of the present English legal system go back to the seventh century. The common law, as it is now known, was based on local customs and from this early time are reported instances of the law awarding compensation to the kin of a murdered man or for injuries, including hair pulling, to the sufferer. After the Norman invasion of 1066, England became united under one king and the common law became modified and unified throughout the country. The king set up courts around the country with power delegated to royal judges.

Another later source of English law was equity. It was felt that certain powerless individuals, for example children, suffered under the common law and equity considered petitions on the basis of right and conscience rather than formal rules. During the seventeenth to the nineteenth centuries equity evolved set principles which took precedence over common law and eventually the two systems were fused.

The development of Scottish law was rather different. Historically, Scotland had strong links with the rest of Europe rather than England and its legal system was much more in line with Europe and based on Roman law. A feature of this legal system was a systematic and codified collection of laws imposed by government so that inconsistency and overlapping were avoided. This contrasted with the English system where law arose from customs and much was unwritten.

In 1707, the Union with Scotland Act was passed and since then differences have become less marked. However, some terminology is still different, for example for courts and court officials, and, as with Northern Ireland, some legislation has to be made specifically for Scotland.

## Judicial precedent and case law

Common law and equity are often said to be 'judge made'. One way of making the law consistent is for judges to refer back to previous decisions involving similar cases (and certain legal principles in Scotland). This case law, also known as judicial precedent, is a complicated process and its proper use requires great skill and knowledge.

Judicial precedent also allows for some flexibility in the law. Whole new areas can be created by case law, for example that involving professional negligence, or the judge can use his position to clarify areas of the law that are unclear. However, the sheer bulk of case law can lead to illogical distinctions superseding the main intention of the law and to time-consuming procedures in the courts.

Case law is still important today in the development of English law, although other sources have greatly increased in importance, most notably legislation.

## Parliament and the process of legislation

As mentioned before, the early kings were able to influence the law. However, it was not until the seventeenth century that Parliament had forged its position as a separate power, and only in the latter part of the nineteenth century that the balance of the legal system shifted markedly towards the use of detailed Acts of Parliament. At that time numerous laws concerning social welfare were passed, and since then, much of common law has been clarified by legislation.

The legislative process today can be complicated and lengthy. Although Members of Parliament can introduce a private member's bill, the background to legislation often involves interested pressure groups putting forward suggestions. A Green Paper, a consultative document, may be issued to test public reaction. Interested pressure groups can at

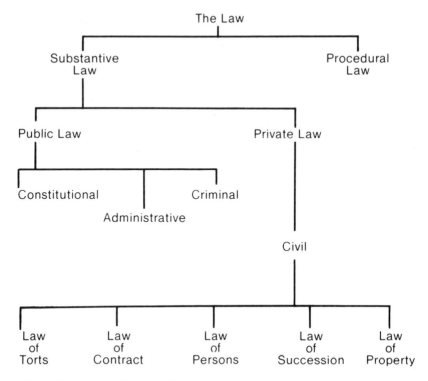

**Figure 1.1** A classification of law.

this stage have a marked influence on the formation of the final Act. A White Paper making detailed proposals follows, still allowing room for changes, before the bill itself is drafted and presented to Parliament.

The bill passes through certain stages in Parliament: first through the House of Commons in three readings and a committee stage, then through the House of Lords. A bill becomes an Act on receipt of Royal Assent. The National Health Service Act (1946), which came into operation in 1948, passed through these stages several times over, as the situation at the time was complicated by a change in Government. Acts of Parliament may apply to all the countries of the United Kingdom but, as already mentioned, separate Acts may need to be passed for the special needs of Scotland or Northern Ireland.

As well as Acts of Parliament, or statutes, being a means of initiating law, the United Kingdom also has a system of delegated legislation. This is essential to implement changes as parliamentary time can in some sessions be extremely limited. Delegated legislation is most often

*I Civil Courts*

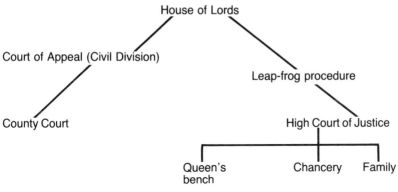

*II Criminal Courts*

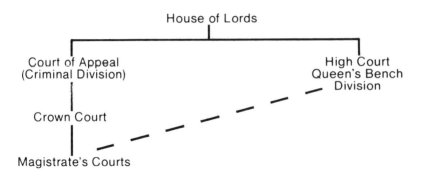

*III Coroner's Courts*

*IV Tribunals*

**Figure 1.2** The courts in England, Wales and N. Ireland.

encountered as Statutory Instruments, Rules or Orders. Parliament, through an enabling Act, will allow certain named authorities to formulate these instruments. For example, the Nurses' Rules, Approval Instrument 1983, were made by the United Kingdom Central Council through the power delegated in the Nurses' Act, 1979. The rules were then approved for implementation by the Secretary of State.

Some Acts of Parliament do not apply to health service premises as these are crown property. This is known as crown immunity. This unsatisfactory state of affairs has now been limited by the National Health Service (Amendment) Act (1986), which came into force in February 1987. Two areas of legislation, those involving food, and health and safety, are now no longer immune from prosecution.

## A classification of law

Not surprisingly, the law has evolved over the centuries into an unwieldy and rather nebulous structure. There are a number of different ways of classifying the components that make up the law, but the one that follows is fairly workable as regards the nurse's involvement (Figure 1.1).

A major division of the law is made between criminal and civil law. A criminal offence is committed against the state and is punishable by the state, for example, the theft of drugs from a pharmacy may be penalised by imprisonment. In civil law, the rights and duties of individuals towards each other are considered in terms of some monetary compensation. Legal action is taken by a private citizen, rather than the state. An example would be failure of an employee to give the employer proper notice of leaving. There are areas of overlap, of course, where some action may give rise to a criminal charge as well as a civil action, for example, assault and battery. This division of the law is enlarged on in Chapter 2.

Another division of the law is the difference between substantive and procedural law. Substantive law lays down the rules according to which the law functions, whereas procedural law is the manner in which the law is enforced through the courts. The nurse may particularly be involved here if she has to appear in court and give evidence (see page 15).

## 1.2 THE COURTS

A number of different courts have developed over the years, which play a central part in the implementation of the law (Figures 1.2 and 1.3). The nurse needs some knowledge of these courts as she may be required to give evidence, for example as a health visitor in the Juvenile Court, or in the Coroner's Court as the nurse who attended a patient at the time of his death. She may have to appear in a criminal court if charged with a

*I Civil Courts*

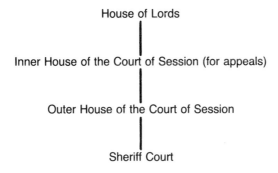

House of Lords

Inner House of the Court of Session (for appeals)

Outer House of the Court of Session

Sheriff Court

*II Criminal Courts*

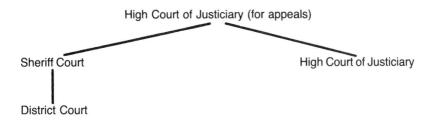

High Court of Justiciary (for appeals)

Sheriff Court

High Court of Justiciary

District Court

*III Tribunals*

**Figure 1.3**  The courts in Scotland.

crime, for example, the theft of drugs, or in a civil court if there is a question of a patient suffering on account of her negligence. Either as a member of management or as the employee, she may become involved in an industrial tribunal, a relatively recent development of the UK legal system.

## Criminal Courts

An individual can be brought to trial in a criminal court by means of a summons or a warrant. A summons is used for relatively minor crimes and orders the accused person to appear in court. A warrant is an authorisation of arrest and is issued to the police by a justice of the peace or magistrate, ordering the accused to be brought to court (see page 18).

The trial can take place in various criminal courts, depending on the severity of the crime. The Magistrate's Court is the lowest-level criminal court functioning locally. It is usually staffed by lay justices of the peace with the advice of a legally qualified clerk, if required. Minor offences can be tried in these courts, particularly ones that cannot be punished by more than three months' imprisonment. Occasionally a more serious crime can be heard if both the accused and the magistrate agree. There is no jury in a Magistrate's Court.

Crimes that may involve heavier sentences must be heard at a higher court. However, the accused first appears briefly in the Magistrate's Court and is there committed for trial in the Crown Court. Here trial is by jury and High Court judges and circuit judges preside.

An important part of the legal system is the possibility of appeal to a higher court. Most appeals are heard by the Criminal Division of the Court of Appeal, although the Queen's Bench Divisional Court may be involved in an appeal on a point of law. The final level of an appeal is the House of Lords. In Scotland, the structure and function of the courts is very different. The lowest court is the District Court presided over by lay justices. More major crimes are referred to the Sheriff's Court which has a full-time Sheriff Principal and a staff of sheriffs. The High Court of Justiciary can be used in the first instance and is used for all appeals. Cases are brought to the courts by the Procurator Fiscal or in the name of HM Advocate in solemn cases.

It is worth noting at this stage that the individual can be required to attend a court, not necessarily as the accused person, but as a witness, for which a subpoena summons will be sent. This applies to both civil and criminal courts, and the nurse can be involved in this capacity, particularly the health visitor in cases of child abuse.

## Civil Courts

The range of cases heard in the civil courts covers claims for damages in relation to breach of contract, negligence and nuisance, landlord and tenant disputes and divorces. The nature of these courts, unlike the criminal courts, is adversarial in nature: thus the terms, plaintiff and defendant. A number of stages must be followed in bringing a civil action and time may be prolonged into years before the case even comes to court. Efforts are often made to settle 'out of court'.

The County Court deals with many of these civil actions, the only restriction being the amount of compensation being claimed. Where large amounts of money are involved (claims for damages exceeding £5,000), the Queen's Bench Division of the High Court must handle the action.

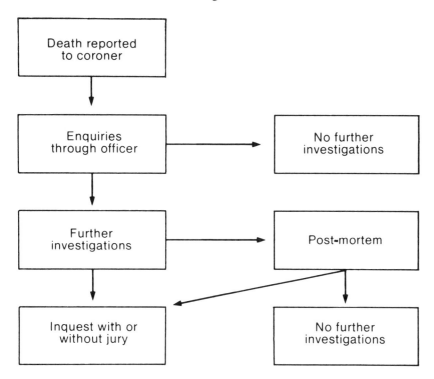

**Figure 1.4** The coroner's investigation.

As in the criminal courts, there is a system of appeals, this time to the Civil Division of the Court of Appeal and finally to the House of Lords.

Again, in Scotland the court system is different (see Figure 1.3).

## Coroner's Courts

The Coroner's Court (Figure 1.4) is an offshoot of the criminal courts and over the years it has evolved its special function in relation to deaths where there are certain factors to be taken into consideration.

There are 12 instances in which the doctor should notify the coroner:

- Violent death.
- Sudden death where, though the terminal cause is known, the underlying causes are not.
- Death from poisoning.
- Death from industrial disease.
- Death from drug addiction, including alcoholism.
- Death where there was no doctor in attendance.
- Where doubt exists as to whether a child was live or stillborn.
- Death resulting from abortion.
- Death of foster children.
- Death to which an accident has materially contributed.
- Death which has been contributed to by an operation or anaesthetic.
- Death where patients' relatives have criticised the medical and/or nursing care provided.

The nurse is therefore quite likely to be involved in a Coroner's Court at some time in her career.

The coroner can be a barrister, solicitor or a medical practitioner of at least five years' standing. He will instigate enquiries through an appointed officer, usually the police. If further investigations are considered necessary, a post-mortem may be ordered, and the results may be brought to an inquest to bring in a verdict as to the cause of death. This includes murder, manslaughter, lack of care or self-neglect, chronic addiction to drugs, want of attention at birth, accident or misadventure, suicide, natural causes or open.

The coroner may call a jury in some cases, most commonly where death has occurred in suspicious circumstances.

The process of investigation into sudden, unexpected and suspicious death is rather different in Scotland. The Procurator Fiscal is responsible. Initial enquiries are always private. These are reported to the Crown Office in Edinburgh and a public enquiry before a sheriff (acting similarly to a coroner) may then be held. The Procurator Fiscal presents the circumstances by leading the witnesses. As well as cause of death, the sheriff reaches a determination on any reasonable precautions which might have prevented death or any defects of any associated system of working.

## Juvenile Courts

Juvenile Courts exist for young people under the age of 17 years. Children are classified as those under the age of 14 years, and young people as 14 to 17 years. Each court has three lay justices, one of whom must be a woman, and the courts are not open to the public.

Their purpose in most cases is to decide what course of action is in the best interests of the child concerned. For example, where there has been child abuse by the parents, the court must consider whether the best course of action is to take the child into care or to leave him with his parents (the guilt of the family is immaterial).

Under the Children and Young Persons Act (1969), the police are entitled to detain a child in a place of safety if they consider that his proper development or health is being impaired.

Health visitors are frequently called to these juvenile courts to give information.

Once again, the situation is different in Scotland. Classifications of children and young people are as follows:

● A pupil is under 14 years for a boy, under 12 years for a girl. A child of this age lacks 'mischievous intention' unless proved otherwise.
● A minor is 14–18 years for a boy, 12–18 years for a girl. No child under 16 years may be prosecuted except on the instructions of the Lord Advocate. A 'Children's Hearing' does not involve prosecution.

## Tribunals

Tribunals are a fairly recent addition to the UK legal system and they can involve wide areas of our lives. They include tribunals for national insurance, rent, industrial injuries, industrial tribunals relating to employment law, domestic tribunals relating to certain professions including tribunals for doctors and midwives.

Their aim is to provide a forum for settling disputes between an individual and the relevant authority. The executive panel attempts to avoid taking a position of authority and therefore hopefully the tribunal appears less daunting than the civil courts.

The officials present at a tribunal hearing include a chairman, usually with legal experience, who has been appointed by the Lord Chancellor, and a clerk who is usually appointed by the appropriate Ministry concerned. Otherwise, the tribunals tend to vary in constitution and procedure. As with other courts, there is an appeals procedure.

# European Court of Justice and Commission of Human Rights

As a member of the EEC, the United Kingdom is affected by two more legal institutions.

The European Court of Justice is the supreme court in Europe for matters which affect people or property in the EEC but separate from their own country. It cannot touch matters which concern only the UK and its people. Twelve judges, each of whom is an eminent judge in his own country, are appointed for six-year terms and assisted by six Advocates-General. This court is not bound by judicial precedent.

The European Commission of Human Rights was established under the auspices of the Council of Europe in 1950. It is possible for UK subjects dissatisfied with decisions of their own courts to petition the Commission. These disputes may then ultimately be heard by the Court of Human Rights at Strasbourg.

# Legal personnel

When involved in legal actions the nurse will encounter a number of different legal personnel with specific roles.

Solicitors are general legal advisers accessible to the public. They may be advocates in the inferior courts, for example, the Magistrates Court, but not in the higher courts. They are to some extent controlled by the Law Society. Remuneration is not fixed but must be fair and reasonable.

Barristers have the exclusive right of audience in all the superior courts and are known as 'counsel' for either the prosecution or the defence. As well as appearing in court they are also involved with the production of written evidence, known as 'taking counsel's opinion'. A barrister is only accessible via a solicitor.

Judges are appointed from experienced barristers. A High Court judge must have a minimum of ten years' experience, and an appeal court judge, fifteen years', but very often it is longer. Rarely, a solicitor can become a circuit judge by gaining a minimum of three years' experience as a court recorder. Judges are appointed by the Queen and cannot be members of Parliament. An independent judiciary is seen as being very important. The role of the judge is to preside at a trial, conduct the hearing according to accepted rules and points of law, sum up factual evidence and give a judgment.

Magistrates or justices of the peace are lay people who receive no remuneration but are reimbursed travelling expenses and subsistence. There is a compulsory training programme and they are assisted by a legally qualified clerk to the court.

# Giving evidence in court

The nurse giving evidence in court will find that there are two stages to this event.

The first is the preparation of a written statement. In criminal cases, the police will usually be involved in helping to draw up this statement; in civil cases, the barrister will give assistance. However, there may still be some instances where the witness has to draw up her statement alone.

First, make sure that the statement is relevant to the court hearing but at the same time is as detailed as possible. Secondly, the nurse should include her name, qualifications and where and in what job she works. The events under discussion should then be written in chronological order, for example from the nurse's first contact with patient or client through details of all subsequent contacts.

Prior to appearing in court, it is extremely useful for the nurse to talk over the case with her legal representative. He can help the nurse to refresh her memory and may be able to give some indication of what questions the nurse may face during cross-examination.

When giving evidence, the nurse should follow certain guidelines. She should speak slowly and clearly so that she can be heard throughout the court. Information should be given in everyday language and where medical terms have to be used, the nurse must be prepared to explain these in lay terms. She should avoid medical abbreviations and jargon, and confine herself to facts, avoiding inferences, opinions and exaggerations.

Her evidence should be from memory as far as possible, although a witness is allowed to refer to her statement or some entry in a record made by herself as long as this was made at or shortly after the event recorded. However, the nurse must be aware that any material thus used must be produced and shown if required, although in practice this is rarely demanded. She should listen carefully to any questions and answer them concisely, but avoiding a simple 'yes' or 'no'. She must answer only what is asked unless it is necessary to introduce new material to explain her answer. She should never lose her temper or become flustered under cross-examination and should always reply politely.

Occasionally, a nurse may be called to give an opinion in the course of giving evidence. This is acceptable if it is in relation to her professional expertise and experience and it is made quite clear that it is not a factual part of the evidence.

A nurse is often concerned about whether she has any privilege in court to decline to give evidence on certain matters. In fact, any communications between nurse and patient, and doctor and patient, although confidential, are not privileged and therefore must be disclosed in evidence if required. (See page 239.)

# Legal services available

The nurse involved in any legal proceedings may need to know what services are available to assist with the costs involved.

The statutory services were set up by the Legal Aid Acts (1974) and (1979), and consist of legal advice, civil legal advice and criminal legal advice.

### Legal advice (also called the Green Form Scheme)
Legal advice is administered by the Law Society and financed from the Legal Aid Fund, subject to the finances of the client. It enables a solicitor to give advice and do legal work for a client up to a set figure.

Application for full legal aid can be made later if necessary but this scheme means that there is no delay in giving advice.

### Civil legal aid
Civil legal aid covers civil proceedings (except defamation, but including tribunals) and any associated work. It is administered by the Law Society which has fourteen Area Committees and 112 Local Committees. The applicant submits an application to the local committee and it is advisable to consult a solicitor for help with this. The local committee will accept the application if there appear to be reasonable grounds for legal action and will issue a legal aid certificate. The applicant's financial means are then assessed on the basis of disposable annual income (gross income less rent, tax, etc.) and disposable capital (gross capital less the value of residence and furniture). A sliding scale of aid is then decided ranging from free legal aid through some contribution required to no aid. An offer is made to the applicant regarding the contribution he will have to make and the instalments by which payment can be made, and he has 28 days in which to accept this offer. The applicant can then

choose a solicitor (and barrister if applicable) off the panel kept by the local committee. Payments are made to the Legal Aid Fund, not the solicitor.

### Criminal legal aid

Criminal legal aid is dealt with in a different way from civil cases because of the need for speed. Power is given to almost all criminal courts to grant a legal aid order when 'desirable to do so in the interests of justice'. In certain cases the granting of this order is automatic, i.e. for murder or an appeal to the House of Lords, but some magistrates have been criticised for inconsistency in granting or refusing legal aid. After trial, the financial means of the person concerned are examined and the court can order a contribution towards legal costs, the amount being at the discretion of the court.

Voluntary services may also be available for the provision of legal aid. In some areas there are legal advice centres or neighbourhood law centres. The nurse should also approach her trade union or professional organisation.

The Government has recently suggested some changes to the statutory services here outlined. A major change would be the bringing together of the various avenues of legal aid under one body, the Legal Aid Board (already in operation in Scotland). The use of voluntary agencies (well informed but legally unqualified) would be increased for giving advice, particularly in the area of welfare law. Other changes would affect the mechanics of applications and contributions required. It is not yet known when these suggestions are likely to be put to Parliament.

## 1.3 THE POLICE

During the course of their work, nurses are likely to come into contact with the police in a number of different ways. The nurse in the accident and emergency department may need to call the police to evict a violent person, or the police may have accompanied to the hospital a person injured in the course of the committing of a crime. The nurse may also be asked to assist the police by making statements or the nurse may face arrest for some suspected crime. This section aims to clarify police powers and the limitations to these powers. Matters involving trespass and confidentiality are discussed in a later section (see pages 186 and 238).

## Powers of arrest

A person suspected of an offence can be brought to court in one of three ways. The first is the use of a summons requiring an individual to appear in court, and the police are encouraged to use this route whenever possible. The other two ways involve arrest of the suspect either with or without a warrant.

A warrant is a written authority signed by a justice of the peace directing the arrest of the offender. The warrant should state the offence charged, the authority under which the arrest is to be made, the persons who are to execute it and the person to be arrested. Where immediate arrest is not necessary, it is much wiser for the police to obtain a warrant as a safeguard against accusations of false imprisonment.

Police powers to arrest without a warrant have been clarified under the Police and Criminal Evidence Act (1984) to four different circumstances:

- If the police suspect an arrestable offence has been, is being or is about to be committed. An offence is arrestable if it carries a sentence of at least five years' imprisonment, for example unlawful possession of drugs, rape and most offences of violence, or if it is designated as arrestable by the Act although carrying a lesser sentence, for example indecent assault on a woman and going equipped for theft.
- If the police have a statutory power of arrest, including Public Order Act offences and driving while unfit.
- If a general arrest condition applies although the offence is not covered by the two points above, for example the suspect refuses to give his name or the police believe the name to be false, the police consider the arrest necessary to prevent the person harming himself or someone else, suffering injury or causing damage to property, or the arrest is necessary to protect a child.
- If the police require the fingerprints of a convicted person. This power will apply in very few cases.

The 1984 Act also states clearly that a police arrest will not be lawful unless the police officer making the arrest informs the person that he is under arrest and states the grounds for the arrest even though these may appear to be obvious. If being arrested by warrant, the suspect may ask to see it and must be shown it as soon as is practicable. The police officer does not have to have the warrant with him at the time of the arrest.

# Powers of detention

After arrest, the individual should be taken to a police station as soon as is practicable, and the custody officer must decide whether there is sufficient evidence to charge him. The maximum period that a person can be detained without charge is 24 hours from arrival at the police station or from arrest, whichever is the earlier. At the end of 24 hours, the individual must be charged or released unless special circumstances apply.

Under the 1984 Act, the concept of a 'serious arrestable offence' is introduced. Some arrestable offences are always 'serious', for cxample murder, rape, and firearms and explosives offences. Other arrestable offences may be treated as 'serious' if leading to consequences such as serious harm to national security, serious interference with the courts or serious injury to a victim. In the case of a 'serious arrestable offence', an individual can be detained for up to 96 hours before being charged (36 hours initially during which access to a solicitor can be denied, followed by further periods of 36 hours and 24 hours if authorised by a magistrate).

Once an individual is charged, he must be released with or without bail to appear in court, and the police are not allowed to continue to question the person in relation to that offence. However, an individual may be held after being charged if the custody officer does not know his name or address, or believes the ones given to be false, if detention is necessary to protect the individual or someone else or if the individual may well fail to appear in court as required.

# Powers of search

The police have a number of powers regarding search of the individual and of property.

First the police may stop and search someone reasonably suspected of carrying illegal drugs, stolen goods, firearms, items connected with terrorism, prohibited articles such as an offensive weapon or an item for use in committing burglary or theft. Before carrying out the search, the police officer must identify himself and state the object of the search. He can require the removal of a jacket, coat and gloves only, and the search can be carried out in a public place or in the garden or yard of property which is not the residence of the person concerned.

Police can enter premises without a warrant to search for a person who is suspected of an arrestable offence. Otherwise a search warrant is required to allow police to enter and search a named place and take away any articles that may be evidence of any offence. Reasonable grounds for suspicion are necessary before a search warrant is granted by the Justice of the Peace. A warrant must only be used on one occasion and the occupier is entitled to a copy.

Thirdly, search can take place at a police station. A search of a person's clothing and personal effects will be carried out by a police officer of the same sex. If any items are seized, the person should be told why. A strip search (removal of more than outer clothing) should only be carried out if the custody officer considers it necessary to remove an item which the person would not be allowed to keep.

An intimate search of body orifices can be authorised if the person may have concealed an item to injure himself or others or for drugs, this latter being carried out by a doctor or registered nurse at a hospital or other medical premises. Police can use reasonable force in carrying out an intimate search. Body samples can be taken, although the consent of the individual is usually required. In some circumstances samples can be taken forcibly, or a refusal to give consent can be treated as corroborating evidence.

## Answering questions and making statements

The police are entitled to question any person from whom useful information may be obtained. This applies whether or not the person questioned has been taken into custody. If the police officer suspects that a person has committed an offence, he should caution that person before putting any questions to him, and a further caution should be given if the person is actually charged. Codes of practice have been formulated to give guidance on how a prisoner should be questioned by the police and also spelled out are prisoners' rights regarding access to legal advice and to have someone told of his whereabouts. However, these rights are subject to qualification and the police have no legal obligation to inform a suspect of them.

The nurse should bear in mind that, although every citizen has a duty to assist the police, no police officer can, other than by arrest, compel any person against his will to come to or remain in a police station.

Making a statement to the police must be done voluntarily. It may be written down by the person concerned or by a police officer taking down the exact words spoken by the person making the statement, without any prompting. If these rules are not followed, the evidence thus obtained may be rendered inadmissible in subsequent criminal proceedings.

## The police and the Crown Prosecution Service

The police have the right to institute proceedings and normally do so in all routine matters. However, detailed provisions exist which govern the taking over of prosecutions by the Crown Prosecution Service with specific responsibility being put on the Director of Public Prosecutions. For example, he can take action in cases of particular importance or difficulty and he must also become involved in any case referred to him by a government department where he considers criminal proceedings should be instituted.

## Questions on Chapter 1

*see page*

1. Briefly describe the differences between criminal and civil law.  8

2. In what ways is statute law different from common law?  5

3. Explain how the Nurses' Rules are a product of the legislative process.  6

4. With which courts is the nurse most likely to become involved?  8

5. Is the nurse legally able to refuse to give evidence in court about a patient on the grounds that the information is confidential?  16

6. How may legal aid be obtained?  16

7. In what circumstances may the police arrest without a warrant?  18

8. If the nurse is asked to accompany a police constable to the police station for questioning, is she bound to go?  20

## REFERENCES

Bell, K. (1969). *Tribunals in the Social Services*, Routledge and Kegan Paul, London.
Department of Health and Social Security (1986). Health Circular HC8614, DHSS, London.

Eddey, K. (1982). *The English Legal System*, 3rd edn, Sweet and Maxwell, London.

Editorial (1987). Legal aid: The new framework, *New Law Journal*, Vol. 137 (6299), p. 305.

English, J. and Card, R. (1985). *Police Law*, Butterworths, London.

National Council for Civil Liberties (1986). Civil Liberty Briefing No. 1, *Police and Criminal Evidence Act*, NCCL, London.

Padfield, C. (1983). *Law Made Simple*, revised by F. E. Smith, 6th edn, Heinemann, London.

Williams, E. (1986). *ABC Guide to the Practice of the Magistrates' Courts*, Sweet and Maxwell, London.

# 2. Criminal and Civil Law

## 2.1 CRIMINAL LAW

Criminal offences are committed against the State, either in the performance of some act which the law forbids, or in the omission of some act which the law requires (see page 8).

The concept of criminal responsibility is an important one. Under common law, for a crime to have been committed, there must normally, as well as the act concerned, exist *mens rea* or a guilty mind. For example, a nurse who gives a drug that has not been prescribed to a patient who dies as a result would be guilty of a crime, as she voluntarily gave the drug to the patient and she had sufficient knowledge to know the dangers of this action. Thus for *mens rea* there must be intention, recklessness or negligence. The State presumes that every person committing an act is sane and doing so voluntarily until or unless this is proved otherwise.

### Classification of crimes

Crimes vary in severity and the previous chapter described how a summons or a warrant can bring a person to a criminal court depending on the severity of the crime. A summary offence is one that is relatively petty and can be dealt with in a Magistrate's Court, the maximum penalty normally being three months' imprisonment. An indictable offence is one that normally involves a warrant for the person's arrest or is an 'arrestable offence' (see page 18). The frequent result is a term of imprisonment after trial in a Crown Court. However, this differentiation is not rigid. In Scotland, crimes are classified into 'true' crimes or offences (similar to indictable and summary offences). Unlike in English Law, three verdicts are possible—guilty, not guilty and not proven, rather than just guilty or not guilty.

Offences can be against the State, the person or property. The first group includes treason, unlawful picketing, bribery of a public officer, perjury and contempt of court. Offences against the person include homicide (murder or manslaughter), illegal abortion, sexual offences, assault, wounding and poisoning. Examples of the final group of offences against property are arson, criminal damage to property, stealing (obtaining by deception, robbery, blackmail and burglary), handling stolen goods and forgery.

# Defences

A defence is a legally recognised reason for the act committed not to have been a crime.

There may be lack of the capacity to form the necessary intention. In raising the defence of insanity the accused must show that he was 'suffering from such a defect of reason, due to disease of the mind, as not to know the nature and quality of the act he was doing, or (if he did know this) not to know that what he was doing was wrong'. If this defence is proved, the accused will be found 'not guilty by reason of insanity'.

Children may also be held to lack the necessary intention, although the law recognises that this varies with age. However, an assumption has to be made as regards the age at which intention is possible, although children vary widely in development. The law states that a child under 8 years cannot be guilty of a crime, and from 8 to 14 years has no 'mischievous intention' unless proved otherwise. For example, a boy younger than 14 is *legally* incapable of rape. Classifications of children and young people are different in Scotland.

- A pupil is under 14 years for a boy, under 12 years for a girl. A child of this age lacks 'mischievous intention' unless proved otherwise.
- A minor is 14–18 years for a boy, 12–18 years for a girl. No child under 16 years may be prosecuted except on the instructions of the Lord Advocate. A 'Children's Hearing' does not involve prosecution.

There could also be lack of intention in the performance of some act when compelled by force or violent threats, or in the case of a genuine mistake.

A further legal response is self-defence. For example, a nurse may defend herself from an attack and bodily harm by a violent patient, or a householder could try to defend his property against an intruder. Thus, if an act is committed against another in the defence of one's person or property, there would be no crime as long as the amount of force used is necessary and reasonably proportionate. For the nurse to hit back at the patient so hard that he died as a result of his injuries might well not be considered reasonable force in self-defence, but unnecessarily exccssive.

It cannot be emphasised too strongly that ignorance of the law is not a defence.

## Sentences

Sentence varies with the severity of the crime and with the criminal history of the convicted person.

For a minor crime, the person may receive a conditional or unconditional discharge, be bound over, put on probation or fined. For serious crimes, or where there has been a long criminal history, a period of imprisonment is likely. For certain crimes, extremely heavy fines are possible, for example if an industrial concern has persistently failed to abide by health and safety regulations for its workers.

## 2.2 CIVIL LAW

Civil law involves the rights and duties of individuals towards each other. It can be subdivided into a number of parts, but the nurse is only likely to be involved in the course of her work with the law of tort, of contract, of persons and of succession.

## The law of tort

This is a very large part of civil law and particularly affects the nurse. A tort (delict in Scotland) is a civil wrong and results in a common law action for damages. Payment of compensation to the affected parties contrasts with the outcome of criminal proceedings (see page 8). A crime is, generally speaking, a wrong so grave that it goes beyond mere compensation between citizens and amounts to a wrong against the community at large.

A legal action involving tort arises when one person suffers unwarranted harm or damage at the hands of another. However, the law of tort is not completely comprehensive, and harm may be sustained where the law is unable to provide a remedy. On the other hand, there is sometimes a legal wrong where no damage is necessarily done, for example in trespass and libel. In such cases, the unwarranted interference with the individual's rights is presumed to amount to damage deserving of compensation.

The length of time before legal action is taken can be long. In the case of personal injury, the writ concerning the tort must be issued within three years of the event, but there may be further delay before it comes to court. It is worth the nurse remembering this when compiling her records as memories are fallible and legal actions fail more often due to faulty records than to legal arguments.

There are also factors concerning the directness of cause and effect in awarding compensation, and a line has to be drawn somewhere as to the remoteness of damage suffered. Courts will consider these factors and an individual will only be found liable for the damage that could reasonably have been foreseen, depending on the particular circumstances.

### Vicarious liability

A nurse employed in the health service is legally the employee of the health authority, and where this relationship exists the employer is vicariously liable for the torts of the employee during the course of her employment. This liability exists whether the acts were authorised or not, unless the act was solely for the employee's own purpose.

It must be stressed that the employee is, of course, personally liable for her own torts, but it is often the employer who is sued, either with or without the employee, as an employing authority is more likely to be able to pay the damages. If the employee is not included at this stage, the employer is entitled to recover some contribution from her but this practice is seldom followed in the National Health Service, which is self-insuring.

### Defences

Some important defences in the law of tort are as follows.

First, *volenti non fit injuria*, no legal wrong can be committed against a consenting person. Therefore, if consent is expressed, orally or in writing, or implied by circumstances, a tort has not been committed. The nurse is likely to come across one particular difficulty in this context. Where there is a sense of urgency to save life or to prevent worsening of a serious threat to health, the nurse will feel that she has an obligation to act even if she is unable to get consent. The law states that as long as an act is such as could be expected of a person of 'ordinary courage and ability', no tort will have occurred even if damage results. This is enlarged upon in Part III.

As in criminal law, self-defence is acceptable as long as the force used is reasonable. However, persons of unsound mind may be liable, even though this is a defence in criminal law (see page 24).

Necessity is occasionally a defence, but only where prevention of a greater evil is necessary. For example, a nurse pushing a patient out of the way of a falling tree in the hospital grounds would not be liable for a tort if the patient suffered some injury from being pushed.

## Trespass

The tort of trespass can be committed to the person, goods or land. The nurse is involved with the law regarding trespass to the person and this is known as assault or battery (also a crime). Assault is an attempt or threat to apply unlawful force to the person of another whereby that other person is put in fear of immediate violence or at least bodily contact. Words alone are insufficient threat. Battery is the actual application of force, however slight, to the person of another against his will.

However, the nurse will usually find she has sufficient defence. Consent of the plaintiff usually applies to the patient undergoing some treatment or care. Other defences are self-defence, parental, judicial or other authority, inevitable accident or preservation of the peace.

The nurse may occasionally be involved in trespass to land. Damage need not be proved, and the tort is committed when a person enters or remains on the land of another without authority. The land concerned could be National Health Service property (see Chapter 7).

## Negligence

Negligence is one of the most important torts, and is the one that most concerns the nurse. Negligence has to be proved on three points:

- That the defendant was under a duty of care to the plaintiff.
- That there had been a breach of that duty.
- That as a result the plaintiff had suffered damage.

(In Scotland the defendant is known as the defender and the plaintiff, the pursuer.) The concept of duty of care is central to any case of negligence.

In law, a person must take reasonable care to avoid acts or omissions which he can reasonably foresee as being likely to injure his neighbour. The legal definition of neighbour in this context is 'a person who is so closely and directly affected by one's act that one ought reasonably to have them in contemplation as being so affected when one is directing one's mind to the acts or omissions being called in question'.

This legal definition has been included in full because of the importance of duty of care in the nurse's work in relation to her patients and colleagues. The standard of care, though usually being taken as that of an ordinary prudent man, for any professional person must be of a higher level. Thus the nurse is expected to exhibit the expertise normally demonstrated by competent nurses.

As well as professional people having recognised duties, employers have a liability to provide a reasonably safe system of work and competent fellow employees (see page 67). For example, a nurse lifting a patient must be able to trust that the nurse with whom she is working is also competent in this skill.

Other points for the nurse to remember are that as well as negligent acts or omissions, she could also be sued for negligent mis-statement (see page 243). Thus the nurse should be careful of the accuracy of what she tells patients and their relatives. Finally, there may be contributory negligence by the plaintiff. This plea, however, serves not as a defence but as a reduction of damages payable by the defendant.

### Defamation
Defamation is a statement which exposes a person to hatred, ridicule or contempt, or causes him to be shunned or avoided by right-thinking members of society. There are two forms of defamation:

- Libel—when a statement is made in permanent form, usually in writing. It may also be a crime if it leads to a breach of the peace.
- Slander—where a statement is made in transitory form, usually spoken. Actual damage must be shown to occur except when the slanderer gives an imputation of crime, venereal disease, unchastity in a woman or unfitness for any office, profession or trade carried out at that time by the plaintiff.

In Scotland, these two terms are used in a slightly different way. Slander is a verbal injury comparable to battery in assault. It therefore appears to have wider implications than in England. Libel and slander also seem sometimes to be interchangeable.

The nurse may be faced with fear of this tort when writing reports on junior nurses, or when making complaints about other members of staff. However, defences for this tort are justification, fair comment, privilege, apology or offers of amend. Thus, if the comments made by the nurse are true, she need have no fear of legal action being taken against her (see page 79).

### Nuisance and occupiers' liability

A further tort is nuisance, which can be public or private. A private nuisance is the unlawful interference with a person's use of his property, health, comfort or convenience, and damage must result. The health authority may be involved here, rather than the nurse. The nuisance must have a marked effect as one defence is triviality, the law having no concern with trifles. In Scotland, nuisances are classified as common law, statutory and conventional.

An occupier has a duty of care to all his visitors, and even to trespassers, and therefore must give warning of any dangers on the premises. This liability of an occupier applies to hospitals and health centres.

## The law of contract

The nurse as an employee will need to be aware of the law of contract. A contract is an agreement between two or more parties which is intended to have legal consequences, and may be made orally, in writing or implied by conduct. By Scottish law, certain contracts must be written, for example those concerning land or property. In the National Health Service, contracts are always made in writing.

For a contract to be valid, a number of points must be observed, the most important for the nurse being:

- Offer and acceptance.
- Capacity of the parties involved.
- Genuine agreement.
- The object of the contract must be legal.
- The contract must be possible to perform.

A contract can be terminated by agreement, by performance of what-ever the contract required, or breached in some way. All these points are enlarged on in Part II and Part III (pages 54 and 140).

## The law of persons

An individual's legal personality starts at birth and ends at death, though certain areas of criminal law protect the fetus. Thus, birth, death, guardianship, infants and minors, marriage and divorce can all be included in the law of persons. The midwife, paediatric nurse and health visitor are most likely to be concerned here.

The legal existence of trade unions may also be included in this part of the law. A trade union is a combination of work people or employers or both, whose principal object is collective bargaining for wages and conditions of work. A union can enter into contracts, sue and be sued, the union and the employee joining in a contract between them. The principle of trade unions is of importance to any employee and the nurse should explore the role of unions in her own field of work (see Chapter 4).

## The law of succession

A brief outline of the law concerning wills and gifts is included here.

A will is a declaration of a person's intentions concerning his property after his death. It must be made by a person of full age and sound mind, but can be cancelled or altered. There are certain formalities necessary for a will to be valid: it must be in writing, dated, have the person's signature at the foot of the will and be witnessed by two or more people present together. (See page 132 for the different requirements in Scotland.) Because there are so many complexities involved, nurses are always strongly advised to call on the administrative staff of the health authority if a patient wishes to make a will. Further details are given in Part III, page 130.

Gifts are the transfer of property when the person giving has received no valuable consideration from the recipient. Once the recipient has full possession of the gift, the matter has been completed. Most health authorities lay down guidelines for accepting gifts from patients to preclude later accusations of bribery and corruption.

## Questions on Chapter 2

*see page*

1. What is meant by the defences in criminal law of lack of necessary intention, and necessity?                                                24

# REFERENCES

Eddey, K. (1982). *The English Legal System*, 3rd edn, Sweet and Maxwell, London.

Padfield, C. (1983). *Law Made Simple*, revised by F. E. Smith, 6th edn, Heinemann, London.

# Part II
# Law and Employment

# 3. The Nurse as a Professional Person

The nurse is both a member of a profession and an employee. This section explains the background legislation controlling the nurse's professional role and enlarges on the legal implications of professional accountability.

Acts and statutory instruments:

Nurses, Midwives and Health Visitors Act (1979)
Nurses, Midwives and Health Visitors Rules (1983)

## 3.1  DEFINITION OF A NURSE

### Who is a nurse?

Mrs Graham in bed 9 called out, 'Nurse Jones, could you get me a bedpan?' Nurse Jones duly brought a bedpan and helped Mrs Graham on to it.

Nurse Jones was a student in training. Was she really entitled to use the prefix 'nurse' to her name?

In fact, the Nurses' Acts lay down a number of restrictions on the use of the title 'nurse', and the wearing of badges and uniform. Miss Jones, in the above example, is not legally a nurse as she is not registered or enrolled, and if she passes herself off as a nurse, she is committing an offence, as she would also be doing by wearing the uniform or badge of a registered or enrolled nurse. However, the majority of hospitals where individuals are trained for the register or roll allow nurses in training to use the title 'nurse' as a courtesy, while on duty, but the legal position should be made quite clear to them.

It is a sad fact that every year a number of offences come to light of individuals claiming to be nurses who are, in fact, not so. Offences are usually discovered through potential employers seeking to confirm that people are who they claim to be. In the past nursing agencies have not exercised as much caution as they should, but with the benefit of hindsight, checking is now carried out much more carefully.

Some offenders possess apparently valid documents and badges, which, if checking is thorough, are found to have been reported lost some time previously. Therefore, it is clearly insufficient for the prospective employer to ask to view documents. An incident occurred only recently of a nurse employed by a psychiatric hospital being suspected of cruelty to patients, but he disappeared before action could be taken. When the employing authority attempted to discover the whereabouts of this individual via the United Kingdom Central Council (UKCC) it was found that the documents belonging to the 'nurse' had been reported lost some years before. New documents and registration number had since been issued. The employee was therefore an impostor using someone else's name. If the employer had checked with the UKCC before taking on the individual, the offence could have been discovered then, rather than some time later after unnecessary suffering to patients. The UKCC has set aside certain telephone lines purely for this purpose, and all employers are strongly urged to make use of this facility.

It is interesting to note that the first fine for the offence was £10 in 1919. It was only in 1977 that the maximum penalty for a first attempt was increased to £500. However, the individual could also be prosecuted as she has obtained the salary of a nurse by deception.

## What is a nurse allowed to do?

Once registered, a nurse will practise as an independent practitioner and be accountable for her actions.

Legally the term 'accountability' equates closely with the concept duty of care as used in negligence (page 27). What actions the nurse is accountable for is a rather more complex issue. The Nurses, Midwives and Health Visitors Rules (1983) are statutory instruments drawn up by the UKCC and approved by Government. Section 18 of these rules gives a framework of competencies that must be acquired for admission to the various parts of the register (see page 40) and these are reproduced below:

1. Competencies for admission to Parts 1, 3, 5 or 8
   (a) advise on the promotion of health and the prevention of illness;
   (b) recognise situations that may be detrimental to the health and well-being of the individual;
   (c) carry out those activities involved when conducting the comprehensive assessment of a person's nursing requirements;
   (d) recognise the significance of the observations made and use these to develop an initial nursing assessment;
   (e) devise a plan of nursing care based on the assessment with the co-operation of the patient, to the extent that this is possible, taking into account the medical prescription;
   (f) implement the planned programme of nursing care and where appropriate teach and co-ordinate other members of the caring team who may be responsible for implementing specific aspects of the nursing care;
   (g) review the effectiveness of the nursing care provided, and where appropriate, initiate any action that may be required;
   (h) work in a team with other nurses, and with medical and paramedical staff and social workers;
   (i) undertake the management of the care of a group of patients over a period of time and organise the appropriate support services;

   related to the care of the particular type of patient with whom the nurse is likely to come into contact when registered in that Part of the register.

2. Competencies for admission to Parts 2, 4, 6 or 7
   (a) assist in carrying out comprehensive observation of the patient and help in assessing her care requirements;
   (b) develop skills to enable her to assist in the implementation of nursing care under the direction of a person registered in Part 1, 3, 5 or 8 of the register;
   (c) accept delegated nursing tasks;
   (d) assist in reviewing the effectiveness of the care provided;
   (e) work in a team with other nurses, and with medical and paramedical staff and social workers;

   related to the care of the particular type of patient with whom the nurse is likely to come into contact when registered in that Part of the register.

The detailed breakdown of skills expected of a registered nurse is nowhere legally spelled out. This is useful in that nursing is continually changing and it would be dangerously restrictive to be too precise. Therefore, the nurse has to rely on other sources to identify the expectations laid on her. These are the content of her training, the curriculum guidelines drawn up by the National Boards, the overall consensus of what skills are expected of a registered nurse with no further training by both her professional organisation and her employer, and the reverse of this, what skills are seen as an extension of the nurse's role and therefore require extra training and approval (page 230).

However, no person's training is going to be identical with another's due to the variable nature of the practical experience gained. Therefore the question, 'What is a nurse allowed to do?' must also be phrased as 'What can a nurse do?' If a registered nurse does not feel competent to carry out a particular skill, being accountable means ensuring that she receives the training and supervision needed to carry out that skill safely (page 112).

## Question and concluding comments on 3.1

*Question:* Miss Roberts did a three year student nurse training with Hospital X, and passed her state final examinations at the end of this time. She then applied for a staff nurse post with the same hospital. References were checked and, after interview, Miss Roberts was appointed as staff nurse on a medical ward. Six months later, she applied for a second staff nurse post.

This time the employer checked with the Council about Miss Roberts' registration; her name was not on the Register. What had been Miss Roberts' legal position during the preceding six months?

*Comments:* This is a relatively common situation. Legally Miss Roberts, as an unregistered nurse, had committed an offence in practising despite having completed her training satisfactorily (see page 36). Newly qualified nurses do not always realise the legal implications of not sending off their registration forms and fee to the Council, and often delay such matters as financial considerations are also present! The hospital authorities concerned are usually unwilling to take any legal action as long as the nurse concerned registers as soon as possible. There is rarely any intent to defraud the employer.

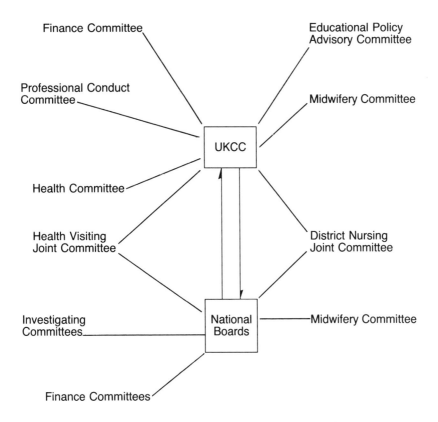

**Figure 3.1**  Committees of the UKCC and National Boards.

## 3.2  STATUTORY CONTROLS OF NURSING

In order to maintain professional standards nursing has been subject to the controls of various Nurses' Acts. The most recent of these, the Nurses, Midwives and Health Visitors Act 1979, legislated for a number of potentially far-reaching changes for the profession. The United Kingdom Central Council (UKCC) and National Boards set up by the Act took over in July 1983 from nine bodies, including the General Nursing Council (GNC) for England and Wales, and for Scotland, the

Northern Ireland Council for Nurses and Midwives, the Central Midwives Board, the Council for the Education and Training of Health Visitors and the Joint Board of Clinical Nursing Studies.

### United Kingdom Central Council

This Council has four major functions:

- To establish and improve standards of training and professional conduct for nurses, midwives and health visitors.
- To determine the rules for registration and maintain the single professional register.
- To provide guidance to the profession on standards of professional conduct.
- To act, through the appropriate committees, to protect the public from unsafe members of the profession (see page 44).

In order to fulfil these functions, the UKCC is empowered to draw up rules through delegated legislation.

A single professional register has been set up. This has involved a massive computerised exercise and includes a periodic fee system which will assist in keeping the register up to date as well as enabling the UKCC to be self-supporting. Rules have been drawn up to define which qualifications are to be registered and how, as well as who may have access to the register and how. The register is divided into 11 parts as follows:

Part 1   First-level nurses trained in general nursing
Part 2   Second-level nurses trained in general nursing (England and Wales)
Part 3   First-level nurses trained in the nursing of persons suffering from mental illness
Part 4   Second-level nurses trained in the nursing of persons suffering from mental illness (England and Wales)
Part 5   First-level nurses trained in the nursing of persons suffering from mental handicap
Part 6   Second-level nurses trained in the nursing of persons suffering from mental handicap (England and Wales)
Part 7   Second-level nurses (Scotland and Northern Ireland)
Part 8   Persons trained in the nursing of sick children
Part 9   Nurses trained in the nursing of persons suffering from fever
Part 10   Midwives
Part 11   Health visitors

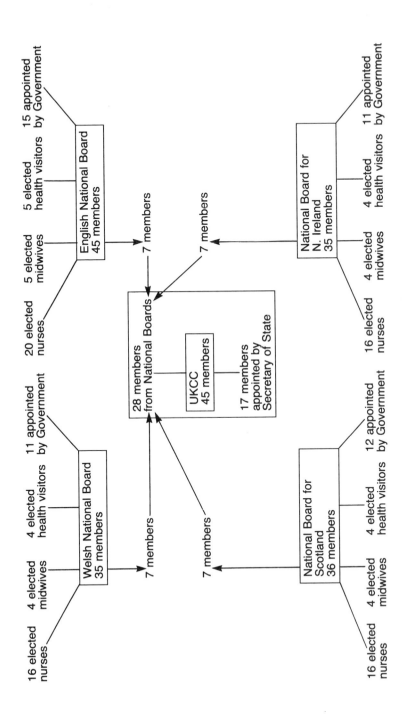

**Figure 3.2** Membership of the UKCC and National Boards.

A number of proposals concerning the future of nurse education and training have been published. Initially the emphasis was on basic nurse training, and Project 2000 has been agreed in principle by Government although much consultation is still required. Mandatory periodic refreshment for those already registered is at present being discussed.

The UKCC has published a Professional Code of Conduct to give guidance to nurses, midwives and health visitors and this is reviewed regularly (see page 205).

Ways that the UKCC acts in order to safeguard the public is discussed in subsection 3.3 (page 46).

The 1979 Act specifically builds in consultation between the Council and representatives of groups likely to be affected. Certain committees are specifically required by the Act, others can be set up as they are needed. The Council at present has three standing committees on midwifery, finance and educational policy. A health visiting joint committee and a district nursing joint committee service Council and National Boards jointly. In order to maintain professional discipline, a professional conduct committee and health committee play an important role (see Figure 3.1).

From July 1983 membership of the UKCC is made up of 28 members of the National Boards and 17 appointed by the Secretary of State (see Figure 3.2).

### The National Boards
There are four National Boards, for England, Scotland, Wales and Northern Ireland. They have the following functions:

● To arrange courses enabling people to qualify for registration and courses of further training meeting the requirements of the Central Council as to their content and standard.
● To arrange for examinations to be held.
● To carry out investigations of cases of alleged misconduct with a view to proceedings before the Central Council (see page 44).
● To work with the Council to promote and improve training methods.

The Nurses' Rules detail a number of controls on nurse training. Training institutions have to be approved and education officers play an important role both initially and in an ongoing capacity. They are concerned with the curriculum in its widest sense and, in addition to the theoretical programme, pay particular attention to the practical experience being used for learners. Staff ratios, adequacy of supervision, teaching programmes in operation and type of clinical experience are just some of the concerns of the National Boards in approving a health district for training. Entry requirements to training relating to length of schooling and academic achievement are also laid down. A minimum entry requirement is set and training schools can set their own higher entry requirements. However, to abide by the law, selection must be without racial or sex discrimination.

The National Boards arrange for theoretical examinations to be set. This may be by centrally set examination papers but for some parts of the register the responsibility is devolved onto Examination Boards set up by the training institution, thus allowing for greater flexibility in response to local requirements. Practical assessments are carried out by approved examiners who have completed an appropriate training course.

Legal requirements can lead to rigidity and limited scope for improvement in nurse education. The UKCC and National Boards therefore encourage experimentation in training. However, it is important to the public and to the profession that standards are upheld, so any experimental schemes, whether concerned with the main programme or methods of assessment, have to be submitted for approval.

## The European Economic Community

July 29, 1979 marked the beginning of a new venture for the UK nurse. From this date, the training of students had to abide by the EEC directives. For most training establishments this meant the provision of a wider training scheme with the inclusion of more specialised experiences than previously legally required. As a basic nurse training should be thought of as a springboard to further learning, giving students a taste of all the main branches of nursing is probably a very good thing.

To date, psychiatric nurse training has not been controlled by EEC directives. Training in this area of nursing has been so diverse and in some countries so minimal that it is likely to be some time before agreement is reached. The UK mental nurse can be assured that her training is well thought of in the European Community.

## Question and concluding comments on 3.2

*Question:* Richard Small, a student nurse in general training, was notified that he had failed the Final Examination. He was very upset by this and consulted a solicitor about appealing against this decision. Would he have any grounds for an appeal?

*Comments:* The responsibility for setting and marking final examination papers for admission to the general part of the register is now devolved onto local Examination Boards. Each Board will have approved regulations drawn up concerning the carrying out of its function. If there was some failure in the way these regulations were observed, then Richard may have grounds for appeal. However if he is objecting to the professional judgement of the person/persons marking his paper, then he has no grounds for appeal. The markers are all experienced nurses and, in addition, the National Board requires that each local Examination Board has external assessors to monitor its functioning and results.

## 3.3 PROFESSIONAL DISCIPLINE

The Nurses, Midwives and Health Visitors Act (1979) lays a clear duty on the UKCC and National Boards to protect the public. In addition, the UKCC has the responsibility of establishing, maintaining and improving professional conduct, and of advising nurses, midwives and health visitors regarding professional standards. In order to carry out these functions in relation to professional discipline, several committees are in operation, the investigating committee, the professional conduct committee and the health committee (see Figure 3.1, page 39).

### The investigating committee

The investigating committee of each National Board acts as a sieve for the large number of incidents brought to the Board's attention. A large proportion of these are the result of nurses being convicted of certain crimes, the police being required by a Home Office Circular to report certain offences to the Board, for example those involving violence, indecency, dishonesty, drugs or excessive alcohol abuse as these may reflect on a person's suitability to continue in her profession. A second large group of allegations received are the result of incidents in professional work situations and have been reported by managers. Other colleagues, patients or relatives may also send complaints to the Board although these usually constitute only a small number.

Only documentary evidence is used by the investigating committee and individuals are not required to appear personally. However, the nurse concerned is informed of the allegation and she is given the opportunity to provide a statement, after consultation with her union,

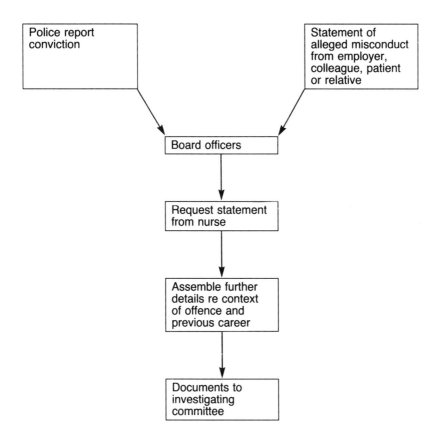

**Figure 3.3**  Investigation by the National Boards of possible misconduct.

professional organisation or solicitor as desired. In addition, supporting evidence regarding the context of the alleged misconduct and relevant information about the nurse's career is collected (see Figure 3.3). The Board officers may themselves take legal advice at this stage, for example concerning the probable credibility of witnesses.

Finally the investigating committee must make a decision on whether to refer the case to the UKCC for possible removal of the nurse from the register or to take no action. The possible options are shown in Figure 3.4. As an example of one Board's investigating committee's actions, the English National Board's annual report 1986–87 stated that of 444

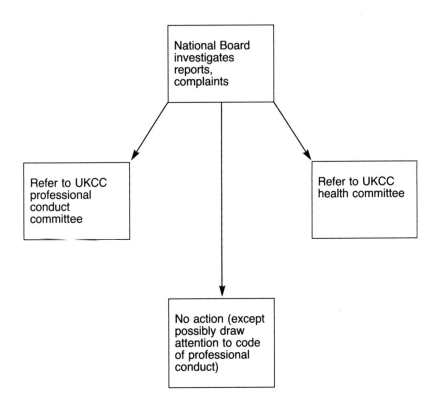

**Figure 3.4** Summary of possible action by National Boards.

cases considered, 27 per cent were forwarded to the UKCC professional conduct committee, 5 per cent to the UKCC health committee, 22 per cent were deferred for further enquiries, 21 per cent had no action taken, and 25 per cent were sent a Code of Professional Conduct with no other action. It was also noted that areas of particular concern were those involving drugs and mental handicap.

## The professional conduct committee

This committee consists of five members drawn from the whole UKCC membership of 45. The members must be selected 'with due regard to

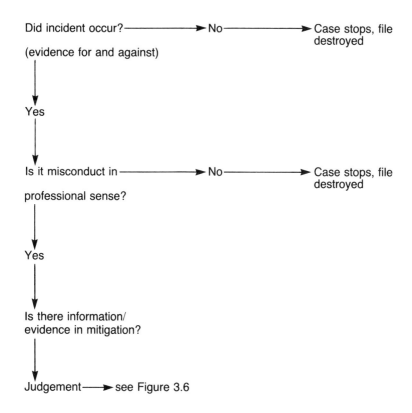

**Figure 3.5** Outline of the UKCC professional conduct committee procedure.

the professional field in which the respondent works or has worked'. This should ensure that the committee has the insight into all relevant circumstances to enable a fairer judgement. Very precise rules control the committee's procedure, and the standard of proof required is very high. A legal assessor (a solicitor or barrister of not less than ten years' experience) is present at any hearing. If necessary, the committee can subpoena witnesses to attend.

Cases are usually referred from a Board's investigating committee, but may come from the UKCC health committee. Sufficient notice (not less than 28 days) must be given to the nurse concerned regarding the

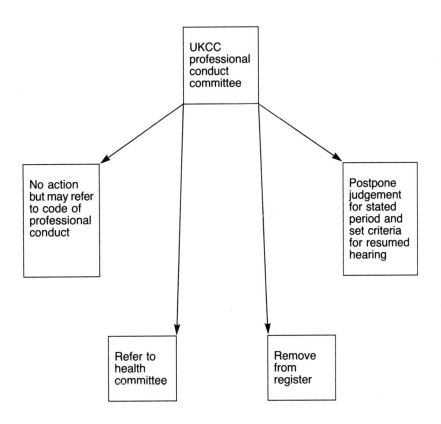

**Figure 3.6** Summary of possible action by professional conduct committee after misconduct found.

date and time of the hearing, and witnesses similarly informed. The committee must hear the evidence and decide whether the alleged misconduct occurred or not, and then, if it did occur, whether it constitutes misconduct in the professional sense. Then any mitigating circumstances must be considered, for example staffing ratios or local policies, and finally character references and any previous criminal convictions or proven misconduct are made public (see Figure 3.5).

The professional conduct committee then passes judgement and has four options available (see Figure 3.6). Postponing judgement involves a delay in making the final judgement until specific references or additional reports, for example from probation officers, are made, and the nurse is required to reattend at the end of a specified period of time. Of the decisions made to remove a person's name from the register, quite a high proportion of the proved misconduct are associated with drugs. There is a right of appeal.

The public by prior arrangement is allowed to observe the professional conduct committee in action. What becomes most apparent to the observer at a hearing is the humanity of the whole proceedings and the attempts made to help the offender to rehabilitation, if possible, either within or outside the nursing profession.

# The health committee

The 1979 Act does not limit removal from the register to those found guilty of misconduct. It requires the UKCC to make rules, in order to protect the public, that allow for removal from the register 'for misconduct or otherwise'. Prior to this Act it was clear that a number of nurses were unsafe because of illness rather than misconduct, and as a result the UKCC health committee was set up.

Access to this committee may be by one of three routes. Usually either an investigating committee or the professional conduct committee makes the referral but direct referral from individuals is possible, for example the nurse's manager, colleague, patient or relative.

A summary of the health committee's functioning is shown in Figure 3.7. A group of 12 council members make up the professional screeners and three of these are convened to consider documentary evidence and make decisions. When referral is from one of the committees, the screeners simply select medical examiners, but if referral is from an individual, they first need to decide if there is cause for concern, and consider the medical examiners reports before proceeding further.

Medical examiners are medical practitioners appointed by the Council following nomination by the BMA or Royal College of Psychiatrists. One must attend the health committee.

The membership of the health committee consists of five members selected from a possible 25 UKCC members. Selection is on the 'due regard' principle as for the professional conduct committee.

The decisions made by the health committee may be one of four (see Figure 3.7). If fitness to practise is shown to be seriously impaired by illness, then removal from the register is a possible option.

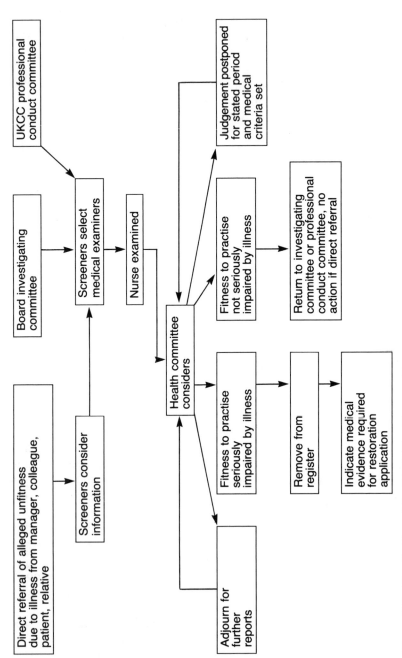

**Figure 3.7** Functioning of the UKCC health committee.

## Student conduct committee

The nurse in training is dealt with in a different way through a student conduct committee. This may decide to discontinue a nurse's training as one among a number of options.

## Question and concluding comments on 3.3

*Question:* Miss Hoskins, RGN, was convicted of theft from a hospital, where she was employed, of pentazocine and hypodermic syringes. The police followed their normal duty of informing the National Board and the case went to the investigating committee. In collecting documentary evidence, it became clear that Miss Hoskins had had bouts of abdominal pain over a period of six years and pentazocine injections had been prescribed for this on a number of occasions. Nine months before the thefts came to light, she took employment with the hospital concerned and for five months was moderately well. However, when the abdominal pain recurred, she feared going to her general practitioner as he was also the medical officer of the occupational health service, and she thought this might jeopardise her job. She therefore took pentazocine from the ward stock at intervals over the following four months. The hospital dismissed her from her job. What action might the investigating committee take?

*Comments:* The nature of Miss Hoskins' misconduct is serious enough to warrant referral to the UKCC. The evidence may point to unfitness due to illness rather than pure misconduct, and the investigating committee may decide on referral to the UKCC health committee rather than professional conduct committee.

## REFERENCES

English National Board (1987). Annual Report 1986–87, ENB, London.
Pyne, R. (1985). The disciplinary process, *Senior Nurse*, Vol. 2 (3), pp. 7–10.
Royal College of Nursing (1981). *Towards Standards: A Discussion Document*, RCN, London.
Statutory Instruments—The Nurses, Midwives and Health Visitors Rules Approval Order No. 873 (1983). HMSO, London.
United Kingdom Central Council (1986). *Introducing the UKCC Health Committee and Explaining Its Role and Procedures*, PC/86/01, UKCC, London.
United Kingdom Central Council (1986). *Project 2000*, UKCC, London.

# 4. The Nurse as an Employee

In this chapter, the reader should realise that there is considerable overlap of the subsections, and the main cross-references are given. However, it is hoped that the method of dividing the subject matter enables the reader to find her way through the particular confusions of employment legislation in as logical and useful a way as possible.

The legal implications to the nurse of holding any posts in the National Health Service are many. She will be involved in the law of contract and the law of torts. More specifically, the main Acts affecting her work are as follows:

The Shops Acts
Young Persons (Employment) Act (1938)
Factories Act (1961)
Contracts of Employment Act (1963)
Offices, Shops and Railway Premises Act (1963)
Health and Safety at Work etc. Act (1974)
Trade Union and Labour Relations Act (1974)
Rehabilitation of Offenders Act (1974)
Employment Protection Act (1975)
Sex Discrimination Act (1975)
Race Relations Act (1976)
Employment Protection (Consolidation) Act (1978)
Employment Act (1980)
Social Security Act (1986)

*sex*
*discrimination*
*act*

No job advertisement which indicates or can reasonably be understood as indicating an intention to discriminate on grounds of sex (e.g. by inviting applications only from males or only from females) may be accepted, unless:
(1) the job is for the purpose of a private householder or
(2) it is in a business employing less than six persons or
(3) it is otherwise exempt from the requirements of the Sex Discrimination Act.
A statement must be made at the time the advertisement is placed saying which one of the exceptions in the Act is considered to apply.

## REHABILITATION OF OFFENDERS ACT 1974

Because of the nature of the work for which you are applying, this post is exempt from the provisions of Section 4(2) of the Rehabilitation of Offenders Act 1974 by virtue of the Rehabilitation of Offenders Act 1974 (Exceptions) Order 1975. Applicants are therefore not entitled to withhold information about convictions which for other purposes are 'spent' under the provisions of the Act, and in the event of employment any failure to disclose such convictions could result in dismissal or disciplinary action by the Authority. Any information given will be completely confidential and will be considered only in relation to an application for positions to which the order applies.

**Figure 4.1**  Statements placed alongside job advertisements.

# 4.1   CONTRACTS

## Becoming an employee

Miss Austin saw the following advertisement in a nursing magazine:

> '... Health District
> A ward sister/charge nurse is required for a busy medical ward at ...
> Hospital. The applicant should preferably have experience of nursing
> patients with chest conditions and be keen to implement the nursing
> process. Closing date for applications ...'

She decided to apply as she had the necessary qualifications and
experience, was interviewed and appointed to the job. On taking up the
post, she received a contract which she read carefully and signed.

The process of becoming an employee or 'servant' of the health
authority commences with the application of the interested nurse.

The law plays a part even in the original advertisement and the
magazines containing these advertisements always carry a reminder of
the Sex Discrimination Act (1975) (see Figure 4.1). This Act also
applics to applicants to nurse training, and all schools of nursing must
now consider men as well as women. As an extension of this, learners
need not have their experience restricted to the care of patients of their
own sex.

With reference to the Equal Opportunities Commission and the
separate but similar Commission for Racial Equality, the prospective
employer also has to be careful not to discriminate on other grounds
such as marital status, race, colour or creed. For example, the nurse
manager who is screening application forms may feel that, other things
being equal, it would be better to employ a single woman rather than a
married one as the latter may become pregnant or take time off work
because of family commitments. Such discrimination would not be
acceptable.

One area where nurse employment is exempt from the law is that of a
nurse's past convictions. Because of the nature of a nurse's work
in relation to the public, the applicant herself and any referees
are required by the Rehabilitation of Offenders Act (1974) (Exemp-
tions) Order (1975) to give details of convictions. Some offences, for
example those involving violence, would make an employer wary of
employing that person, as the employer has a duty to protect the
public.

# Making a contract

When a nurse is appointed to a job, she takes up the role of employee to the health authority and a contract is entered into between them (Figure 4.2). For all appointments in the health service, this contract is now written and most health authorities have a standard form.

For a valid contract, certain details must be included. The names of employer and employee with job title and date of commencement will head the contract. Details relating to conditions of employment will take a major part, with pay scales, hours and place of work, holidays, sick pay entitlement, disciplinary and grievance procedures. Periods of notice required will be set out for both the employer and employee. As a booklet would be required if full details were included, it is common and acceptable practice to give a reference of where the relevant information can be found, for example of sick pay entitlement and disciplinary procedures. The documents concerned are named and a location given of where they can be read. As regards place of work, the contract is usually purposely vague about this. If a definite location is given, there will usually be a rider such as: 'You may be required to work elsewhere in the health authority'.

There are certain requirements regarding giving notice. For example, for the employer to the employee, notice of one week is required after 13 weeks' continuous service, and four weeks after five years; and for the employee to the employer, after 13 weeks, one week's notice is necessary. However, it is likely that the nurse's contract will state different lengths of notice, for example one month on either side. As long as these are not less than the statutory minimum periods, they are legally sound and must be adhered to unless either party wishes to waive his right of notice (see page 93).

All learner nurses are also in the position of employees and require an appropriate contract. Even the small number of student nurses who are true students at a university or college following some kind of degree course require a simple form of contract to enable them to gain work experience in the health authority. The situation may well change if Project 2000 is fully implemented and student nurses given the recommended training grants. However, at this time it is not clear how this would alter the present employee status of student nurses.

# Types of contract

The nurse will meet two main variations in types of contract. As a learner nurse, she will have a fixed-term contract specifying for how

**Figure 4.2**  Sample contract of employment.

GH 952

COST CENTRE ☐ ☐ ☐ ☐                    OCC CODE ☐ ☐ ☐

## Health Authority

## Contract of Employment

THIS CONTRACT SHOULD BE READ IN CONJUNCTION WITH THE STAFF HANDBOOK.

Part 1

Contract of Employment between the Health Authority and

Surname _____ Other names _____

Address _____

_____

Title of Post _____ Post number _____

Location _____ Grade _____

Responsible to _____ Starting date _____

1. **TERMS AND CONDITIONS OF SERVICE**  The appointment is subject to the receipt of satisfactory references, and medical screening, which may involve a medical examination. The terms and conditions of employment are those laid down by the General Council and The . . . . . . . . . . . . . . . . . . . . . . . . . . . . . . . . . . . . . . . . Council of Whitley Councils for the Health Service. Full details of these may be seen on request to the Personnel Department, or your departmental/nurse manager.

   The details set out below are subject to confirmation of previous employment in the National Health Service.

2. **PAYMENT**  The current basic full-time salary scale for your grade is £ . . . . . . . . . . per annum rising by . . . . . . . . . annual increments to £ . . . . . . . per annum. Your starting salary/wage* is at the rate of £ . . . . . . . . p.a./p.w.* (based on a full time rate of £ . . . . . . . . p.a./p.w.* for a . . . . . . . hour week), and will be paid monthly/weekly* in arrears. (The first payment will be made on . . . . . . . . . . . . . . . . . . . . . . . . . . . . . . . . . . . . . . . . . . . . .)

   You will be paid the following allowances:

   £ _____ Per annum/per week* London Weighting

   £ _____ Per annum/per week*

   £ _____ Per annum/per week*

   £ _____ Per annum/per week*

   Bonus payments if/as appropriate* _____

3. **INCREMENTAL DATE**  Your incremental date will be _____

4. **LEAVE**  The leave year runs from _____ to _____

   Your basic entitlement to annual leave with pay is as follows, plus long service entitlement, if appropriate:

   . . . . . . . . . . . . . . days for current leave year

   . . . . . . . . . . . . . . days in the next year

   . . . . . . . . . . . . . . days in subsequent leave years

   Public and . . . . . . . . . . . . . . extra statutory holidays are additional to the above (if you are full-time, or part-time and would normally be required to work them. To be taken as they fall or days off in lieu, dependent on your department.
   *Part-time Nursing Staff*
   Your entitlement is inclusive/exclusive of public and statutory holidays, dependant on option chosen. (Option forms are attached for relevant staff).

5. **TERMINATION OF EMPLOYMENT**  Termination of employment is subject to . . . . . . . . . . . . . . . . . . . . . . . . . . . . . . . . . . . . notice, to be given in writing by either party. Your entitlement to additional periods of notice is contained in the 'Staff Handbook'.

   (For this purpose your employment with (and subsequent to) . . . . . . . . . . . . . . . . . . . . . . . . . . . . . . . . . . . . . . . . . . . which commenced on . . . . . . . . . . . . . . . . . . . . . . . has been counted continuous with this post).

6. **HOURS OF DUTY**  Your basic hours of duty will be . . . . . . . . to be worked over a . . . . . . . . day week/fortnight* inclusive/exclusive of meal breaks.

7. **RESIDENCE**  You will initially be resident/non-resident. If resident, the appropriate charge will be deducted from your pay. (Details of the Whitley accommodation charges may be seen on request at the local administrators office, or the Home Wardens.)

8. **SICK PAY**  Details of your entitlement are contained in the Staff Handbook.

9. **SUPERANNUATION**  Details of the scheme are contained in the Staff Handbook and the N.H.S. Superannuation booklet. Your position is that you are required to join the scheme/on commencement of employment/when you reach 18 years of age/on completion of two years' service/you are already a member of the scheme/membership of the scheme is optional.

   (Further details may be obtained on request from the Salaries and Wages Department. N.B. Staff for whom membership is optional will not be included on the scheme unless Salaries and Wages are requested otherwise.)

10. **DISCIPLINARY POLICY**  The disciplinary rules and appeals procedure which apply to you are contained in the Staff Handbook.

11. **GRIEVANCE**  Any grievance which you may have about your employment should be raised either orally or in writing with your immediate supervisor in the first instance. Further details about the grievance procedure are contained in the Staff Handbook.

**12. LOCATION** There may be occasions when you will be required to perform your duties at other locations within the Health Authority.

**13. UNIFORM** Uniform and protective clothing, where provided, should be worn, as necessary, when on duty.

**14. OTHER DETAILS:**

Signed _____   Name _____

Designation _____   Date _____

On behalf of _____ Health Authority

**Part 2** *(To be completed by the employee)*

Marital status _____  Maiden name (Married woman) _____

Address _____   Tel No. _____

Permanent address _____   Tel No. _____

Date of birth _____   Nat. Ins. No. [ ][ ][ ][ ]

Disabled person?   YES/NO   If Yes give RDP No. _____

Next of kin _____   Relationship _____

Address _____   Tel No. _____

Nationality _____   Passport No. (If not British) _____   Work Permit No. _____

Professional Qualifications _____

Details of all service with Hospitals, Universities, Local Government Authorities or Nationalised undertakings.
If none, write 'NONE'

| POSITION HELD | DATES From | DATES To | NAME AND ADDRESS OF EMPLOYER | FOR OFFICE USE ONLY |
|---|---|---|---|---|
| | | | | |
| | | | | |

I authorise _____ Health Authority to deduct from my remuneration any amount which shall at any time become due from me in respect of meals, board, lodging, laundering of uniform or any other miscellaneous charges.

I appreciate that I may have access to confidential information in my post and that disclosure of this information or any information about patients or former patients is not permitted.

I appreciate the need to accept any necessary medical, diagnostic or preventive measures designed for the protection of particular staff or patients.

I authorise _____ Health Authority to pay my wage/salary* to the credit of:

Account of (Name) _____   Account No. (If known) _____

Name of bank _____   Branch of bank _____

I accept your offer of appointment on the Terms and Conditions referred to in this statement and confirm that I have received a copy of the Staff Handbook.

Signed _____   Mr/Mrs/Miss/Ms*   Date _____

*Delete as appropriate

I have engaged the above-named who commenced employment w.e.f. ...........................................

Signed ..................................... Title .....................................

long it will run. For example, the pupil nurse's contract will run for 98 working weeks, as this is the statutory length of training for enrolment. The student nurse's contract may state some period over the 146 working weeks required for registration, as she may not have received the results of the state final examination at the exact end of this time. The contract will allow for this and carry on to the date the examination results are published.

A newly qualified staff nurse may also be given a fixed-term contract. To ensure a continuing supply of jobs for the newly qualified in the health authority of their training, there can be a certain number of staff nurse posts for which only six- or four-month contracts are given. This is a good way of allowing for rotation of staff so that they can gain experience in a number of areas.

A temporary member of staff may also be given a fixed-term contract if the vacancy is only going to exist for a limited period. However, if another similar vacancy arose during that period, the employee may wish to be put on an open contract. If for some reason the employing authority did not wish to continue this person's employment, it could give rise to difficulties. The use of the fixed-term contract in these circumstances should be approached with caution and with full legal advice.

For most employment in nursing, the open contract is the norm. No time-span is specified.

## An invalid contract

As was seen in Part I, there are certain prerequisites for a contract to be valid.

Failure of the nurse to declare information required by the prospective employer would invalidate the contract. For example, it was pointed out that past convictions must be declared (see page 54). Failure to do so could in certain circumstances invalidate the contract or make the terms within it unenforceable by the person who gave an incomplete or false declaration. Careful medical screening is a common requirement prior to a job being offered. If the nurse failed to declare her past medical history in the belief that it would jeopardise her chances of employment, later discovery by the employer would make the contract void if the history was such that employment would not have been offered.

On the employer's part, failure to specify the conditions of employment as listed above would seriously affect the validity of the contract. In certain spheres, for example a nurse being employed by a private nursing home carrying out abortions, the contract could be made void if the work the nurse was expected to perform was outside the scope of the 1967 Abortion Act.

One area in which one might expect a contract to become invalid but where this is not the case is where an appointment has been made by mistake in excess of the authorised establishment. Also, if the employer makes an error in the details laid out in the contract, once these are discovered, the employer must first terminate the contract and then give the nurse the option of continuing in her employment under the proper regulations.

## Alterations to contracts

Inevitably conditions change during the nurse's employment. Some of these changes are of such a marked nature that they may frustrate the terms of the original contract and a fresh agreement becomes necessary.

For example, learners half-way through their training were faced with a completely different type of assessment for their practical work. As they had originally agreed to the normal Board assessments, it was felt that such an important change should have the learner's written agreement. Therefore each learner was given the option of signing an amendment to her contract agreeing to this change.

A fairly common situation arises when a learner fails her state final examination at the end of the three years. If the school of nursing agrees to allow her to resit it while remaining employed, it may be found that her fixed-term contract has expired if the examination has been sat near the end of training. In these circumstances, an extension to the contract will need to be drawn up and signed by both parties, carrying on employment as a student nurse until the result of the next examination is made known.

Sometimes it is wiser to issue a completely new contract rather than amend a previous one. A nurse who has had a break in employment, even if taking up a similar position, should have a fresh contract, as some conditions of service may have changed, at least marginally.

## Agency nurses

Nurses supplied by an agency to work in a health authority do not have a written contract with that authority. However, although for tax purposes classified as self-employed, the agency nurse is usually working in a short-term post on a fixed commission without final profit sharing. In these circumstances, she can still be regarded as an employee of the health authority. In effect, she has an unwritten contract to provide her services as a nurse and abide by the employing authority's requirements as regards conduct. However, there are no legal obligations regarding notice, holidays, sickness and superannuation, and her status as employee, or otherwise, of the health authority will depend on the precise terms and conditions of the engagement agreement. It is therefore worth noting that the health authority may not accept the same liability for the actions of an agency nurse as it will for its own employee.

## Questions and concluding comments on 4.1

*Question:* On applying for a job as an enrolled nurse, the applicant failed to note on the medical screening form that she had suffered from anorexia nervosa. As it was over two years since she had been ill, she did not consider it relevant and therefore did not mention it, in spite of the form particularly requesting this information. Does this omission invalidate her contract?

*Comments:* If the nurse concerned had a recurrence of this condition, it is possible that the information regarding her previous medical history would come to light. The question of validity of the contract would certainly be considered as a medical screening form will include a declaration regarding the accuracy and honesty of the information given.

*Question:* Due to staff shortage in one particular area a nurse was moved from her own ward for two weeks to provide adequate cover. However, the type of experience was not identical. Did the nurse have any grounds of complaint in relation to breach of contract?

*Comments:* Most contracts will make some statement relating to place of work such as 'There may be occasions when you will be required to perform your duties at other locations within the Health District'. Therefore the nurse would have to adapt to this situation as well as she can. However, if she was moved repeatedly, she would be advised to discuss the situation with her manager and even her union representative, as it could impede her own development and may be damaging to the quality of the service she can give. Her manager should be aware of possible complaints of victimisation if other nurses are not moved as often, while at the same time doing her best to maintain an adequate service.

# 4.2 TRADE UNIONS AND PROFESSIONAL ORGANISATIONS

## Trade unions and nursing

Nursing has traditionally been a female occupation and women are known to be far less unionised than men. However, the importance of unions and professional organisations is becoming recognised by nurses, mainly for the provision of legal insurance.

There are a number of organisations that nurses can join. The Royal College of Nursing and the Royal College of Midwives are professional organisations that have, under the Trade Union Labour Relations Acts (1974) and (1976), also taken on the role of trade unions. Nurses can also become members of COHSE (Confederation of Health Service Employees) and NUPE (National Union of Public Employees), the two main unions involved.

Nursing has no closed-shop policy and it is likely that a large number of nurses still opt out of any union membership. It is difficult to obtain accurate figures of membership as it is known that a number of nurses join both a union and a professional organisation, so one nurse is counted twice. COHSE and NUPE do not always provide separate figures for nurses apart from their other members. The latest approximate figures suggest that the professional organisations have a much higher membership than COHSE and NUPE. Traditionally the unions have tended to recruit well in the psychiatric area where the proportion of male nurses is very much higher than in the general area. Female nurses, part-time nurses and nurse managers appear to be attracted in higher numbers to the professional organisations.

This situation does not lead to great solidarity of nurse workers and in fact there is an element of competition between the different organisations. A certain degree of instability in the field of industrial relations in nursing tends to occur.

### The role of trade unions and professional organisations

There are several reasons for a nurse wishing to belong to a trade union or professional organisation:

- For legal protection and advice on professional matters.
- To play a part in decisions on pay and conditions of service through representatives negotiating with the Whitley Council and other bodies on her behalf.
- For settling grievances according to the Whitley Council rulings (see subsection 4.5, page 83).

As previously mentioned, the first point is the commonest reason for nurses becoming members. By far the largest number of queries dealt with by the relevant legal departments concern injuries received during the course of employment, for example back injuries. The nurse wishes to have advice regarding the possibility of compensation. The unions with a higher membership in the psychiatric areas may have to deal with injuries received as a result of a patient attacking a nurse, and a certain number of cases are referred by the unions' legal advisers to the Criminal Injuries Compensation Board (see page 75).

Other occasions when legal help is given to a nurse concern complaints by a patient or a patient's relatives about the nurse's professional competence.

Members are able to voice their opinions about conditions through their shop steward who will attend staff meetings at a local level. There is a system of representation at regional and national level, including a number of seats for unions and professional organisations on the Nurses and Midwives Whitley Council.

### Appointment of shop stewards
In most trade unions and professional organisations, the central administrative figure of a branch is the secretary, supported by shop stewards.

The number of shop stewards required in an area should be agreed between unions and management (see below) and the work group for which each individual steward is responsible should also be clarified. The conditions for the selection and appointment of shop stewards will be decided by each union and professional organisation, although such factors as limited staffing on certain shifts and in certain areas would influence the selection process. Stewards are elected to office and, once appointed, the union should notify management.

Certain details need to be clarified regarding the powers and duties of the shop stewards and these should be given in writing to the individual concerned.

When a steward ceases to be employed by the authority, it is perhaps stating the obvious to point out that the nurse's appointment as a steward would automatically be terminated. However, in the light of recent events in an area of industry, it does sometimes become a relevant point. Equally the appointment would be terminated if the person's membership of the union lapsed or was terminated.

### Time off for union matters

Much of what is being discussed in this subsection is drawn up by codes of practice rather than by an Act of Parliament. There are in fact three codes of practice concerning the rights of the employee in relation to trade unions. Although these codes are not legally enforceable, they do give the employer and employee guidelines in interpreting the relevant Acts, in this case the Employment Protection (Consolidation) Act (1978) and the Employment Act (1980) in a sensible and workable way.

One area often seen as a problem is when nurses as shop stewards require time off in order to deal with union matters. The law states that 'reasonable' time off should be given. The code suggests that the steward should be allowed paid leave where union activities are directly related to the employment, for example when dealing with grievance or disciplinary issues for a union member and when required to attend union meetings such as joint staff consultative committee meetings. Unpaid leave is more likely for attendance at conferences or for union activities not directly related to employment. The steward will also require time off for training.

It is therefore possible that the extra work load for the nurse steward may be considerable. One way around this is for the union or professional organisation to maintain adequate numbers of stewards so that shop steward commitments do not unduly impose on the nurse's professional commitments.

Further problems commonly arise as a result of the interpretation of the word 'reasonable' regarding time off. Nurse managers are encouraged to allow time off, but in the real situation, perhaps with staff shortage, it is tempting to say, 'Yes, by all means—if you can find someone to cover for you'. However, the code of practice puts the onus very definitely onto nurse management to make time off possible and to be responsible for arranging cover if necessary. Because a nurse is basically concerned about the care of her patients, she will most likely feel the conflict between her professional and union duties most keenly. This situation is particularly acute for the community nurse. The end result can often be the nurse's withdrawal from her shop steward responsibilities leaving a vacuum to be filled, possibly by someone feeling less of a commitment to patient care. It is up to nurse managers to encourage responsible stewardship by making it possible for the nurse to take time off.

As a final perspective on the amount of time off required, it is useful to compare this with the amount of time lost by absenteeism. If sickness particularly could be reduced, the small amount of time taken by the shop steward in comparison would seem relatively less important.

### Industrial action

Industrial action by nurses is a very emotive subject and needs some discussion and clarification.

The term 'industrial action' can cover a wide range of circumstances, including withdrawal of labour, the takeover by nurses and other workers of the running of a hospital, taking part in demonstrations or picketing. Basically, it can be defined as any union action in opposition to management, and therefore 'going on strike' is only one small part of this. As long as a nurse genuinely has the welfare of patients at heart and carefully considers any industrial action in relation to this and as long as she is acting within the law, she should feel free to carry out this action without fear of reprisals.

The code of practice expands on the responsibilities of individuals by stating that some employees have special obligations arising from membership of a profession. A nurse should not be called upon by her union to take action conflicting with the standards of work or conduct laid down for her profession. This would relate to action endangering the health and wellbeing of an individual needing treatment and care or risking public health and safety.

The UKCC has drawn the attention of nurses contemplating industrial action to items (1) and (2) of the UKCC Code of Professional Conduct. Each registered nurse, midwife and health visitor shall:

'Act always in such a way as to promote and safeguard the wellbeing and interests of patients/clients.

Ensure that no action or omission on her part or within her sphere of influence is detrimental to the condition or safety of patients/clients.'

Thus, the nurse taking industrial action must be aware that she could be guilty of professional misconduct unless she ensures that the safety and welfare of her patients is not jeopardised by her actions (see page 44). Strong mitigating circumstances would be when the nurse is motivated to industrial action by concern for the patient.

The law has some specific requirements for industrial action to be taken. Official strike action is only legal if the union or professional body has held a properly run private ballot of its members. Any other strike action is unofficial and if a nurse was absent from duty because she was unofficially on strike, disciplinary action could be taken against her by her employer. The law also lays down some controls on picketing. This must be peaceful and relate to the employee's place of work. Secondary picketing, that is picketing at a place other than the employee's own place of work, is illegal.

### Consultative committees

Recently there has been a development in joint staff consultative committees. Their name is perhaps misleading as these committees are very near to being negotiating committees.

They consist of a staff side and a management side, the staff side consisting of representatives of unions and professional organisations. Nurses are involved in these committees together with representatives of other groups of staff within the health authority. It is important to have a nurse input when decisions are made concerning health authority procedures so that these may also be applicable to nursing structure.

In some authorities, an offshoot of the joint staff consultative committee is the nursing staff consultative committee. Its format is similar but it consists entirely of nurses. Hopefully, it will provide a forum for discussion and resolution of matters relevant to general employment conditions but which require a particular nursing perspective.

# Health and safety at work

Nurses are frequently working in areas where their health and safety are likely to be put at risk. The nurse comes into contact with numerous infections, some of which can adversely affect her whole career, such as AIDS and hepatitis B (serum hepatitis) contracted from infected needles (see page 70). The nurse is also exposed to radiation unless she takes stringent precautions (see subsection 8.2). Fire hazards are always present in a hospital from the use of oxygen, from patients smoking in unauthorised places and from equipment carelessly placed against fire exits. The use of electrical equipment, if faulty, may cause burns to the operator.

The list of hazards is a long one and only a few affecting the nurse's health and safety have been mentioned. The Health and Safety at Work (etc.) Act (1974) sought to initiate a system of inspection and worker involvement that would help to make people's work places safer. The main requirements of the Act (now exempt from Crown Immunity) are as follows:

- The creation of two new bodies, the Health and Safety Commission and Executive, the former being responsible for policy, and the latter for the enforcement of the Act.
- A system of inspectors who have wide powers under the Act to inspect premises and even to prosecute.
- An employer responsibility to ensure the furtherance of health and safety in relation to the work-force, machinery and substances involved. This requires the employer to give appropriate information, instruction and supervision, as well as to carry out maintenance and ensure safe entry and exit points.
- An employee responsibility towards himself and others. The Act requires the employee to co-operate with the employer in health and safety matters and this includes a responsibility to use safety equipment provided, for example hoists. The trade unions involved should appoint safety representatives who can form a safety committee if the employer or the representatives so wish. Very often the shop steward will take on these duties as well as her other ones, increasing her need for extra time off.

The learner nurse is in a peculiar situation here. There is no reason for her not to be appointed as a representative, but the National Boards lay down the amount of time off allowed during training and any excess has to be made up before training is completed.

## Questions and concluding comments on 4.2

*Question:* There has been much discussion on the value of members of certain occupations giving up the 'right to strike' in return for protection of their pay. Is this necessary in nursing in order to protect patients?

*Comments:* The interpretation of the relevant Employment Acts is clarified in several codes of practice. Although these codes are not enforceable in the same way as an Act of Parliament, their guidelines make it clear that no union should expect its members to act in a way contrary to their professional code. In addition, the UKCC disciplinary function could be initiated if a nurse takes industrial action endangering a patient, and the nurse may even face civil liability if harm resulted.

Such controls in theory sound sufficient and in practice rely on the nurse's attitude to her work and her patients. Whether this reliance is well placed can only be answered by each individual concerned.

*Question:* A third-year student nurse is given the possibility of becoming a health and safety representative. What advice should be given to her?

*Comment:* It should be carefully explained that the extra work-time spent on health and safety duties will have to be made up before she can register, in order to abide by her training requirements. It would also be worthwhile to remind her that this commitment may also encroach on her own time and she may be wise to consider this if her state final examinations are looming near.

# 4.3  INJURY, SICKNESS AND PENSIONS

## Injury to nurses

Nurse Matthews was a staff nurse on a female geriatric ward. There were 26 patients in the ward on this particular evening. Staff nurse had one enrolled nurse on duty with her, the third member of staff for this rota being sick.

As the two nurses were helping patients back to bed for the night, the enrolled nurse was called to the opposite end of the ward by a patient. Nurse Matthews continued working on her own. As she attempted to lift a rather heavy hemiplegic patient into bed, she felt a pain in her back. By the next morning, her back was stiff and painful. She reported to her doctor and was placed sick with a back injury.

This was just the start of a long history of back trouble for Nurse Matthews. She had recurrent episodes of sickness due to this injury and eventually gave up nursing. She wondered, by this time, whether she should have sued the hospital in the first place.

The above example is, unfortunately, only too common, but the end result is rarely the award of damages to the injured nurse.

The position of the health authority is as follows. Under the law of torts relating to negligence, the employer would be liable if there was a failure to take reasonable care to provide proper tools and a safe system of working. Proper tools in this instance would be mechanical lifting aids, and it would be unlikely that staff on a geriatric ward would not have access to a hoist, even if it were shared between two adjacent wards.

Perhaps even more relevant in the above example is the provision of a safe system of working. Several factors are pertinent here. First, the employing authority must include proper training in lifting techniques and point out the dangers of not following the taught procedures. All training schools will include teaching in lifting and handling patients during a nurse's training. Sufficient training must be given prior to the learner starting to work full time on the wards, to ensure her safety and that of others, but ongoing training and practice must be incorporated throughout training so that the student becomes increasingly confident in dealing with a number of different situations, with decreasing levels of supervision. For the trained member of staff, the question has been asked as to whether the employer can presume that this nurse has received adequate training in lifting during previous employment and training. The answer here is that it is potentially dangerous for the employer to make such assumptions and it is best to arrange for refresher courses for all newly appointed members of staff. For un-trained members of staff, the hospital must provide training in lifting if this is part of the employee's duties, or face liability for back injuries. Again, most auxiliary nurses receive some induction training to include lifting. In the community, nurses face a special problem in that they are very often working on their own in a patient's home. In these circum-stances, extra training is needed in the special skills required. For each employee, the tuition received must be carefully documented.

Second, a safe system of working also entails the provision of adequate staff to cope with the physical demands of nursing. Nurse Matthews may have complained that the ward was left short staffed due to staff sickness and she was placed in the position of having to lift unaided. However, it is rare that a nurse is left completely on her own in the hospital situation, and this argument would only apply if an emergency arose which required the nurse to lift on her own as she could not wait for assistance. Nurse Matthews was not working on her own and the situaton was such that she could have found some other task until the enrolled nurse was free to assist her. The employing authority may face some liability if the nurses are required to look after an abnormally heavy patient, such that three or four nurses are required merely to lift the patient up the bed, but this is an unusual circumstance. However, there is some evidence that the courts are beginning to look at the weight of patients being lifted by comparison with the recommended maximum load for women in industry which is 55 lb (25 kg). Although this weight could not be directly applied to the health service, health authorities are advised to pay more attention to the whole issue of weights being lifted by their female employees.

LNS 1006

COPY TO

1. Central Administration – white
2. Head of Department – yellow
3. Occupational Health Department – pink

**Health Authority**

TO BE COMPLETED BY CENTRAL ADMINISTRATION
Was it reported under RIDDOR Regulations 1986?
YES NO

**ACCIDENT REPORT FORM FOR ALL EMPLOYEES**

To be used to report all accidents; and dangerous occurrences (whether or not anyone is injured); or any disease contracted; as a result of Health Authority activities. All fatal accidents, major injuries or notifiable dangerous occurrences are to be reported in accordance with the Unit's serious incidents procedure.

USE BLOCK CAPITALS and please tick appropriate boxes.

TO BE COMPLETED IMMEDIATELY

SURNAME: ______ OTHER NAMES: ______ MALE ☐ FEMALE ☐ DOB ______

PLACE OF WORK: ______ DEPT: ______ JOB TITLE: ______

LOCATION OF ACCIDENT: WARD ☐ DEPT ☐ PATIENTS HOME ☐ PRIORITY CARE ☐ OTHER ☐

DESCRIPTION OF ACCIDENT INCLUDING POSSIBLE CAUSE (Specify accurately) ______

PART OF BODY INJURED ______

DATE OF INJURY ______ TIME (24 hr clock) ☐☐☐☐ HRS

NAME TO WHOM REPORTED ______ DESIGNATION ______

DATE REPORTED ______ TIME (24 hr clock) ☐☐☐☐ HRS

NORMAL WORKING HOURS FOR THAT DAY ______ REMAINED ON DUTY

HOURS ACTUALLY WORKED ______ YES ☐ NO ☐

NAME OF WITNESS 1. ______ 2. ______

ADDRESS ______

SIGNATURE OF EMPLOYEE ______ DATE OF SIGNING FORM ______

SIGNATURE OF MANAGER ______ DATE OF SIGNING FORM ______

NAME OF MANAGER (IN BLOCK CAPITALS) ______

| INJURY | YES | NO |
|---|---|---|
| Did it involve needle-stick or other sharp instrument? | | |
| Was it an injury inflicted by a patient or visitor? | | |
| Did it involve tripping or falling on the same level? | | |

Did it involve lifting? YES ☐ NO ☐

IF YES

Type of load ______

Weight of load ______

If PATIENT involved

Name of Patient: ______

Type of manual lift selected: ______

No. of staff involved in lift ______

Was lifting equipment available YES ☐ NO ☐

If lifting equipment used, name of equipment ______

TREATMENT

If yes, given by: OHD ☐ A&E DEPT ☐

First Aider ☐ If so Name: ______

If admitted to hospital - name of hospital ______

Over/Under 24 hours admission YES ☐ NO ☐

Who was informed: ______ Date ______

Follow-up date ______

FEBRUARY 1988

**Figure 4.3** Sample employee accident form.

Nurses who have to be off sick for a lengthy period due to back injury should note that the DHSS give an extra allowance for an injury sustained at work.

### Hepatitis B, AIDS and HIV infection

A completely different injury to which the nurse is exposed is the pricking of a finger on a syringe needle or intravenous infusion cannula. This seemingly slight injury could, in certain circumstances, lead to the nurse contracting hepatitis B (serum hepatitis). She may suffer prolonged illness or have to give up nursing. This disease is now recognised as an industrial injury, and compensation can be granted if evidence of the nurse contracting this disease while on duty is clear. Therefore, any incidents of this nature must be reported clearly and fully, including details of the patient concerned. Most hospitals have appropriate forms for this purpose (e.g. Figure 4.3).

With this type of injury, the employer is very unlikely to be responsible for negligence; rather it is the nurse's own carelessness in handling equipment. As accidents of this nature can occur very easily, however, it seems only fair that she should not be financially penalised.

AIDS and HIV infection are relatively new and represent frightening threats to health in today's society. They are transmitted in ways similar to hepatitis B and therefore nurses are at risk by contact with blood, particularly through needle-stick injuries, but only to a very limited extent through contact with other body fluids dealt with during the course of their work.

Nurses have several responsibilities when caring for these patients—towards themselves, their colleagues and the patients.

It is important that the nurse is well educated about the risks, that the information she has about the disease is up to date and that she is trained in the precautions to be taken to prevent transmission. As long as these precautions are carefully followed the chance of HIV transmission is negligible.

In caring for these patients, nurses must ensure that patients' rights are maintained, for example in the gaining of consent for taking blood samples for testing. Nurses must also be aware that they can never be selective about which patients they nurse (except in relation to abortion—see page 208).

If a nurse is found to be HIV-positive or even to have clinical manifestations of AIDS, it does not necessarily mean a termination of employment. The nurse's clinical work will need to be considered, but in some environments, as long as sound techniques are carried out, the nurse should not be an infection risk.

**Violent patients**

Another possible source of a nurse's injuries is an attack by a violent patient.

Violence can be expressed in several ways. Verbal abuse is relatively common, and the patient may threaten physical violence without then taking it any further. Occasionally, physical violence does occur, with varying results, depending on the strength and anger of the assailant.

For either verbal or physical violence, the underlying cause is often frustration. Illness and admission to hospital are both stressful occurrences, and the resulting anger and fear may be difficult for the patient to cope with. It is important for nurses to be aware of this, and, if possible, to try to reduce this stress and frustration by building up trust and mutual understanding, even in brief encounters. It may even be wiser for a nurse to avoid a possible inflammatory situation with which she would be unable to cope and to go for help. She should not feel a coward!

It is also useful for the nurse to have some idea of which patients are most likely to resort to physical violence. This is difficult to specify as it is an area where impressions are readily offered and hard facts are difficult to come by. However, the following categories identify those most commonly encountered.

The acutely disturbed patient is usually found in the psychiatric area, is often overactive, restless prior to an aggressive outburst and very quick to react to veiled hostility. The nurse should make efforts to appear tolerant and helpful and try to find appropriate outlets for the patient's aggression. The patient with an undisclosed history of aggression presents a problem and highlights the importance of careful observation at all times.

Patients may become violent due to confusion, possibly of a physical origin, for example cerebral anoxia, electrolyte imbalance or the after-effects of anaesthesia. Such patients have difficulty in communicating and therefore become easily frustrated and afraid. This situation will be found most often amongst the elderly, and repeated reassurance and reorientation are necessary.

Some patients are unco-operative when faced with impending treatment or investigations. Fear and lack of understanding often play a part in triggering violence and if possible treatment should be postponed until staff have spent more time in giving information required. Obviously the nurse must ensure that consent to treatment is gained where this is a legal necessity (see pages 102 and 233).

The areas where violence most often occurs are also difficult to

**Figure 4.4** Sample report on violent incident form.

| | Ward/Clinic | Consultant |
|---|---|---|
| **Health Authority**<br>**REPORT ON VIOLENT INCIDENT** | Surname<br>First Name<br>Date of Birth<br>Address | Unit No.<br><br>Sex |

This report is CONFIDENTIAL

1.  It is intended to ensure that violent incidents are notified with the least possible delay.

2.  It is NOT intended to replace the present STATEMENT OF INCIDENT TO PATIENTS OR VISITORS form, which will also be required, and should be routed as at present.

A quarterly summary of violent incidents will be given to the Medical Committee Executive.

Affix documentation label to, or complete manually, data box above. In addition complete status details as follows:

Inpatient.................... Day Patient ................ Out Patient (current)............

Out Patient (old)............ Informal............ Formal ............

The following should be completed for all incidents:

Hospital ............ Ward/Dept............

Room/area............ Consultant............

Date of Incident............ Time of Incident............

Name of Person Making Report ............ Status ............

Was violence threatened?............ Inflicted ............

Was damage/injury done (or threatened) to (yes or tick where appropriate)

Property............ Nurses............ Doctors............

Other staff (specify) ............ Others (specify) ............

Was Statement of Accident (or Incident) completed............ Was weapon used (specify)............

How much warning of violence was given ............

Were drugs a factor in the incident............

Was the patient under the influence of alcohol............

Was there a history of violence............

Was this history known to those involved............

Was help called from: other staff on the ward/dept............

Nursing Officer/Night Sister............ Staff on other wards............

Patients Doctor/Duty Doctor............ Police/Fire Brigade............

Others (specify)............

Was medication given............ With consent ............ Without consent ............

Was physical restraint necessary............ How many staff/helpers were there............

Was the incident satisfactorily resolved............

Was the patient transferred/discharged (specify)............

Date of staff discussion ............

WPD 765

Description of the incident

_____

Signed .................................................... Nursing Officer ...........................................(date)

Signed .................................................... Consultant ...................................................(date)

_____

1.  The completed form should be sent to the Sector or Unit Administrator who will check the details, register receipt and forward it to the Assistant Administrator—Patient Services. The latter should be informed if staff are absent sick subsequent to an individual incident.

2.  The form should **not** be held locally while enquiries are pending. A photocopy may be taken and the original sent on.

specify. Psychiatric wards and accident and emergency departments are usually quoted, but general, geriatric and even paediatric wards (parents included here) are found to have some violent incidents. Probably the main difference between these areas is in the actual physical damage, as a geriatric patient is usually too weak to inflict any injuries, whereas a physically strong psychiatric patient could cause serious damage (see page 176).

Community-based staff are particularly vulnerable because of the nature and location of their work. Violent incidents may occur in clinics, patients' homes or on the street.

Legal repercussions tend to occur only when the nurse actually sustains injuries serious enough to require time off sick or to result in some permanent disability. The nurse has several possibilities open to her in these circumstances.

She could sue the employing authority for negligence in the provision of a safe system of working, but this is not often successful. The duties of the employer are limited to providing reasonable precautions for the safety of nurses where the work is of a dangerous character. As violent incidents are not a frequent occurrence, even in psychiatric units, the employer's explanation of what is 'reasonable' is frequently upheld. However, health authorities are beginning to respond to the demands of staff for greater assistance in avoiding violent incidents. This is tackled in two ways. First, the employer can provide training in preventing and minimising violence, although the employee has a responsibility to follow this advice. For the community nurse this involves ensuring other staff know her whereabouts, visiting in pairs if a family or area poses particular risks, erring on the side of caution by leaving if a situation shows signs of becoming tense, and by being 'streetwise'. In the hospital setting, the nurse facing a violent or potentially violent situation should seek help, appear calm and confident, attempt to ensure the safety of the environment and only use physical restraint if absolutely necessary (see page 126). Secondly, the employer should provide equipment and safe working environments, for example the installation of non-verbal call systems in high-risk areas, the provision of personal alarms to community nurses and the fitting of shatterproof glass in units for the acutely disturbed. Monitoring violent incidents is also useful to the employer in planning prevention. However, none of these measures is legally required (see section 2.2 for wider issues).

The nurse could, in some circumstances, sue the patient. Violence from one person to another is assault and battery, both in criminal law and under the law of tort. The patient is, in fact, liable in civil law, even if lacking the necessary intention to be guilty under criminal law due to his confusion or mental disorder. However, in most instances this is not helpful to the nurse, even if her case is good, as an elderly or mentally disordered patient is unlikely to have the financial resources to pay any compensation awarded.

Thus, the nurse is limited in what she can do to receive damages. However, some financial assistance is possible through several other channels. She may receive an injury allowance at the discretion of the Secretary of State as provided in the NHS Superannuation Regulations. Most usefully, where the injuries sustained are serious, the nurse can apply to the Criminal Injuries Compensation Board. A sum of £2,000 or more can be awarded from this Board, there being no necessity for a charge to have been brought against the patient or for a conviction.

For the above claims, careful and detailed reporting of the incident leading to the nurse's injury is vital. The nurse should report the incident to a senior member of staff and complete the appropriate form as soon as possible (Figure 4.3), as claims are often settled only after some considerable time lapse. For compensation from the Criminal Injuries Compensation Board, the police must also be notified, and the nurse concerned should check that her senior officer has done this, or she should do so herself.

## Sickness and maternity leave

When a nurse is off sick, the employer is responsible for payment of sickness benefit for the first 20 weeks of sickness in any tax year. This is statutory sick pay (SSP). At the end of this time, the responsibility for payment of sickness benefit reverts to the DHSS and the nurse must claim this as the employer will automatically deduct from the gross pay the amount of benefits presumably received by the nurse.

The amount of time for which the nurse off sick receives full pay and then half pay before pay is stopped depends on length of service. Details are set out by the Whitley Council and summarised below.

- During first year of continuous service: full pay one month, half pay one month
- During second year of continuous service: full pay two months, half pay two months
- During third year of continuous service: full pay four months, half pay four months

- During fourth and fifth year of continuous service: full pay five months, half pay five months
- After completing five years of continuous service: full pay six months, half pay six months

Maternity leave, while rather a different situation, also involves absence from work, and there are various regulations concerning this. The legal situation is now fairly clear, and no woman should face dismissal because of pregnancy. Exceptionally, associated illness during the time she should be working may become a factor, as the employer in certain circumstances may dismiss the nurse if she is incapable of doing her job properly.

From April 1987 Statutory Maternity Pay (SMP) is payable to employees who satisfy certain conditions. There are two rates of SMP, higher rate or lower rate depending on length of employment and weekly hours worked. For a summary of SMP see Figure 4.5. The woman must inform her manager in writing of her intentions regarding return to work and the date her absence will begin, as well as providing the maternity certificate with the expected date of confinement. During her pregnancy she is entitled to paid time off in order to receive antenatal care.

The woman has the right to the same work or a similar job on her return. She does not have any right to part-time work, when previously employed on a full-time basis. The woman's manager can write to her at any time later than 49 days after the confinement or the expected date of confinement asking for written confirmation of her intention to return to work. Failure to comply with this request within 14 days will result in loss of the right to return to work.

## Pensions

Nurses are protected financially in sickness, retirement and death by the usual state pensions. They may also receive benefits from the National Health Service superannuation scheme which was initially set up by Act of Parliament when the Health Service was created in 1948. It is now authorised by the Superannuation Act (1972) amended 1988. The Department of Health is responsible for its administration.

Nurses have three choices regarding membership of a pension scheme, the NHS superannuation scheme (plus payment of the lower contracted out National Insurance contributions), a personal pension scheme (plus

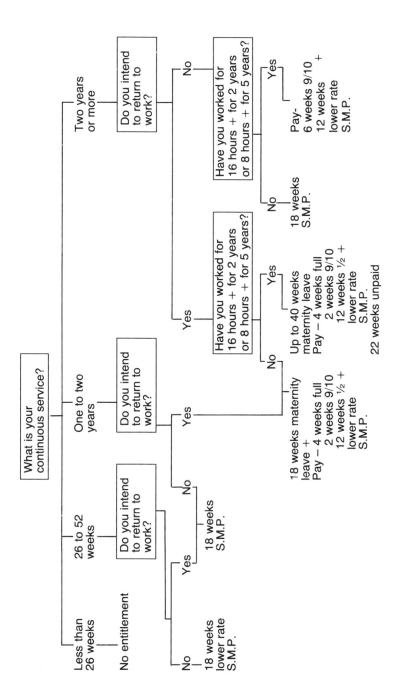

**Figure 4.5** Summary of Statutory Maternity Pay.

lower National Insurance contributions) or the State earnings-related pension scheme with full National Insurance contributions. The NHS superannuation scheme is available to those who work more than half time and are over 16 but under 60 years old. The value of the scheme is that both the nurse and her employer pay contributions so that the employee can qualify for benefits. The contributions are deducted from the nurse's pay on a percentage rate and rank for full income tax relief.

If a nurse leaves the scheme before retirement, she may be able to preserve her pension rights or transfer them to a different occupational pension scheme if this has been approved by the Inland Revenue. Only if the employee has paid less than two years' contributions is it possible to get a refund of contributions and it gives a very poor return as income tax then has to be deducted on the employee's contributions, and the employer's contributions are not included.

The benefits of the scheme are payable on retirement or death of the nurse concerned. For retirement benefits the nurse must have completed at least five years' service, and they consist of a lump sum and a pension, calculated on the nurse's final pay. Retirement benefits will also be given if the nurse has to leave work on the grounds of ill health. A valuable safeguard of the scheme is an annual review of the cost of living index, with pensions and allowances being increased in line with this.

## Questions and concluding comments on 4.3

*Question:* Nurse Brown and student nurse Green were on night duty in a busy surgical ward. About 01.00, Nurse Brown sent Nurse Green off the ward for a meal break of 30 minutes. Shortly afterwards, several patients called out urgently. A heavy ill patient was hanging half out of bed. In a confused state, he had tried to get out of bed. Nurse Brown rushed to his assistance and managed to lift him back to safety. She later found that she had injured her back. Could she sue the hospital?

*Comments:* The hospital is responsible for providing a safe system of working, and there is a possibility that in this case, there is some liability. The nurse had to lift the patient as it was an emergency situation. It is also only reasonable that nurses have some break during the night and this resulted in the ward being left with only one nurse. The question arises as to why a night sister did not come to relieve the ward for half an hour. Did Nurse Brown inform her? If so, Nurse Brown is certainly not responsible for her injury, although the employer may still not be liable. Was the hospital so short staffed that relief was not possible? In this case it would appear that the hospital authority had some liability (see page 68).

*Question:* Nurse Seymour was working in a medical ward with mainly single rooms and a few larger bays. She was called to one of the single rooms by a patient's buzzer. The male patient concerned was abusive to Nurse Seymour and threatened violence. Nurse Seymour had the sense to keep between the door and the patient and managed to edge to the door and get out of the room. If she had been injured, what would have been the legal outcome?

*Comments:* Single rooms do present an extra problem in that it is difficult to call for help if there is no call system installed for nursing staff. If she had been attacked and seriously injured, she would probably have been best advised to claim some compensation from the Criminal Injuries Compensation Board via the police. The hospital could scarcely be held negligent as violence is rare on a medical ward and the hospital need only carry out reasonable precautions. Nurse Seymour could sue the patient, but though the action would most likely be successful, getting the money awarded for damages from a private individual is extremely uncertain (see page 74).

# 4.4   STAFF REPORTS

Nurse Simmonds was staff nurse on the gynaecology ward. She had been qualified for three years and took charge of the ward in sister's absence. One afternoon, the sister, newly on duty, had reason to use the controlled drugs book, and noticed an amendment to one of the morning premedications. This was signed by Nurse Simmonds and a student nurse. As the staff nurse had the afternoon off, the sister asked the student nurse what had happened. In a rather distressed state, the student admitted that the patient had received the wrong dose of a drug, but that she herself had been to the operating theatre and admitted the error to the anaesthetist. The staff nurse's attitude when sister spoke to her the next day was that 'no harm was done'.

From then on, sister observed Staff Nurse Simmonds' work rather more closely. On a number of occasions this was below standard, and she also upset the patients by her offhand manner and by giving inaccurate information. Her work failed to improve in spite of the sister reprimanding her for her errors.

After about a month, the nursing officer suggested that the ward sister should write a report on Nurse Simmonds so that further action could be taken. The sister carefully constructed her report and interviewed Nurse Simmonds to discuss it, prior to the nursing officer taking action.

In the above situation, it was clear that some action was needed to safeguard the patients, and the outcome was the writing of a staff report. Reports may be required on a regular basis or as an isolated event when someone's work is unsatisfactory, as with Nurse Simmonds. In both situations, but particularly the latter, the person doing the reporting frequently fears libel or slander actions under the law of tort. Writing staff reports is not surprisingly found to be stressful, particularly when the person reporting is inexperienced and may worry about the repercussions to patients and other more junior members of staff.

However, as long as certain considerations are kept in mind, writing these reports should not involve the laws of defamation (see page 28). A report can only be defamatory if it is false, and if it is made honestly and without malice, by a person having a duty to make it, then the writer can feel easy that no libel action will be successful. In legal terms, the report is subject to privilege. Similarly, any legal action for negligence in the writing of the report would also fail.

In practice, any nurse manager is likely to find herself in the position of writing a report about a subordinate at some time. The ward sister will be required to report regularly on any learners in her area, and the school of nursing usually provides a specific form for this. It is always wise to use the forms provided, as the wording has been carefully considered particularly to counter any defamatory overtones. Many hospitals are implementing an appraisal system for trained staff and the completion of some form is included as part of the process, usually on an annual basis. Thus the nurse manager, by the very nature of her job, will have a duty regularly to make staff reports.

Her duty will also extend to the making of 'one off' reports when a nurse's work is unsatisfactory. As illustrated by Nurse Simmonds, the duty may be necessary to safeguard the patients. In other areas where patients are not perhaps the central concern, the duty to make a report may hinge on maintaining certain professional standards of behaviour. For example, if a member of staff is repeatedly unpunctual and fails to complete her work, to such an extent that colleagues suffer, her superior would feel it her duty to report on these shortcomings.

In some instances, it would be appropriate for the nurse making the report to consult with others who have also been involved before she completes it. This is not in any way a legal requirement but where there is a risk of legal action when behaviour has been unsatisfactory, it is always wise to gather facts and opinions from other responsible members of staff to rule out personal bias. This may be particularly useful when assessing progress made by a learner when the sister has been on holiday or off sick for some of the time. The person actually constructing the report does, of course, take the ultimate responsibility even if there has been consultation.

The main factor protecting the person reporting from successful legal action is that the report is made honestly and is true. Several factors will aid the individual here. The first is the sensible use of vocabulary, and the second, the keeping of some record of times, dates and incidents when adverse comments have to be made.

Even if the ward sister writing a report on Nurse Simmonds felt that she could quite accurately describe the staff nurse as a danger to her patients and unfeeling and untrustworthy in her dealings with them, it would be unwise legally to use such definite language. The reaction of a court of law to extreme language is that no one can be really that bad all the time, and the standing and integrity of the person reporting may be somewhat undermined. However, it is interesting to note that it is practically unheard of for courts to question a nurse's professional judgement. Below is a list of words and terms that reduce the risk of legal action:

| | |
|---|---|
| usually<br>has on several occasions | } instead of always |
| tends to<br>appears to be | } instead of is |

as far as can be judged
as far as can be ascertained
avoid such strong words as disloyal, dishonest and untrustworthy
    unless definite proof.

Making a note of specific occurrences is also a valuable way of reducing the legal risks. In the example at the beginning of this section, the ward sister would have been well advised to write a brief outline of any incidents and also to make a note of the date and time of each. It is unwise to rely on memory, as even an inaccuracy of date will undermine the validity of the report, however accurate the description of a particular incident. Often the person writing the report would not want to include all these details, but only give the gist of them. However, if the nurse receiving the adverse report threatens to take legal action, the situation can usually be rapidly resolved by quoting actual events.

A further precaution regarding staff reports is the careful control of confidentiality. The report, as mentioned above, is subject to privilege. It should be communicated only to the proper person and unauthorised persons should not have access to it. The proper person is usually the report writer's immediate superior, and on no account should the report be discussed when other members of staff are present. There is no legal requirement for the individual to see any report written about her, but most employers, because of ethical considerations, do specify that the report should be read by its subject, and discussed with her. Of course, there is theoretically an increased risk of legal action in these circumstances, but in practice, the nurse having a report made on her work usually realises that this is for her benefit. Any areas of incompetence are pointed out and she knows in which directions she needs to improve. (See also section 4.5 on disciplinary action.)

A further legal safety factor is the careful signing and dating of the report both by the person writing it and the person on whom it is made, after she has had the opportunity to read and discuss it. She is not signing that she agrees with it! For some reports, there is also space for a senior member of staff to countersign, for example on some appraisal forms where there may be anxiety regarding personal bias.

Finally, it is vital to the maintenance of professional standards that, where necessary, adverse staff reports are made. It is unhelpful both to the individual at fault and to the profession as a whole to be over-generous in making allowances for poor performance. Hopefully, senior staff are helpful and supportive when reports have to be made, and it is certainly important to keep them well informed as disciplinary action may result. It is reassuring to remind oneself that although a nurse may threaten legal action in the emotional upset of receiving an adverse report, she is unlikely to take it further. By reporting honestly and carefully, the risk is minimal.

## Question and concluding comments on 4.4

*Question:* Consider the report below. What are the legal pitfalls in it?

Report on first year student at the end of her ward placing:

| | |
|---|---|
| Application to work: | Has frequently been unpunctual, appears uninterested. |
| Quality of work: | Has been slapdash and unreliable in carrying out instructions competently; is usually observant. |

| Attitude to patients: | Does not always show sympathy and understanding. |
|---|---|
| Attitude to co-workers: | Offhand manner, resents criticism. |
| Professional behaviour: | Usually neat and poised. |
| Overall comments: | This student could not be trusted to carry out competent nursing care. Much improvement required. |

Signed

*Comments:* Although the report follows a prescribed pattern, some of the statements are perhaps too definite, for example 'has been slapdash and unreliable ...', 'could not be trusted ...'. If such statements are true, the actual occasions when unsatisfactory behaviour occurred should be stated. Otherwise, the writer of the report should considerably modify the language used.

# 4.5  DISCIPLINARY ACTION AND APPEALS

## Situations involving disciplinary action

Staff Nurse Beamish, working on night duty, had had a particularly trying night with several emergency admissions and a very confused and noisy patient. She was also worrying about her nine-year-old son who had been feeling unwell when she left for work. At 06.00, she took the second-year student nurse with her to do the drug round. To her horror, she realised, too late, that Mr M had received Mr P's medications. She reported the incident and fortunately the drugs concerned did not cause any untoward reactions.

Three nights later, tired through not sleeping well, Nurse Beamish checked an analgesic drug with the junior nurse. On checking the drug charts in the morning, she found that the patient had received the wrong dose of the drug.

Student Nurse Shannon was due two weeks' annual leave. The day before her holiday was due to start, she failed to turn up for work and the ward sister had to mark her as absent as no message was received.

Enrolled Nurse Turner was due on duty at 08.00 but she did not appear until 08.45. She appeared confused and was walking unsteadily. Her breath smelt of alcohol and she seemed not to hear what was said to her. Without being given any instructions, she started assisting a patient

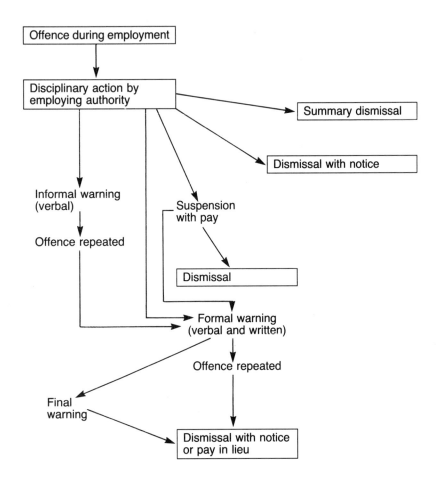

**Figure 4.6** Disciplinary action procedure.

out of bed. As this patient was to remain on bedrest, this action was completely inappropriate and possibly dangerous to the patient.

All the three examples above require some sort of disciplinary action, although the situations vary considerably in severity. It is important for other members of staff and the patients' safety that the action taken is adequate, carefully carried out and gives the nurse concerned appropriate help to improve. Disciplinary action can vary from a system of warnings to suspension or even dismissal.

The legal framework is the Nurses' Rules and the relevant employment legislation, and may sometimes include the law of tort regarding defamation or negligence.

## Disciplinary action by the employing authority

Most disciplinary action is in the hands of the employing authority, although it will become apparent later where other agencies may become involved (Figure 4.6).

The nature of the disciplinary action will depend on the severity of the offence. The main classification is of general or gross misconduct, although where general misconduct becomes habitual, it is sometimes difficult to differentiate between the two. Probably the clearest way of seeing how disciplinary action works in practice is to follow through the examples given at the start of this section.

Student Nurse Shannon's single incident of absence without leave could be an example of fairly minor general misconduct. It is an area where there are clearly grounds for concern and some action is needed, but this should be fairly low key and be aimed at helping the individual rather than being seen as punitive. Nurse Shannon should be seen by her immediate superior, in this case her tutor, and an informal warning given. This informal warning is purely verbal and not documented in the employee's personal file, although it would be wise for the person giving the warning to make a note of it in some other place with details of any particular action that is to follow. For example, in the case of absence in relation to annual leave, it may be as well to monitor any further episodes of absence as to when they occur.

This type of disciplinary action is appropriate to many situations and may be all that is necessary. For example, unpunctuality, inaccurate wearing of uniform and isolated incidents of rudeness, may be dealt with in this way on the first occasion of their occurring. The individual concerned should be warned of the more serious consequences arising if the offence is repeated, but there is no need to incorporate any appeals machinery into the proceedings at this stage. As many informal warnings may be given to the individual as the manager decides are appropriate and useful, but obviously more formal procedures must be considered if informal warnings fail to bring about the required improvement.

Sometimes misconduct is so serious that, although not gross misconduct, it is clearly detrimental to the effective running of the health service. Nurse Beamish's drug errors would be in this category. In this and similarly serious situations, it may be necessary to instigate formal disciplinary procedures without having an initial informal warning. The procedure for a formal warning would be as follows. Nurse Beamish would be seen by the appropriate nurse manager, probably the senior nursing officer, and given notice of formal disciplinary action. This notice is important because the employee must be informed of her right to call in her trade union representative or a friend. A time that is mutually acceptable would be arranged for a meeting, but this should be within seven days of the alleged offence. At that meeting, the senior nursing officer, with another manager acting as a witness, makes the allegations to Nurse Beamish, gives her a chance to reply, summarises the meeting and verbally issues a formal warning that any recurrence within a stated period of time (for example, six months) could result in further disciplinary action (for example, dismissal). If new facts come to light during the meeting, the senior nursing officer should stop the meeting in order to explore and clarify these facts further. Before the meeting with Nurse Beamish is terminated, she should be told of her rights of appeal and, where relevant, that she will receive a written warning.

The formal written warning follows a formal verbal warning where the facts are perfectly clear, and no further investigations have to take place. Nurse Beamish would certainly receive one, probably on the following lines:

By hand to Staff Nurse A. Beamish

Date

Dear Mrs Beamish

FORMAL WARNING

Further to our discussion on . . . regarding the two drug errors you made on . . . and . . ., I have to inform you that a formal warning has been issued that if you make any further drug errors within the next twelve months, further disciplinary action will be necessary.

Please do not hesitate to ask for any help that you feel you require in this area.

Yours sincerely

. . . ,

It is important to ascertain that the employee has actually received the formal written warning and it would be very foolish to trust the post. Usually, the manager will personally hand the written warning to the employee, with a copy which the nurse should sign as evidence of having received the warning. This copy will be retained in the nurse's personal file. The nurse has a stated number of working days from receipt of the written warning in which to appeal if she so wishes. (For appeals procedure, see page 89.)

After the formal warning, it is wise for the manager to check regularly on the nurse's performance and to give appropriate help if the nurse will accept it. The employee's performance should be finally checked at the termination of the time set for improvement.

Most formal situations arise after informal warnings have failed to bring about improvement. For example, if Nurse Shannon in the second example had had further periods of absence without leave, the senior nurse would be well advised to turn to formal action. Once this decision is made, the above sequence of events should follow.

In the third example at the beginning of this section, the situation is very much more serious. This would be an example of gross misconduct where the nurse's behaviour is markedly irresponsible. Other examples are theft of hospital or patients' property, fraud, insubordination, unauthorised sleeping on duty, physical violence or menacing behaviour on the premises, and wilful negligence or unauthorised absence seriously endangering health and safety.

Where there are no further enquiries to be made, dismissal may quickly follow instances of gross misconduct, but only authorised senior officers can act in this way. Each health authority will specify who has the power to dismiss, for example, the district nursing officer. Dismissal may be with notice, with pay in lieu of notice or summary dismissal (no notice or pay).

Much more commonly, suspension with pay will follow gross misconduct. This will give time for a full investigation of the facts where there is a possibility of some doubt, and for senior managers to consult prior to taking action. Again, the health authority will specify who may suspend, for example nursing officer level and above, although in practice suspension will need to be instigated in an emergency by the most senior person present at the time. For example, Nurse Turner will be suspended prior to further investigations into her behaviour, and the proper person in the circumstances would most likely be the nursing officer who could easily be bleeped and quickly be available. (See page 84 for summary, and section 4.6 re dismissal.)

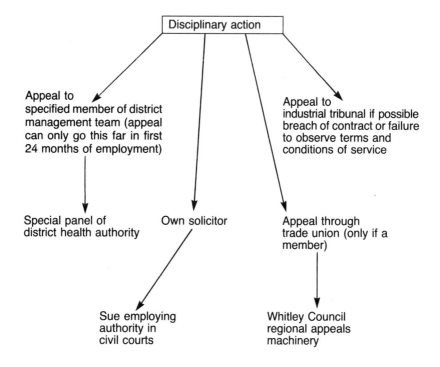

**Figure 4.7** The appeals procedure.

Since the implementation of the new (Griffiths) management struc-ture, there is a query as to who is the nurse's manager in the disciplinary setting. Although health districts have implemented the proposals in many different ways, matters requiring disciplinary action of nurses are nearly always concerned with professional behaviour. It is therefore usual for nurse managers to deal with disciplinary action rather than, for example, non-nursing unit managers.

# Methods of appeal

When formal disciplinary action has been taken against a nurse, she has several possible methods of appeal (Figure 4.7).

For example, a nurse receiving a formal warning regarding her repeated unpunctuality on duty may feel that she has been unfairly treated. Perhaps she feels that the facts of the case have not been considered carefully enough although she had explained that the unreliability of public transport from her home to the hospital made occasional unpunctuality unavoidable. In the first instance, she may use the appeals procedure within the health district. The appeal must be lodged within a stated number of working days (21 days is suggested by Whitley) from the date of receipt of the formal warning letter and made to the appropriate member of the district management team, usually the district nursing officer for a nurse employee. Normally, an appeal hearing should be held within the following 21 days, with sufficient notice (for example 14 days) being given to the nurse and her manager so that appropriate statements can be prepared.

After this district appeal hearing, if the employee is still unsatisfied, she may appeal to members of the district health authority who will establish an appeal committee following certain lines of procedure. A final appeal from the aggrieved employee can be made to the regional health authority but only at this authority's discretion depending on the merits of the case. The employee herself has no statutory right of appeal at this level. Also, an employee has limited rights of appeal within the first 24 months of employment. Within this time, she can only appeal to the district management team and is unable to take the matter any further.

Less commonly, the nurse can employ her own solicitor to seek redress in the civil courts. Third, she may apply to the indistrial courts where there has been a breach of contract or a failure to observe the terms and conditions of service binding under the NHS regulations (see page 13).

Finally, if she is a member of a trade union or professional organis-ation, she may apply through them to the Whitley Council Regional Appeals machinery. The national Whitley structure consists of nine functional councils, including one for nurse and midwives, and these deal with conditions of service. Each council has a management and a staff side. In addition, there is a system of regional appeals committees and the procedure of referring disputes is carefully laid down in Section 22 of the General Council Handbook. However, it must be emphasised that the nurse alone cannot appeal to this committee.

# Sickness

A not infrequent situation is when a nurse is so often unavailable to work due to sickness that the manager feels that some action is necessary. Genuine sickness is not a disciplinary matter but may still lead to dismissal in certain conditions (see page 94).

Two examples may clarify the problems encountered.

Student Nurse Peterson had been in training for two years. On checking her sickness record, it was found that she had had 53 days of sickness, all as short periods of between one and three days' duration, totalling 22 occasions.

Staff Nurse Bingley had injured her back and been off sick for one month as a result. She returned to work for two days, then went off sick again and was still off sick six months later with no improvement to her back problem.

In the first example it would be advisable for the student's tutor to discuss the situation with the student to see what her problems are and if any measures can be taken to improve her health. Regular monitoring of the student's sickness record would follow.

If the repeated short-term sickness continued, referral to the Occupational Health Department for advice and possible medical examination may be advisable. This would certainly be appropriate in the second example. Following comments from the occupational health doctor the nurse manager must decide on what action to take. With Nurse Peterson this may involve a follow-up formal interview in one month's time. Often such supervision and discussion can help the nurse to help herself. In Nurse Bingley's case, the only conclusion may be dismissal (see page 93).

## Question and concluding comments on 4.5

*Question:* Sister Howard is in charge of a surgical ward of 28 beds and she has been in the post for two years. It first became apparent that all was not well when a senior student nurse went to her tutor in a very distressed state because of the 'cruelty' that she felt she had witnessed by the ward sister towards the patients, and the lack of supervision of the junior nurses working on the ward. The student was advised that the tutor was unable to intervene as she had not actually witnessed the occurrences described, but it was strongly suggested that the student make an appointment to see the nursing officer and senior nursing officer concerned. As a result of this, other nurses on the ward and some patients were interviewed, and it appeared likely that there was some truth in the initial allegations of mental cruelty and inadequate supervision, leading to poor nursing standards being practised. What action could the nurse managers take in these circumstances?

*Comments:* This is an area where disciplinary action is difficult to take, as attitudes rather than clear-cut actions are concerned. However, it is obviously a matter of great concern warranting some kind of action.

Before any kind of warning can be given, it is imperative to collect proof of the allegations made and here the nurse manager will run into a problem. First, patients are very unwilling to make statements, written or verbal, that criticise the nursing staff. Many are afraid of victimisation, and, on the whole, are prepared to suffer in the short term knowing that their stay in hospital is not likely to be prolonged. Once away from the situation, they are only too happy to forget about it. Secondly, nurses dislike making adverse statements against senior nursing staff, particularly a ward sister. Loyalty can cloud the issue and nurses fear victimisation, particularly learners who feel that an adverse ward report will seriously affect their training and careers.

However, assuming that some statements can be collected of specific instances, the nurse manager can then proceed. Because of the serious nature of the allegations, it is likely that formal action would be instigated. This would probably take some time to finalise, with adjournments for clarification of the issues involved and the collection of further statements. The load on nurses giving evidence is great and they require continuing support to stand firm rather than withdraw.

If the end result is a formal written warning that the ward sister's behaviour must improve over, for example, the following three months, she has the option to appeal to the district management team and, if necessary, to the district health authority. She could also seek redress in the civil courts on the grounds of defamation, and with her union representative, to the Whitley Appeals Committee.

Because of the serious professional nature of the complaint, the district management team would have a duty to inform the National Board. The investigating committee would probably refer the matter to the professional conduct committee for the necessary proof of professional misconduct and appropriate judgement (see page 44).

# 4.6 TERMINATION, DISMISSAL AND REFERENCES

## Termination of contract

To the Director of Nurse Education

Dear

It is with regret that I have decided not to continue with my nurse training. I have for some time felt unhappy with nursing and feel that I would be better suited to some other career.

I therefore give one month's notice of leaving.

Yours sincerely

V M Bloggs

To Miss J Wiseman

1 April 19 . . .

Dear Nurse Wiseman

I have to bring to your notice that you have had a further 13 days' absence on eight occasions. With reference to the letter of warning that you received on 10 March 19 . . . , it clearly stated therein that you must not exceed 10 days or seven separate periods of absence in the next two months.

I therefore have to terminate your employment in this hospital, giving you one month's notice or salary in lieu.

Yours sincerely

Senior Nurse

For numerous reasons, employees decide that they wish to leave their present employment. Legally this is perfectly acceptable as long as the proper notice is given as laid down in the employee's contract (see page 55).

The usual period of notice required is one month and as seen in the first letter above, this has been adhered to. For some senior members of the nursing staff, the periods of notice required may be longer, and for certain specialist posts, perhaps associated with research, the contract may contain a clause that the individual is expected to stay in the job for, for example, two years. However, if personal circumstances arose that made this impossible, it would be doubtful if the employing authority could keep the individual to this part of the contract. The same would apply for other fixed-term contracts.

In some cases, it may be humanitarian to waive the month's notice from an employee. For example, if a nurse's mother living at the other side of the country was taken seriously ill, it would be only sensible to allow the nurse to leave immediately in order to help care for her. In other cases, it may be merely realistic not to pursue the working of a month's notice by someone who has decided to leave. For example, if Nurse Bloggs, in the first example, failed to complete the full month's notice, it would be legally possible to sue her for breaking her contract. As well as being scarcely worthwhile financially, it would be rather pointless to try to make a person unhappy in her job continue working and giving less than her best to the patients.

If the employee is working to a fixed contract, it is not strictly necessary to write a letter giving notice of leaving when the contract expires. For example, the student nurse's contract will expire at the end of three years approximately (depending on examination results and sickness). There is no question of her continuing to work in this capacity even though the employing authority will probably like to be informed of any intention to work as a staff nurse in the district. Therefore there is no legal requirement to give notice.

## Dismissal

Dismissal has already been mentioned in conjunction with disciplinary action (see page 84) but it is worthwhile summarising some of the different reasons for dismissal in this section.

Four main reasons for dismissal are described: misconduct, incapability, constructive dismissal and redundancy, although the reader should be aware that there is sometimes overlap between them.

Dismissal due to misconduct will usually follow the disciplinary system of warnings, or, if gross misconduct, it will lead directly to dismissal. In any of these cases, the employer must have acted reasonably in treating the incident as a ground for dismissal. For example, if a nurse was found eating food that had been provided for patients in the ward kitchen, the employing authority may dismiss her for theft, but this would probably not be reasonable if it was the first occasion that this had occurred. A warning would be more appropriate.

The nurse may be found to be incapable of doing the job on a number of grounds that may lead to dismissal. In the last section it was pointed out how drug errors could lead to disciplinary action. If the nurse continued to make errors of this kind, it would be reasonable to assume that she was incapable of performing safely as a nurse, giving grounds for dismissal.

Another special area involves examinations. Recently, a student nurse appealed against dismissal following failure of the National Board practical assessment. In another example, a student failed the hospital intermediate examination in spite of resitting it and appealed against the resulting dismissal. In both these examples, the learners had very little grounds for appeal as it is inherent in nurse training that the learner must reach certain standards and pass examinations in order to proceed with training. These conditions should be made quite clear in the nurse's contract. Although wise to give the learner some kind of warning before she takes an examination for the final attempt, it is difficult to see how dismissal in these circumstances could be unfair as long as the examinations are properly conducted (see page 43).

Repeated absence from work due to ill health is another problem area that can lead to dismissal, because the nurse is incapable of performing the job for which she has been employed. It is unusual and only occasionally fair to dismiss a nurse while on sick leave unless this has been protracted and the job cannot be filled by another while the ill person remains employed. However, it may be possible to offer the employee some other job within her capabilities rather than outright dismissal, but the needs of the individual have to be balanced against the needs of the employer and the law recognises this. The commonest problem is repeated short-term sickness and it is important that normal sickness procedures are followed, with full medical back-up, before dismissal can reasonably occur. An example of this situation was given on page 90.

The nurse has the right to maternity leave and cannot be dismissed merely because she is pregnant. However, if the pregnancy renders the nurse incapable of performing her duties, the employing authority cannot be found liable for unfair dismissal. For example, a nurse suffered a threatened miscarriage at about three months, having previously lost a baby. The doctor told her that she must take things easy and not be on her feet all day or be involved in heavy work. The hospital authority quite fairly dismissed her as she would have been unable to perform her duties as a nurse because of the pregnancy.

A different kind of situation is as follows. Sister Wright was ward sister of a medical ward for a number of years. Due to ward closures and reorganisation within the hospital, her ward was incorporated with another, and she was told that she must take a night sister's post as this was all that was available. Although she did go on night duty for a few months, she found it adversely affected her health and she resigned. She later claimed that she had been constructively dismissed.

Constructive dismissal is a difficult and fairly new concept under the law. There is no formal act of dismissal by the employing authority but because of the employer's behaviour, the employee feels compelled to hand in her notice. This behaviour must be seen to be directed towards the nurse concerned, although it may not consciously be intended to drive her out. It should normally involve some breach of contract, but could also arise where the employee has suffered marked loss of responsibility. In the above example, it is not clear whether the ward sister could claim constructive dismissal for the reasons mentioned as it would depend on the actual local conditions. Grounds involving constructive dismissal are often difficult to clarify, and each complaint must consequently be assessed (if necessary by an employment tribunal) on its own merits and particular circumstances.

# Redundancy

Redundancies never featured very much in nurse employment. However, the picture has changed with health service financial cuts leading to ward and hospital closures. Most health authorities try, in these circumstances, to redeploy staff to areas where there are shortages, but if this is impossible, redundancies can occur.

This particular type of dismissal must follow certain procedures as laid down by the law. Prior to any action, the employing authority must supply the unions and professional organisations with information of the reasons for redundancy, numbers involved and what grades, and the proposed methods of selection and dismissal. Individuals are usually selected on the basis of those last employed are the first to lose their jobs, and if agreed procedures are not followed, the nurse could possibly claim that she had been unfairly dismissed. It is useful to note that the employee has a right to a trial period of four weeks in another job if available without commitment on either side or loss of redundancy pay.

## The role of the industrial tribunal

As discussed in section 4.5 the nurse has several possible methods of appeal following disciplinary action, and these also apply to cases of dismissal if this is thought to be unfair.

The industrial tribunal acts as the outside agency in a dispute between employer and employee who has a minimum of two years' continuous service, although to the employee the situation may appear rather formal and authoritarian. However, it does seem useful to have this extra means of appeal, particularly as the onus of proof for the dismissal being fair rests on the employer.

If the tribunal finds that the employee has been unfairly dismissed, two courses of action are possible. Re-employment or reinstatement can be recommended but the tribunal has no power of enforcement here. However, the tribunal can enforce payment of compensation, either in line with redundancy pay or as a larger compensatory award (see page 13).

## References from employers

On leaving employment, a nurse may require a reference or testimonial. Two examples are given below:

> Miss A M Wills has been employed as a staff nurse on a medical ward for the last six months.
>
> She is a pleasant person with a cheerful manner. She works conscientiously in all she undertakes and sets a good example to others. She is particularly able in building good relationships with her patients and shows great sensitivity and understanding. She can be very supportive to her colleagues. She is able to take responsibility for organising the ward but still tends to be lacking in confidence.

Overall, she is a likeable and caring nurse who should do well with further management experience.

Miss R N Ball was a student nurse in training for 15 months from . . . to . . . She was a sensitive and caring person who was well liked by others. However, on the wards she appeared to have difficulty in concentrating and carrying out instructions accurately although she related well to her patients. It gradually became apparent that she was not really happy in the job or suited to nursing. This had a serious effect on her health as the amount of absence from duty was high. Eventually she realised that nursing was not the career for her. She always gave the appearance of working conscientiously in any area in which she felt real commitment, and I feel sure that in another job, her warm and gentle nature will be an asset.

As with writing reports on nurses, a reference or testimonial is the subject of qualified privilege. Even in a non-privileged situation, if it is true, it cannot be defamatory. However, as pointed out in section 4.4, it is wise for the person writing the reference to keep the language moderate. If a nurse has not performed well, it is also important to remember that if a favourable reference is given and results in harm to another individual in the nurse's next employment, the giver of that reference would have some legal liability.

## Question and concluding comments on 4.6

*Question:* Nurse Rose had been working for four months since qualifying as a state registered nurse. She failed to come on duty one afternoon and instead telephoned the nursing officer to say that she was leaving. The nursing officer insisted that Nurse Rose came to the hospital to see her. How could the nursing officer handle this situation? What should be done regarding references?

*Comments:* Nurse Rose is legally breaking her contract by not giving a month's notice. The nursing officer could try to insist that she works for the month but, if the nurse is determined to leave, it is more practical to accept the nurse's resignation from that day (see page 93).

It is tempting in these circumstances to threaten not to supply a reference to the next potential employer but it is not a really fair action, even though legal, to withhold a reference, particularly if the nurse's work has been satisfactory prior to the final resignation. There is no reason, though, for the facts involving the termination of employment not to be made known.

# REFERENCES

Department of Health and Social Security (1987). Conference on Violence to Staff, DHSS, London.

Department of Health and Social Security (1988). *NHS Superannuation Scheme*, Leaflet SDC, DHSS, London.

General Nursing Council (1973). Health and Safety at Work Act (1973), 76/5, 78/27, GNC, London.

General Nursing Council (1975). Sex Discrimination Act (1975), Equal Opportunities Commission, 78/31, GNC, London.

Rea, K. (1987). Negligence, *Nursing* (Oxford), Vol. 3 (14), p. 533.

Rowden, R. (1987). Employment law and nurses, *Nursing* (Oxford), Vol. 3 (14), p. 530.

United Kingdom Central Council (1984). *Code of Professional Conduct*, 2nd edn, UKCC, London.

United Kingdom Central Council (1985). *Griffiths Review: Implementation and Implications*, Admin 85/03, UKCC, London.

United Kingdom Central Council (1986). Implementation of the General Management Function within the NHS, Implications for Nursing and Midwifery Education, 1986/8/APS, UKCC, London.

United Kingdom Central Council (1986). *Project 2000*, UKCC, London.

United Kingdom Central Council (1988). *AIDS and HIV Infection*, PC/88/03, UKCC, London.

United Kingdom Central Council (1988). *Register, Issue Two*, UKCC, London.

Whincup, M. (1982). *Legal Aspects of Medical and Nursing Service*, 3rd edn, Ravenswood, Beckenham, Kent.

# Part III
# Law and the Practice of Nursing

# 5. The Nurse and the Patient

The nurse's main concern is her patient. Occasionally this concern breaks down for one reason or another, and the nurse becomes involved under the law of tort, quite apart from any ethical considerations. The major part of this law concerns negligence, though the nurse may also be involved with the law on trespass. The law of succession and criminal law may also have a place.

Acts:
  Fatal Accidents Act (1846–1977)
  Offences against the Person Act (1861)
  Children and Young Persons Act (1933)
  Public Health Act (1936), amended 1961, 1968
  Young Person's Act (Scotland) (1937)
  Occupiers Liability Act (1957)
  Mental Health Act (N. Ireland) (1961)
  Children and Young Persons Act (N. Ireland) (1968)
  Family Law Reform Act (1969)
  NHS Act (1977)
  NHS (Scotland) Act (1978)
  Supply of Goods and Services Act (1982)
  Mental Health Act (1983)
  Mental Health (Scotland) Amendment Act (1983)
  Public Health (Control of Diseases) Act (1984)
  Hospital Complaints Procedure Act (1985)

Cases:
   Chatterton *v*. Gerson (1981)
   Whitehouse *v*. Jordan (1981)
   Sidaway *v*. Bethlem Royal (1982) and (1985)
   Hills *v*. Potter and others (1983)
   Wilsher *v*. Essex AHA (1986)

# 5.1   THE PATIENT'S CONSENT TO TREATMENT

Mr Howard was admitted to hospital for an operation to repair his inguinal hernia, which was to take place the following day. He was seen by the doctor shortly after admission and the operation was explained to him. Mr Howard then signed the consent form. Later in the day, a nurse checked that Mr Howard had fully understood the implications of the operation.

Finally, before the patient received his premedication the next morning, the staff nurse checked that Mr Howard had in fact signed the consent form.

Mrs Bones was to have a mastectomy. She signed the consent form after having the operation explained to her. On the day of operation, student nurse Long went to Mrs Bones to prepare her for theatre, the premedication being due in 15 minutes. She was rather surprised to find Mrs Bones very agitated and saying that she had decided she couldn't go through with it. Nurse Long fetched the staff nurse in charge of the ward who explained the reasons for the operation and tried to alleviate Mrs Bones' fears. However, the patient remained adamant in her refusal to go for the operation. The staff nurse therefore informed the doctor, and the premedication and operation were postponed.

Giving consent is vital to enable doctors, nurses and other staff to carry out the care required by a patient. If a patient does not give consent for treatment performed, the member of staff concerned and the health authority could be liable for assault and battery, and find themselves being sued in court for damages (see page 27).

Both examples above involved the patient giving written consent, but consent may be expressed in other ways or merely be implied by circumstances.

The patient, except in rare situations, enters hospital voluntarily, and it is fair to imply from this that he is willing to undergo various investigations and treatments. Similarly, the patient who allows the district nurse into his home shows a willingness for the nurse to minister to his needs. For example, the nurse performing a dressing on a patient's leg ulcers does not need to make any further efforts to obtain the patient's consent. The patient may also imply consent by his actions. The nurse approaching the patient with an injection will assume the patient consents when she sees him roll over in readiness.

Consent can also be given verbally. The doctor who is about to perform an internal examination on a female patient will ask her if she is willing for this to be done. The student nurse who has to write a patient care study as part of her training will tell the patient she has selected about this project and ask if he minds if she writes about him. Consent can, of course, be refused orally, and in the example of Mrs Bones above, the staff nurse quite rightly accepted this verbal refusal as superseding the written consent previously gained.

The health authority requires written consent in a number of instances to make legally sure that the patient has agreed to any investigations or treatments involving a marked risk. For example, any operation or investigation under a general anaesthetic would require written consent. Health authorities use a standard form for this purpose and details of the specific operation or procedure must be included (Figure 5.1). A broadly worded consent allowing the medical staff to proceed to any treatment considered necessary would have very little value. However, it is usual to include a proviso that the doctor can proceed to any treatment considered necessary, arising from the procedure to which the patient has given consent. This further treatment would have to be seen as really necessary. It would be insufficient for a female patient, for example, to consent to a breast biopsy and further necessary treatment, without it being made clear in writing that this might involve a mastectomy.

This particular legal area mainly involves the medical staff who have the responsibility of explaining the procedure to the patient and gaining his consent. However, it is important for the nurse to understand the underlying principles of consent.

First, the patient must be given sufficient information to enable him to decide whether to undergo the procedure or not. There have been a number of legal cases in this country which show clearly that the doctor must inform the patient in broad terms as to the nature of the procedure and about those risks that are reasonably probable and serious in their consequences. Remote risks do not need to be revealed. The amount of information given by the doctor will depend on a number of factors, namely:

**Figure 5.1** Sample consent form.

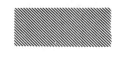

<u>FOR NOTES ON THE COMPLETION OF THIS FORM, SEE OVERLEAF</u>

HEALTH AUTHORITY

Any deletions, insertions or amendments to the form are to be made before the explanation is given and the form submitted for signature.

FORM I. OPERATIONS AND PROCEDURES UNDER ANAESTHESIA

CONSENT BY PATIENT/PARENT/GUARDIAN*

............................................................................................................................ Hospital

I ...................................................................................of .................................................

.........................................................................................................................

hereby consent to *undergo ...................................................................
                    the submission of my   *child to undergo
                                     ward ...................................................................

the procedure or operation of................................................................................
the nature and purpose of which have been explained to me.

I also consent to such further or alternative operative measures as may be found necessary during the course of the operation and to the administration of a general, local or other anaesthetics for any of these purposes. (see note overleaf)

I understand that no assurance has been given to me that the operation will be performed by any particular practitioner.

Date................................................. (Signed).........................................................
                                                  * (Patient/Parent/Guardian)

I confirm that I have explained to the patient the nature and purpose of this *procedure/operation to the *patient/parent/guardian.

Date................................................. (Signed).........................................................
                                                  (Medical Practitioner)

*Delete as applicable

FORM I

NOTES FOR HOSPITAL STAFF ON THE COMPLETION OF THIS FORM

The patient must sign this form before any operation or treatment under any form of anaesthetic is performed.

Before any operation or treatment under anaesthetic is carried out on a child, one of the parents must sign this form (except in emergency). A child is a patient who has not reached his or her sixteenth birthday.

'Treatment under anaesthetic' includes the intended use of drugs such as Ketamine.

Please make sure this form is completed fully and with care.

The name of the Hospital                                   should be entered at the head of the form.

Specify the nature of the operation or treatment as precisely as possible.

In the event of a course of treatment or procedures being decided upon following an operation the parents consent would be needed a second time for the course of treatment. This form suitably modified can be used but no attempt must be made to combine both consents i.e. a consent given for an operation would not extend to a later course of treatment.

The nature and purpose of the operation or treatment should be explained to the patient in simple language by a medical practitioner, who should sign his name at the foot of the form. A person who is not a medical practitioner is not competent to do this.

Maternity Patients   It is not necessary to obtain the patient's written consent to any of the operative or manipulative procedures normally associated with childbirth. This includes induction.

- The patient's capacity to understand and reach a decision; this may be restricted by his medical condition, intelligence or education. However, there are some doctors who will make a particular effort to explain to and educate their patients regarding their condition and treatment, and the nurse can play an important role in reinforcing this information.

- The extent to which the patient wishes to be informed; the more the patient asks, the more the doctor should tell him. Again the nurse can play a part in supporting the patient, either by respecting his wishes for a limited amount of information, or in assisting him in phrasing questions and by clarifying medical terminology. The patient may have felt too much in awe of the medical establishment to question the doctor at the appropriate time, and, if the nurse feels satisfied that she can clarify some of these points for the patient, then she is free to do so, but if the patient clearly wants more information regarding treatment or surgery than the nurse is competent to give, then she must refer these queries back to the doctor. The gaining of the patient's consent is, after all, his responsibility. The nurse must always remember that there is a possibility of her being sued by the patient for giving wrong information.

- The importance of the procedure; generally the less essential the procedure is to the health of the patient, the greater the obligation to give detailed information. Similarly, the greater the risks, the greater the obligation to disclose sufficient information. However, the decision as to how much information to give in any specific case still rests with the doctor.

- The likely effect of information on the patient. If the doctor is concerned that detailed information could have a direct detrimental effect on the patient's health, he may limit the amount of information given. Potentially the nurse may be of assistance here in sharing her assessment of the patient with the medical staff.

  It is interesting to note that although giving inadequate information could invalidate the consent given and lead to the patient suing for assault, another possible legal outcome is a legal action against the doctor and health authority for negligence of the doctor in failing to disclose relevant information.

A second important principle is the right of the patient to change his mind. It is the nurse who is going to be with the patient from the time he has given his consent to the actual procedure taking place. Thus, if the patient has any reservations, or even decides to change his mind, she will have to know how to deal with the situation. As was clear from the example of Mrs Bones, the nurse in charge of the ward has a duty to inform the doctor of any change of mind, and also if the patient expresses any reservations about proceeding or has any further queries that the nurse is not competent to answer. In any of these instances, a written note should be made by the nurse in the patient's records of what transpired in case of later legal queries.

## Accident and emergency cases

Accident and emergency cases may involve not only the nurse in hospital but also the nurse called out to any accident where there is some delay in getting a seriously injured casualty to hospital.

In an emergency situation where the patient is unconscious or semiconscious, the medical team can assume the patient's consent to any treatment urgently needed to save life, to relieve great pain or for the ultimate wellbeing of the patient, for example to save a limb. The consent of the patient's nearest relative is not necessary as there is no general rule that gives this person authority to consent on behalf of another adult. However, the agreement of the nearest relative is often considered desirable; it may reduce the risk of later legal action. A failure to gain this agreement will never prevent the doctor or nurse from carrying out life-saving procedures if there is no medical reason against them.

The commonest reason for a relative refusing 'consent' is on religious grounds, saying that the patient would not have wished for certain treatment. The law takes the view that it is impossible to know what a person's choice would be if faced with possible death. It is therefore acceptable for attempts to help the patient to be made as long as these are urgently required, and the opinions of the nearest relative can be put aside. The legal defence of necessity can be employed here.

## Gynaecological operations and sterilisations

Nurses and doctors may be uncertain about consent for certain gynae-cological operations on married women, for example, an operation involving loss of the woman's ability to have children. If such an operation is to be carried out, the doctor will explain, and gain the written consent of the patient and may well decide to include the patient's husband. This inclusion of the husband in such discussion may ensure his support and co-operation but is merely a courtesy and has no legal necessity. A husband has no right of veto and if he were asked for and refused his consent, the nurse should be aware that this is no reason for not continuing with the operation and that it was quite unnecessary to raise the question of consent with him at all. The only possible exception to this may be in certain cultures where the ability of the wife to bear children may have serious repercussions on the marriage. This usually only applies to visitors from other countries, in which case the gaining of the husband's consent may become legally more important.

Consent for a therapeutic abortion can also be given by the woman alone, although hopefully the husband's agreement can be procured. In one documented case, a husband went through the courts in an attempt to stop his wife from having an abortion. He failed in this attempt on the grounds that no husband can legally interfere with his wife's decisions regarding her own body. However, the couple were estranged at the time. (For further aspects of abortion see Part IV, page 208.)

Similarly, procedures resulting in the sterilisation of either husband or wife can proceed with the consent of the partner concerned without recourse to the other partner. Again the doctor may prefer to gain the agreement of the other partner but there is no legal necessity even though the procedure is unlikely to be medically necessary or urgent. (See Part IV, page 211.)

## Children

As a general rule, for children under a certain age the consent of a parent, guardian or judge (if the child is a ward of court) is required. In England, Wales and Northern Ireland this age is 16 years and parents cannot veto any treatment that the 16- or 17-year-old is willing to accept, in spite of the fact that the legal age of majority is 18 years old. In Scotland, parental consent is needed for girls under 12 years and boys under 14 years. From that age up to 16 years, consent of the parent or guardian should be sought if possible but consent of the patient can be sufficient. Over the age of 16 years, the consent of the patient usually suffices. However, although the 16- or 17-year-old can give consent in his own right, the doctor breaking his young patient's confidence to the parent or guardian appears to incur no legal consequences (see Part IV, page 238).

The nurse is likely to meet several problems regarding children's consent. In an emergency, there may be inadequate time to contact the parents. The child's consent can be considered sufficient as long as the circumstances are urgent.

Another situation that the paediatric nurse, and sometimes the community nurse, may encounter is the refusal of parents or guardians to give consent. However, the nurse should bear in mind that the law, although giving parents custody and control over their children, also lays down that they have a duty to provide the necessary medical aid. Thus, if care is required to save life or to prevent some marked disability that would seriously affect the child's life, the parents' refusal can be overridden. The best-known example of this situation is of parents who are Jehovah's Witnesses refusing a life-saving blood transfusion. If the situation is such that the nurse has to act alone, the urgency of the case would be her defence. However, the general rule is that the medical officer in charge takes responsibility for giving consent where the matter is urgent.

Where the situation is less urgent, a care and protection order is obtained (in Scotland, a place of safety order which, on review by a children's panel, is amended to a supervision order). The health authority usually has an arrangement whereby such orders can be obtained rapidly to make sure that legal problems are minimised. A further legal action would be to prosecute the parents for neglect.

Having stated the possible outcome of parents' refusal, it should be emphasised that these steps are only taken as a last resort. It is usually the mother who spends more time with her child and therefore the doctor or nurse finds it easier to get the mother's consent. However, if the mother refuses consent, the reason is often that the father has instructed her to this effect and, in spite of reasoning, she feels that she must abide by her husband's instructions. Staff should therefore try to see the father as it is often possible to persuade him of the seriousness of the situation.

Caution is required if the parents are separated or divorced. It may be difficult to ascertain who has legal custody of the child, or frequently custody may be joint. In these situations, the consent of one parent is sufficient and the onus is not on the nurse or doctor to find out custody arrangements.

One further difficulty with which the nurse may become involved is if a child under 16 years asks for advice regarding contraception. Two legal problems exist here. The first is that sexual intercourse with a girl under 16 years is a criminal offence and a girl considering this action should be aware of this. The second is that, as already explained, parental consent is needed for any treatment prescribed for a patient under 16 years old. The DHSS suggest that the doctor should always seek to persuade the child to involve parents or guardian but the final decision for prescribing must be left to the doctor's professional judgement. Legal advice from the BMA states that if a doctor acted in good faith to protect a girl against the potentially harmful effects of intercourse, the doctor would not be acting illegally.

Finally, children may be involved in experimental procedures or research that do not directly benefit the child. In these cases the parents or guardian must consent if the child is under 18 years (this also applies for blood or organ donation). The parents must act reasonably in safeguarding the child's interests and only consent if the likelihood of risk or discomfort is negligible (see Part IV, page 222).

## Questions and concluding comments on 5.1

*Question:* Mrs Summers was being examined by the doctor prior to an angiogram scheduled for the following day when he was called away by an emergency. As he left the ward, he asked the staff nurse to get the patient to sign the consent form. Staff nurse took the consent form to the patient and showed her where to sign it. Mrs Summers, before signing, asked if there were any risks, to which the staff nurse answered, 'No'.

Shortly after the angiogram, the patient haemorrhaged and suffered some brain damage. As a result, she had some residual paralysis. Has Mrs Summers any grounds for suing the hospital?

*Comments:* The consent the patient gave was gained by misrepresentation. There is known risk of haemorrhage during or after an angiogram and the nurse completely failed to explain this. Therefore, the written consent was invalid and the nurse herself could be sued as well as the hospital authority (see page 106).

*Question:* A baby with hydrocephalus was seen at intervals by the health visitor. The baby was well cared for by his parents, but in spite of persuasion from the health visitor and general practitioner, the parents steadfastly refused to allow his admission to hospital for treatment. The health visitor became increasingly worried as signs of impaired development started to appear. She informed the doctor of her observations. What action would be possible in these circumstances?

*Comments:* The failure of the parents to allow their child to be treated would ultimately have severe effects on the child. It may be possible for a care and protection order to be made as parents are by law required to provide any necessary medical care for their child. However, the severity of the child's condition must be clearly demonstrated for such a drastic step to be taken (see page 109).

## 5.2  INJURIES TO PATIENTS

### Injuries and negligence

Nurse Yates, a third-year student nurse, was in charge of a medical ward on night duty. She had a first-year pupil nurse on duty with her. At 01.00, they were caring for a very ill patient when they heard a crash from the other side of the ward. Mr Peacock, an elderly patient suffering from bronchopneumonia, had fallen out of bed. He was found to have cut his head in the fall.

In retrospect, Nurse Yates was very upset by the accident. She blamed herself for not noting the patient's restlessness and was also concerned that she had been negligent in her care of the patient.

This common example of an accident to a patient illustrates the fear that nurses have of being found guilty of negligence. As shown in Part I (page 27) there are three requirements for negligence which are: that a duty of care is owed; that there has been a breach of this duty; and that there is resulting damage. Clearly, the nurses owed a duty of care to Mr Peacock, and there was resulting damage from the fall. The crux of the matter is whether there has been a breach of that duty. The law looks at whether the care given is reasonable for the people concerned in those particular circumstances. In the above example, the fact that it was night duty with fewer staff on duty and other ill patients to care for would make it somewhat unreasonable to expect Nurse Yates to be watching Mr Peacock all night. On the other hand, if the patient had been restless for some time and had already tried to get out of bed, the nurses should have been more aware of this particular danger and perhaps have put cotsides upon the bed to safeguard the patient. Thus, each incident is going to have to be considered in the light of all the circumstances in order to assess if there has been any negligence. On the whole, if nurses have taken as much care as could be expected of a reasonable nurse, there is no negligence. No one is expected to be perfect.

The sister or staff nurse in charge of an area can be guilty of negligence in delegation. For example, a learner in her first week on her first ward is sent by the ward sister to give a patient an injection and is not observed in carrying this out. If damage resulted, the sister could be sued for negligence as well as the nurse who actually gave the injection. In this example, the sister could not reasonably expect such a new nurse to perform adequately without supervision.

Most training areas now use individualised nursing care (the nursing process) in organising their work. This may create additional legal problems in delegation to learner nurses. The practice of giving the learner four or five patients to care for is legally unsound unless it is clearly specified that an identified trained nurse is supervising this learner and therefore taking ultimate responsibility.

It is important that the learner or inexperienced nurse herself understand that legally she is responsible for care given if this has been wrongly delegated to her. The patient must be protected from mistakes due to lack of experience and should be able to expect safe care from any nurse. Therefore, the nurse has a responsibility to ask for help and guidance.

Negligence in delegation would also be proved if a member of staff was asked to carry out certain procedures which she had previously performed unsafely. This may put the senior nurse in rather a predicament when there is shortage of staff, but she must still show that she has acted reasonably in the delegation of duties (see Figure 5.2). In other cases of delegation to a qualified member of staff, that qualified nurse to a much larger extent stands alone in any later legal action. Thus if some duty is delegated that she feels she is unable to perform, it is her clear professional and legal responsibility not to undertake this duty until she feels she is competent to do so. (See Part II, page 38, and Part IV, page 230.)

In addition, the health authority suffers vicarious liability (see page 26). However, even if the patient decides to sue only the health authority and not the nurse concerned, the authority may, and sometimes does, make the nurse pay the compensation awarded by the court. This is especially likely to happen where the conduct of the nurse is very much at fault. For example, the nurse had to pay the compensation in a case where she cleaned a child's mouth with cotton wool on scissors causing irreparable palate damage. Inadequate staffing levels has already been mentioned as not being an excuse for unsafe delegation. Recently this issue has become increasingly important to the hospital nurse with a higher proportion of very dependent patients occupying hospital beds.

Similarly, the early discharge of patients after treatment and the decision not to admit a number of ill patients to hospital at all has increased the workload on community nurses. In either case, if a patient comes to harm because of inadequate staffing, those nurses may well be

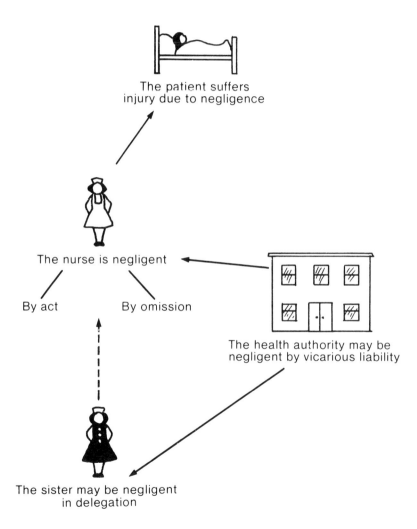

**Figure 5.2**   Negligence and the nurse.

negligent, along with the health authority. It is extremely important that if a nurse is seriously concerned about the safety of her patients due to there being insufficient nurses, that she reports this to her manager who in turn has a responsibility, if there is no immediate remedy, to ensure that the unit general manager or district management team are aware of this danger. If a patient did then suffer harm, it is unlikely that the nurse will be held negligent, only the health authority. Preventative action by the authority may well be to stop further admission to that particular ward or to refuse to take further patients onto the community nurse's case list. Once responsibility for a patient has been accepted, proper care must be taken.

### Accidents in the ward

The possibilities of accidents in the ward are enormous and are the commonest reason for the health authority being sued.

A patient falling over or out of bed is an accident that occurs frequently. The fact that patients are mobilised early after operations and even frail elderly patients are encouraged to get up are reasons for the frequency of these accidents. Also the use of cotsides is now less frequent as they tend to confuse further the already confused patient. Legally it would be safer to encourage patients to stay in bed and put cotsides up on all of them! Medically, of course, such action would be disastrous.

Nurses will therefore continue to face the possibility of these accidents. Many patients can be reminded when the nurse helps them out of bed that they are going to be unsteady on their feet and must ask for the nurse's help before walking to the toilet. Often patients in adjoining beds will call the nurse if the unsteady patient starts walking on his own. However, other patients should be discouraged from actually helping to support a fellow patient, as they both could fall, with extra damage resulting. The nurse has to use her common sense in encouraging patient mobility and in preventing accidents. A good call system or the location of unsteady or restless patients near the nurses' station where it is easier to observe them will be reasonable steps to take in the prevention of falls. The nurse will need to take special care of unconscious, partly paralysed or delirious patients, and the medical staff need to consider the types of sedation used at night, particularly with the elderly, to prevent subsequent confusion.

Scalds and burns are accidents that can result in quite severe damage. A nurse would without fail be negligent if she allowed a patient to enter a bath with excessively hot water. It is not only nurses who should always run some cold water into the bath first, but the nurse is the person who is legally expected to use this safeguard against scalding. In one accident, a nurse had run a bath for a patient and a second nurse placed the patient in the bath. The water was much too hot and the patient received severe scalds. Both nurses were negligent, as the second nurse should have had the sense to check the water temperature.

Patients can receive burns from dropping lighted cigarettes on their clothing. If a seemingly capable patient does this, the nurse cannot be expected to observe all her patients smoking, particularly as this is usually only allowed in a day room. However, if a blind person wishes to smoke, the nurse would be well advised to stay with the patient and ensure that she is the one who has actually to fetch his cigarettes and lighter from his locker. Drinks prepared for patients can also be spilt and cause scalds. If a patient is unsteady, the person giving out the drinks must add extra milk or allow the drink to cool slightly before giving it to the patient. Often it is not the nurse who is giving out drinks and thus she must ensure that other staff or patients realise the importance of these precautions, demonstrating a further extension of care in delegation.

The nurse should also be observant of the overall environment of the ward. A glass urinal that has been dropped and broken will be a hazard for patients walking along the ward, particularly as a number of patients don't wear slippers. Dirty linen, dropped clothing or water spilt on the floor would also provide a dangerous environment. It would not be adequate for the nurse to say that she had not dropped these items or spilt any fluids. Regardless of who was careless in the first place, the nurse has a duty of care to provide a safe environment. Very often, as in the examples given, she can do something about them immediately and could be negligent if she ignored the risks. On other occasions, perhaps where a structural defect provides a danger, she must report it. (See page 63 for further details.)

Most hospitals have a system for reporting accidents (Figure 5.3). A written report must be made as soon as possible after the incident as memories are fallible, staff mobile and the time long before civil actions come to court (see page 26). In writing an accident report, the nurse must ensure that information is factual, accurate and in sufficient detail. The date and time of the accident, which members of staff were on duty and who actually witnessed the accident are all important, as well as which patient was concerned, what actually happened and what damage resulted (completed by the doctor). Any nurses who actually witnessed the accident should write their own accounts in their own words. It is

**Figure 5.3** Sample statement of incident to patients or visitors form.

| | Ward/Clinic | Consultant |
|---|---|---|
| **Health Authority** | Surname<br>First Name<br>Date of Birth<br>Address | Unit No.<br><br>Sex |
| STATEMENT OF INCIDENT TO<br>PATIENTS OR VISITORS | | |

This report is CONFIDENTIAL

It is required for the use of the Service's Solicitors only in order to enable them to advise the District and act on its behalf in any proceedings that result from this incident.

| | |
|---|---|
| PART I<br>(below) | is to be completed in duplicate immediately the incident has occurred.<br>The bottom copy is to be sent as soon as possible to the Nursing Administrative Offices. |
| PART II<br>(overleaf) | The top copy should be kept until Part II is completed by the Medical Officer, then sent as soon as possible to<br>the Nursing Administrative Offices. |

PART I    If patient, affix documentation label to, or complete manually, data box above. All details must be completed.
          If visitor complete biographical details as follows:

Name ...................................................................................    Date of Birth/Age ........................................................

Address ...................................................................................................................................................................

The following should be completed for all incidents:

Clinic/Hospital ...........................................................    Ward/Dept. ...............................................................

Date of Admission ......................................................    Consultant ................................................................

Diagnosis ..................................................................................................................................................................

Date of Incident ........................................................    Time of Incident .........................................................

Persons Involved ......................................................................................................................................................

Account of Incident ...................................................................................................................................................

...................................................................................................................................................................................

...................................................................................................................................................................................

...................................................................................................................................................................................

...................................................................................................................................................................................

...................................................................................................................................................................................

...................................................................................................................................................................................

Names of Witnesses (not directly involved) ...............................................................................................................

...................................................................................................................................................................................

...................................................................................................................................................................................

Addresses of Witnesses ...........................................................................................................................................

...................................................................................................................................................................................

...................................................................................................................................................................................

To which member of staff reported ...........................................................................................................................

Name of Medical Officer informed .............................................................................................................................

Relatives informed: If yes, name/if not, reason ........................................................................................................

...................................................................................................................................................................................

Signature of member of staff in charge at time of incident

                                        ...............................................................................................

PART II

Name of relative informed ....................................................................................................................................................................

Date and Time ..........................................................................................................................................................................................

Medical Officer's Report ........................................................................................................................................................................

........................................................................................................................................................................................................................

........................................................................................................................................................................................................................

........................................................................................................................................................................................................................

........................................................................................................................................................................................................................

Date X-rayed (if not necessary please state) ....................................................................................................................................

X-ray Report .............................................................................................................................................................................................

........................................................................................................................................................................................................................

........................................................................................................................................................................................................................

........................................................................................................................................................................................................................

........................................................................................................................................................................................................................

Signature of Medical Officer ..............................................................

Date ...............................................................

1. Date form received in Nursing Administrative Offices ................................................. ...............................................

   Comments ............................................................................................................................................................................................

   ........................................................................................................................................................................................................................

   ........................................................................................................................................................................................................................

   ........................................................................................................................................................................................................................

   ........................................................................................................................................................................................................................

2. Date form received in Sector/Unit Administrative Offices ....................................................................................................

   Comments ............................................................................................................................................................................................

   ........................................................................................................................................................................................................................

   ........................................................................................................................................................................................................................

   ........................................................................................................................................................................................................................

   ........................................................................................................................................................................................................................

3. Date form received in Clinical Superintendent's Office ............................................................................................................

   Comments ............................................................................................................................................................................................

   ........................................................................................................................................................................................................................

   ........................................................................................................................................................................................................................

   ........................................................................................................................................................................................................................

   ........................................................................................................................................................................................................................

4. Date form received in District Administrative Offices ..............................................................................................................

   Comments ............................................................................................................................................................................................

   ........................................................................................................................................................................................................................

   ........................................................................................................................................................................................................................

   ........................................................................................................................................................................................................................

   ........................................................................................................................................................................................................................

surprising how different details are noticed by several witnesses of one event. The existence of any hazards in the ward should be noted, for example any trailing wires, and whether there are warning notices of these hazards, such as the NO SMOKING notices put up when oxygen is in use. The more detailed the account of the accident, the easier the job of the hospital solicitor in cases of legal action. It may even be unnecessary for the nurse to give evidence in court if her statement is full enough, but of course this will be at the discretion of the legal personnel concerned. In all events, the nurse would be wise, as well as informing the doctor, to call on her senior nurse, for example the nursing officer, for advice in completing the appropriate accident form. (See page 124 for further details on reporting.)

### Accidents in the community

By the nature of her work, the community nurse is not with her patients over the whole 24 hours, neither does she have the same responsibility for the provision of a safe environment, as the patient is obviously responsible for his own home. However, some areas of possible negligence are common to all nurses such as scalds when bathing patients. In addition, the district nurse will have to take particular care to prevent falls in lifting or mobilising patients as she is usually working on her own. For example, she must take extra care in positioning a patient before lifting him out of bed. She will also be exposed to other types of accidents by the fact that she is usually dealing with a family rather than just a patient. Thus, if a nurse takes drugs, needles or syringes into a patient's house or leaves them accessible in an unlocked car, she could be negligent if children took these and harm resulted.

The health visitor could be negligent in quite a different way. All nurses can be negligent in what they tell patients, but the health visitor is in a key position for advising families on health matters. If she gives faulty information on which an individual acts and damage results, she could be sued for negligent mis-statement.

### Accidents in the operating theatre

Accidents in the operating theatre are a particular hazard due to the stressful nature of the work. They most commonly involve swabs and instruments being left inside patients, but the use of faulty electrical equipment resulting in burns to the patient, or carelessness in the use of anaesthetic equipment with subsequent brain damage are also possibilities. As on the wards, the environment itself can provide hazards if equipment or fluids are dropped on the floor and theatre personnel slip on them. Damage to the patient could result if the patient is being handled at the time or the accident leads to the patient being jogged.

However, the main involvement of the theatre nurses regarding negligence is if swabs or instruments are left in the patient. Nurses must check the swabs and instruments laid out before the operation, the scrub nurse will count how many are in use as the operation progresses, and another nurse will have the responsibility of counting the swabs and instruments before the surgeon closes the operation wound.

Accidents tend to occur in this sequence of events when there is an undue emphasis on speed, usually due to the patient being critically ill either at the start of the operation or becoming so during the operation, or where there is excessive pressure due to long operating lists. Inexperienced nurses or nurses with insufficient authority to question the surgeon where there is any doubt are additional problems. The circulation of nurses around several theatres makes further difficulties. All personnel should also be aware of any swabs or instruments being removed from the theatre with a specimen.

The Medical Defence Union jointly with the Royal College of Nursing have issued a pamphlet on *Safeguards against failure to remove swabs and instruments from patients*. Where the nurse is concerned, the recommendations emphasise the importance of careful counting and the fact that the surgeon must allow sufficient time for checks to be made. If there is any doubt, the nurse concerned should inform the senior nurse immediately. Overall, the scrub nurse should be the one who controls the number of swabs, packs and instruments on the table at every stage of the operation. Finally, every hospital should have a set procedure for the care of swabs and instruments which is set out in writing and which is given to all nurses working in the operating theatres.

### Wrong operations

Operations carried out on the wrong patient or on the wrong side of the body, limb or digit will result in the health district being sued for negligence. Unfortunately, the nurse may be involved although the main responsibility rests with the doctor.

It is a strict necessity for nursing staff in both the ward and the operating theatre to check the identity of the patient being collected. The only really safe way of carrying this out is for each patient being admitted to hospital to have an identity bracelet fixed around his wrist. If the nurse in charge of the ward fails to check the patient's hospital number on his wrist band with that on the operating theatre slip, she would be guilty of negligence if the wrong patient was received in the theatre and subsequently had the wrong operation. Similarly, if the patient has no identity band to check, she will also be negligent. It happens fairly frequently that an unconscious patient remains unlabelled or a band is cut off during some procedure, but the nurse has a clear duty to ensure that all patients are properly labelled.

The nurse may also become involved in operations on the wrong part of a patient's body. This type of error is usually due to negligence on the doctor's part but the nurse may become involved, for example in the following situation. The doctor is examining the patient prior to operation the following day. He gets called to an emergency before marking the patient's body and asks the nurse to do this for him. The nurse looks at the patient's notes and thinks that the doctor has written amputation of the right leg, although he has abbreviated the word right. However, it was actually the left leg. The wrong operation is performed as a result of the faulty marking and the nurse is involved in a case of negligence. She would have been much wiser not to have agreed to do the marking.

The ward nurse must also ensure that the correct notes accompany the patient to the operating theatre as in a rush the mistake may not be noticed and the wrong operation performed.

The Medical Defence Union and the Royal College of Nursing have also published a pamphlet to give guidance on preventing wrong operations.

### Wrong treatments

The nurse can be negligent either in carrying out wrong treatments or in failing to perform required care.

Drug errors occur with worrying frequency in hospital. Common errors involve giving drugs to the wrong patient, the wrong dose of a drug being given or the drug being given by the wrong route. Most hospitals have strict rules for double-checking drugs by two nurses and for identifying patients, usually by checking the identity band. If no harm results to the patient, strictly speaking there is no negligence, but the nurse is likely to face disciplinary action (see page 83). In this case, the health authority has additional responsibility in providing the nurse concerned with support and help to prevent further mistakes and the nurse's manager should appreciate the duality of her role here. Nurses should constantly be aware of when such errors are likely to occur, for example when they are nearing the end of a long night shift, or when they have been called away in the middle of a drug round to deal with an emergency. Extra diligence in checking is then required.

The nurse may be involved in negligence in conjunction with the doctor if she has given a prescribed drug that she should have realised would harm the patient. If the doctor has prescribed a drug to which the patient is allergic, the nurse if she has this information, would be negligent to administer it. Similarly, if the doctor has written up the dose of a drug that appears to be abnormal, the nurse has a duty to question this, and, if really dubious, to refuse to give the drug. Errors do occur in drug dosages in the paediatric and geriatric areas. A nurse would be negligent if she gave 0.625 mg of digoxin to an elderly patient, where the normal dose is 0.0625 mg and the drug is a common one that the nurse should know.

Errors can occur with intravenous fluids and blood in a similar manner. In addition, extra vigilance is required in case of 'tissuing', i.e. intravenous fluid being pumped into the subcutaneous tissues. Harm may well result to the patient; two cases occurred in very young children where the subcutaneous dextrosaline caused swelling and blistering. The nurse would only become negligent in such a case if she failed to monitor properly the infusion site, by unbandaging and observing it at regular intervals.

The nurse may be sued by a patient who developed pressure sores which markedly delayed his recovery. There is the possibility of negligence here if the nurses had failed to alter the patient's position frequently. This type of situation does emphasise the importance of careful assessment of the patient on admission to hospital or when the community nurse first visits, as there is always the possibility that the patient was already developing sores prior to passing into the nurses' care. Careful reporting of nursing care is also vital (see page 124).

### Failure of supervision

A 17-year-old patient, known to be a suicide risk, climbed out of the ward's ground-floor window, walked along a grass path, climbed some steps on to a roof and threw himself to the ground. He was seriously injured, becoming paraplegic. The district health authority was held to be negligent.

This example demonstrates an area of negligence where nurses can fail to supervise their patients adequately. Patients who are a suicide risk need extra attention to prevent them from making further attempts. Any patients who are incapable of properly caring for themselves must rely on nurses to safeguard their wellbeing, for example unconscious patients and children. Nurses will observe how children's wards have doors that automatically shut and handles positioned well above the

**Figure 5.4** Sample of nursing process documentation.

| | | |
|---|---|---|
| NAME<br><br>ADDRESS<br><br>TEL. NO.<br>DATE OF BIRTH<br>RELIGION<br>MARITAL STATUS<br>HOSPITAL NO. | PROPERTY RETAINED IN HOSPITAL<br><br>Spectacles     Yes/No<br>Dentures     Yes/No<br>Hearing Aid     Yes/No<br>Prosthesis (specify)  Yes/No<br>Valuables     Yes/No<br>Day Clothes     Yes/No<br>Drugs     Yes/No | DISCHARGE<br><br>Date of Discharge/Transfer/Death<br>Discharged/Transferred to<br>Relatives informed Yes/No<br>Transport needed Yes/No — ordered<br>Escort needed Yes/No — arranged |
| TYPE OF ADMISSION<br>Formal — Informal — Urgent — Routine<br>DATE OF ADMISSION | COMMUNITY STAFF<br><br>G.P<br>ADDRESS | O.P.D. Appointment Yes/No<br>Date<br>O.P.D. Transport needed Yes/No — ordered |
| NEXT OF KIN     RELATIONSHIP<br>NAME<br>ADDRESS<br><br>TEL. NO. | TEL. NO.<br>Other<br>NAME | Day Patient attendance Yes/No<br>Transport needed Yes/No — ordered<br><br>Doctor's Letter sent Yes/No<br>T.T.O's required Yes/No |
| CONTACT IN EMERGENCY<br>NAME<br>ADDRESS | ADDRESS<br><br>TEL. NO. | Written     Dispensed<br>Home Help required Yes/No<br>Home Meals service required Yes/No<br>Community Nurse contacted Yes/No<br>Nurses Letter sent Yes/No |
| ARE NEXT OF KIN AWARE OF ADMISSION<br>Yes/No<br>Comments | HOSPITAL PERSONNEL e.g. Social Worker | DIAGNOSIS ON DISCHARGE |
| RELEVANT MEDICAL HISTORY | | |
| PROVISIONAL DIAGNOSIS/REASON FOR ADMISSION | | WPA 660 |

(i)

| | | |
|---|---|---|
| ASSESSMENT ON ADMISSION<br>OBSERVATIONS<br>T.   P.   R.   B/P<br>Height     Weight<br>Urinalysis | BODILY FUNCTIONS<br>Sight  Good — Poor — Wears spectacles Yes/No<br>Any problems | OCCUPATION |
| GENERAL APPEARANCE<br>Size — Normal — Thin — Emaciated — Obese<br>Mood — Anxious — Miserable — Composed —<br>     Euphoric<br>Remarks | Hearing  Good — Poor — Wears aid  Yes/No<br>Any problems<br>Appetite  Good — Poor<br>Special dietary requirements | HOME SITUATION |
| SKIN CONDITION<br>Broken areas    Yes/No<br>Bruises    Yes/No<br>Rashes    Yes/No<br>Oedema    Yes/No<br>Remarks | Elimination<br>Micturition — Normal — Frequency —<br>     Incontinence — Retention<br>Any problems | DEPENDENTS<br><br>OTHER RELEVANT SOCIAL ASPECTS |
| Condition of Mouth<br><br>MOBILITY — is help required with<br>Walking    Yes/No<br>Bathing    Yes/No<br>Dressing    Yes/No<br>Feeding    Yes/No<br>Other Activities | Defaecation — Regular — Diarrhoea — Constipation<br>Regular use of aperients — Yes/No<br>Any problems<br><br>Menstruation — Regular    Yes/No<br>Blood loss — Normal — Heavy — Light<br>Pain    Yes/No<br>Any problems | History taken by<br>     from<br>Date |
| PAIN    Present  Yes/No<br>Location<br>Analgesic taken (if any)<br>ALLERGIES | Sleep — Normal Pattern<br>Sedation taken<br>What else helps | |

(ii)

INFORMATION SHEET

Please note: 1) any information given to the patient or his relatives concerning treatment, care or after care and
2) any relevant information given to or by the patient

| Date | | Signature |
|------|---|-----------|
| | | |
| | | |
| | | |

(iii)

## NURSING CARE PLAN

| Date | No. | Problem | Patient Goal | Nursing Plan | Signature | Date to be reviewed |
|------|-----|---------|--------------|--------------|-----------|---------------------|
| | | | | | | |
| | | | | | | |
| | | | | | | |

(iv)

WNU 566

## EVALUATION/NURSING PROGRESS NOTES

| Date | No. | | Signature |
|------|-----|---|-----------|
| | | | |
| | | | |
| | | | |
| | | | |
| | | | |
| | | | |
| | | | |
| | | | |
| | | | |
| | | | |
| | | | |
| | | | |
| | | | |
| | | | |
| | | | |
| | | | |
| | | | |
| | | | |
| | | | |
| | | | |
| | | | |
| | | | |
| | | | |
| | | | |
| | | | |
| | | | |
| | | | |
| | | | |
| | | | |
| | | | |
| | | | |
| | | | |
| | | | |
| | | | |

NAME:                    CONSULTANT:                    HOUSE OFFICER:                    HOSPITAL UNIT No.

(v)

height of small children. If a nurse left one of these doors propped open, she would be negligent if one of her small patients fell downstairs. Similarly, extra care to prevent scalding or any other accident is needed where children are concerned.

The nurse may also be negligent in supervising a plaster. If she fails to note the digits of a plastered limb becoming blue and cold, she could be held responsible if the patient later lost that limb. As already mentioned, carefully kept records are vital for contesting later legal action.

### Failure of reporting

The nurse can be negligent in failing to report certain changes in her patient's condition, which if known, would have resulted in a change in treatment prescribed. The best known example is when a patient complains of excessive or unexpected pain.

Further to this, the importance of careful reporting at all times cannot be emphasised too strongly. There is always the possibility of a patient bringing legal action for damages without there having been negligence. With inadequate or poor reporting, it is difficult for the court to assess the real situation. The patient developing pressure sores mentioned above is a good example of the reliance that must be given to the nurses' reports, and all reports and any charts must be considered as possible legal documents.

Most health authorities are now using individualised nursing care (the nursing process). The associated documentation (see Figure 5.4) demonstrates the stages of this process, i.e. assessment, identification of problems and goals, planning of care and evaluation of care. There are legal implications to each of these stages.

Assessment should be comprehensive. The documentation used should record the answers to a wide range of questions and observations. Depending on the circumstances, the nurse can use her own judgement in identifying the questions that are relevent to a particular patient. In addition the nurse will recognise cues from the patient in areas of assessment not specifically covered by the documentation and she should respond to these, if only to record a feeling of uneasiness about a particular area of questioning. In spite of this being a nursing assessment, the patient may well impart important medical information that the doctor is unaware of. For example, a staff nurse was encouraging a patient to tell her about her social activities. These seemed to be centred totally on the local pub, and after more conversation the patient admitted to having a drink problem that was very relevant to her present hospital admission, but which she had hidden from the doctor.

Identification of problems and setting of goals or objectives causes concern to nurses regarding legal repercussions. The way in which this part of the nursing process is carried out will vary considerably from place to place, but this does not matter as long as the nurse bears the following points in mind. First she should remember that these are nursing or patient problems; a medical diagnosis is rarely adequate. Secondly, goals or objectives must be realistic. For example, to prevent shock after surgery is unrealistic for the nurse to achieve, whereas to monitor for shock after surgery is attainable by the nurse. A useful practice is the setting of a review date but the nurse must then make sure that this is done.

The planning and evaluation of nursing care must be reported in sufficient detail. A major problem for the nurse in completing the documentation required for the nursing process is the time required. One way of reducing time is to use abbreviations but those used must be clear to all the nurses concerned. For example, BP, TPR and PA care may be widely understandable but some abbreviations used on specialist wards are unintelligible to a nurse from a different type of ward. Omissions in reporting are particularly dangerous and are most relevant to the evaluation section. 'Usual day', 'Slept as well as could be expected' give no indication of whether the planned care has been implemented. Even 'Wound dressed as required' lacks any useful precision. The nurse must record details of the care given as well as the patient's response to that care or medically prescribed treatment. Any unusual occurrences or observations, even if seemingly unimportant at the time, should be included.

The frequency of writing in these nursing documents is another debatable issue. Legally there is no specific requirement, for example for a daily entry. Instead it is up to the nurse's professional judgement. Thus, in the intensive care unit, updating every four hours may be necessary, whereas on a long-stay ward for the elderly, a weekly evaluation may be sufficient. A legal guideline would be to record an entry when a review date or time occurs, when a patient's condition changes or when there has been some omission of planned care. This last point is of particular importance to the community nurse who is usually working on her own and therefore has no colleague to confirm what has occurred at a later date.

On all records it is vital that the nurse should sign her full name, rather than her initials. It is impossible to trace a nurse for giving evidence when initials are the only guide. When it is the responsibility of a learner nurse to complete the records of a patient whose care has been delegated to her, the same rules apply, but the trained nurse responsible for delegating this task must ensure that the records are completed satisfactorily. In some places it is made a requirement that a trained nurse counter-signs but this is not a legal requirement, the main point being that supervision has been adequate.

If an error is made, this must be treated as carefully as a cheque-book error. Pencil or snowflake must not be used but the mistake carefully crossed through with a single line and signed before rewriting and signing again. The written record must of course be legible.

### Dangers on the premises
Accidents to patients because of dangerous premises or dangerous equipment on the premises are the responsibility of the hospital authority, but the nurse should take what steps she can to remove or have removed any source of danger.

For example, a defective bedpan washer floods the sluice and toilet area of a ward. A patient slips and falls, breaking a leg and prolonging his stay in hospital with the result that he loses his job. The nurses contributed to the accident by not reporting the failure of the bedpan washer or warning patients not to use those particular toilets. The situation has therefore resulted in serious consequences due to the nurses' failure to act.

### Criminal assault and battery
Injuries to patients may occur when a nurse uses force against a patient for self-defence or for the protection of the patient himself or others around him. However, it is important that the nurse only uses the minimal amount of force required to control the patient and if possible does not deal with him single-handedly. If more force is used than is reasonably necessary, the nurse could be guilty of assault and battery. The problem can particularly arise with the mentally disordered, children and the aged (see sections 4.3 on violent patients, and 6.6 on the mentally disordered, and Part IV section 11.2).

An additional problem faced by the male nurse caring for female patients is the possibility of a female patient accusing the nurse of rape, attempted rape or indecency. Generally, health authorities support the principle of professionals caring for patients regardless of sex, but in hospital it may be wise for a male nurse to avoid becoming isolated in a single room with a female patient. Either the work should be allocated differently or the male nurse can ask for a female colleague to be working nearby. The community nurse would be many times more vulnerable and it may well be wiser to allocate male patients to male nurses unless the work is being undertaken with a female colleague. In all cases where the nurse suspects that a patient may make accusations, the importance of full and careful documentation is advised.

## Questions and concluding comments on 5.2

*Question:* What legal problems could arise if the following nurse's report was used in evidence in court?

Kardex — Mrs Rose Watkins   Age 72

2.6  Admitted via casualty having fallen at home onto her Ⓛ hip. Nursed on skin traction. ? for operation mane. To be NBM from breakfast time. Obs. on admission T35$^5$ P100 R20 B/P 180/120. Urine protein 30 NAD.

3.6  Incontinent +++. Please could patient be persuaded to use a bedpan or her bottom will get very sore. NBM after breakfast.
Potassium level too low—op. postponed. Fluids and diet to be encouraged. IVI continues. ? for theatre tomorrow depending on potassium levels.
To be NBM after light breakfast. Commenced effervescent K tablets qds. To be encouraged with fresh orange juice.

4.6  Appears to have a + balance of 1590 ml. Apparently weights fell off skin traction yesterday evening and Ⓛ leg was giving her some pain. Pethidine 75 mg given at 23$^{30}$ to settle with good effect. Continues to pass urine frequently with burning—? UTI—offensive, cloudy urine. ? last time bowels open. NBM after breakfast. Premedication given at 15.00 hr prior to insertion of L pin and plate. Pethidine 75 mg given on return from theatres. IVI. Incontinent of urine and faeces. Obs satisfactory.

5.6  Fair post op night. Obs remain satisfactory. Zimmer drains changed X 2 during night . . .

*Comments:* The above report is particularly likely to lead to legal problems because of inadequate reporting.

1. The weights falling off the traction was not reported at the proper time. This could have been negligent. Fortunately the night staff discovered what had happened.
2. The problem of fluid balance is not mentioned until the day after admission and the amount of fluid to be given is very vague. Clearly, something went wrong as the reporter cannot believe what is

written on the fluid chart—'appears to' is not a statement of careful nursing.

3. The problem of Mrs Watkins' bottom getting sore is realised but the condition of the skin is nowhere mentioned.

4. 'Obs satisfactory' and 'fair post op night' give little indication of the patient's condition.

There are a few other errors of reporting, but the most important to note is the side of the body being abbreviated to ⓛ or L. This should always be written in full.

*Question:* The district nurse has been visiting Mrs West weekly for a number of months in order to redress her leg ulcers. However, on a number of occasions Mrs West has refused to let the nurse in and on other occasions she has refused to let the nurse redo her dressings. What should the nurse document?

*Comments:* It is important that the nurse documents each visit and what happened. It is insufficient to document only those times that she was allowed to redress Mrs West's ulcers. In addition she should document what steps she took to assess Mrs West's condition when she was allowed entry. In this way any possible accusations of failing to give adequate care can be answered.

## 5.3 PATIENTS' PROPERTY

### Patients' property in hospital

Mrs Cray, an 82-year-old woman, was admitted to hospital. She was rather confused and her daughter accompanied her. Her property was checked by two nurses and a list was made. She only had 54 pence in change and a yellow metal wedding ring as valuables.

Five days later, the patient called to a nurse and complained that she could not find £10 that she had had with her. The nurse helped Mrs Cray to look for it but there was no sign of any money apart from a small amount of change. The relatives were not very helpful. Mrs Cray had had numerous visitors who could have brought in the money and the daughter tended to believe her mother. The nurse could only point out that, if in fact Mrs Cray had lost £10, the hospital could not take any responsibility for this.

This tale is not unusual, and the nurse will find herself playing an important part in the care of patients' property. All hospitals take a clear position on people bringing property and valuables into hospital and issue a statement absolving them of responsibility for any loss unless items are handed over to the hospital authority for safe keeping.

Particular care needs to be taken of valuables. These include money, cheque books and cards, pension books and any jewellery. Each hospital has specific procedures to follow and the nurse must always ask the patient if he wishes to hand over his valuables for safe keeping. If he refuses, he should be reminded that he is keeping them on the ward at his own risk. The nurse may be involved in listing valuable items and care must be exercised in how these are described. It should never be assumed that jewellery is of gold or silver or contains precious stones. They must be listed as yellow metal, white metal or as the colour of the particular stone. A patient receiving his valuables on discharge may refuse to accept a yellow alloy ring if the nurse had mistakenly described it as being of gold.

The ward staff must take some responsibility for the valuables of a patient going to the operating theatre or the labour ward. As patients are required to remove jewellery, the ward must have a lockable safe or cupboard in which these items, listed and checked, can be placed safely for the short time that the patient will be unable to take care of them. Dentures should be placed in a carefully labelled container.

If on admission a patient is found to be confused or to have poor sight, it is wise for the nurse to check the property with an accompanying relative or with a second nurse, making a list of all items, including dentures and spectacles, that the patient has brought with him.

### Emergency admissions

Special care must be taken if a patient is admitted unconscious. Two nurses should check the patient's property and valuables as soon as possible after arrival at the accident and emergency department in case there is a later query on whether an item was lost before the patient's arrival at hospital. A list should be made which both nurses sign.

The nurse should be careful about handing items to the relatives accompanying the unconscious patient to hospital. Legally, the nurse has no right to hand over someone's property to another individual, but in practice some discretion is exercised. For example, if a husband or wife has accompanied the patient, it is a reasonable risk to hand over large items of clothing to take home as hospital storage space is so limited. However, handing over money would be extremely risky, especially as it is not unusual for large sums to be involved, particularly on pay day.

There may be additional problems with emergency admissions at night or weekends when finance staff are not available. All hospitals should have a detailed procedure for dealing with valuables in these circumstances, for example, a separate safe for this purpose.

### Discharge

On discharge, a patient receives the belongings he has handed over for safe keeping, signing a receipt for them. He may, of course, ask for his valuables while still an inpatient, in which case he must be reminded that he takes the risk of having these items on the ward.

The nurse should check that the patient has, in fact, received all his property on discharge. It is so easy to forget an overcoat, with resultant cost and time to the staff having to remedy the situation later. Ensuring that the patient receives the correct property is also the nurse's responsibility and depends on how carefully items were checked, stored and labelled in the first place. The initial property list will be useful here, but the nurse will realise that it is unlikely to be accurate as relatives will have brought in extra items during the patient's stay.

### Deaths

In law, a deceased person's property should be handed over only to the person's executors or administrators. The nurse runs a definite risk if she takes on herself the decision as to who should receive the patient's property. The death of a relative does not always bring to light people's better natures and the nurse is advised to keep very well clear of the battles that can erupt between relatives over a deceased person's property. Most hospitals have very strict rules about this situation.

Sometimes a patient or the next of kin makes a particular request that rings are not removed from the body after death. This particularly applies to wedding rings, and such requests should be honoured. The nurse must make a written note in the nursing records to this effect. A note attached to the shroud or body is also a valuable safeguard to ensure that rings are not lost or mistakenly returned to the relative.

## Wills

Nurses may be approached by patients who want to make their wills. People who are seriously ill suddenly realise the importance of sorting out their financial affairs, and the nurse is often the person at hand.

However, it is not wise for nurses to become involved. As pointed out in Part I, there are various requirements for the making of a valid will

This is the last will and testament of me, ......................of
......................in the county of....................

I give and devise all my estate and effects, real and personal, which I may die possessed of or be entitled to, unto .................... absolutely, and I appoint ................ executors of this my will, and I hereby revoke all former wills and codicils.


Dated this .......... day of .......... 19.....


Signed.......................


..........................   Name, address and description
..........................   of witness.


Signed by the testator in the presence of us who thereupon signed our names in his and each other's presence.


..........................   Name, address and description
..........................   of witness.


(There must be 2 witnesses.)

**Figure 5.5**   Sample form of will for use in England, Wales and N. Ireland.

and the nurse cannot be expected to have the necessary legal expertise. If the situation is not too urgent, it should be possible to advise the patient to ask his own solicitor to deal with the matter, but if the patient is in a serious condition, an administrator should be contacted. Even outside office hours, there should be someone on call.

The community nurse is in a more isolated situation and she may find it difficult to contact an administrator. If she feels she has no option but to act as a witness, she must feel sure that the patient is of sound mind. She should check that the signatures of the patient and the two witnesses come right at the end of the document. For the will to be valid, the patient making the will and the two witnesses must sign in each other's presence, so the nurse must ensure that she is not called away in the middle of this procedure. (The law regarding this is different in Scotland—see below.) This is less likely in the community than in hospital. If the nurse is to benefit under the will, she cannot sign (again different in Scotland). If she does, that part of the will becomes invalid unless the nurse was acting as a third witness whose signature is legally unnecessary. A husband or wife cannot act as a witness.

A sample of a very simple will that can be used in England, Wales and N. Ireland is laid out (Figure 5.5) in case the nurse finds herself unable to get hold of a legal expert in an emergency situation.

There are a number of important differences regarding the making of a will in Scotland. For example, if a patient cannot sign, a solicitor, JP or Minister of the Parish can do so on his behalf. A 'holograph' will can be made privately by an individual with no witnesses present. It must be wholly in his own handwriting and dated and signed by him, and if the bequests are straightforward, it is unlikely that any legal difficulties would arise after death. If the will is written by another, the individual signing the will can write above his signature at the end 'adopted as holograph' and date and sign it as before.

There are also differences affecting the witnesses. For example, they need not sign at the same time as the patient provided they saw him sign the will, or heard him acknowledge his signature, and provided they sign during the patient's lifetime. A witness is not necessarily disqualified from taking a legacy under the will. As in England, it is preferable for the nurse to procure the services of a solicitor for the patient.

## Gifts

The law is also involved when nurses receive gifts from patients. Usually, if the gift is of little value, the nurse can safely accept it; to refuse it would probably cause unnecessary hurt and embarrassment. However, a more substantial gift can have serious repercussions. The law takes the view that if a patient makes a gift to his nurse, there is the likelihood of pressure having been brought to bear, not necessarily in an obvious way, but because of excessive feelings of gratitude. This may lead to a patient making a gift that is not in his best interests and which he later regrets and his relatives may contest if he dies.

Thus, nurses should be wary of receiving gifts of money, a piece of jewellery or any item of reasonable value. Most hospitals have regulations concerning nurses receiving gifts, but the situation can be difficult to handle when a patient is very insistent. If the nurse finds it difficult to convince a patient that she cannot receive some gift, she would be wise to ask for a senior nurse to speak to the patient on her behalf.

A patient may give the nurse money in order for the nurse to undertake some shopping for the patient. Such an action makes the nurse vulnerable to later accusations of theft. Theoretically it is not the nurse's responsibility to take on such a task for the patient. If, however, a nurse wishes to help in this way, she does so as an individual. She should buy what the patient requires (small items only) from her own money and be reimbursed by the patient on producing the goods with a receipt.

## Question and concluding comments on 5.3

*Question:* The relative of a very ill, semiconscious patient complains that a valuable silver locket has been stolen from the patient. What should the nurse do in this situation?

*Comments:* The nurse can check the list of property and valuables made on admission to see if there is a record of the locket and whether it was handed over for safe keeping. However, if the patient had at that time been well enough to make the decision to keep the locket around her neck for sentimental reasons, it would not be included on any receipt for valuables, although the nurses admitting the patient should still have made a note of it. With the worsening of the patient's condition, the nurse would have been wise to have arranged for the locket's safe custody, but the hospital authority could still disclaim responsibility. The relative, however, may feel that the patient was not in a fit condition to care for her own valuables.

The nurse should certainly inform a senior nurse of the situation and suggest to the relative that if she wishes to pursue the matter, she should write to the health authority administrator. (See section 5.6 regarding complaints.)

## 5.4  DETENTION OF PATIENTS AGAINST THEIR WILL

Mrs Biggs was a woman of 66 years with atherosclerosis, and she was admitted to a geriatric ward for long-term care as her relatives were unable to cope with looking after her. She was encouraged to dress and stay up all day, but she was very confused as to her whereabouts. She would make repeated visits to the door of the ward and, if not turned round, would leave the ward and start down the stairs. It was usually possible to distract her, but occasionally two nurses would need to lead her back to her chair and sit her in it with a table in front of her to restrain her from leaving the ward. Sometimes it would take 15 to 20 minutes for her to calm down and stop insisting that she must go. Not surprisingly, this worried the nurses who also wondered what their position was legally.

A general rule for nurses to remember is that no one can be detained in hospital without lawful authority. The majority of patients have freedom of choice as to whether to continue with treatment in hospital or not.

## Patients who can be detained

The law lays down certain regulations as to who may be detained. These are as follows:

- Those detained under the Mental Health Act (1983), the Mental Health (Scotland) Amendment Act (1983) or the Mental Health (N. Ireland) Act (1961). In practice these numbers are small (see Chapter 6).
- Those unable to look after themselves with no one to look after them, who have a chronic disease or are old and physically incapacitated, and living in unsanitary conditions. An order made by a justice of the peace or sheriff is required.
- A similar order is also required for those suffering from or carrying certain infectious diseases which would be a danger to others. Under the Public Health Act (1936), amended 1961 and 1968, and the public Health (Control of Diseases) Act (1984), certain diseases are notifiable:

| | |
|---|---|
| acute encephalitis | cholera |
| acute meningitis | diphtheria |
| acute poliomyelitis | food poisoning |
| amoebic dysentery | infective jaundice |
| anthrax | lassa fever |
| bacillary dysentery | leprosy |

leptospirosis

malaria

Marburg disease

measles

ophthalmia neonatorum

paratyphoid fever

plague

rabies

relapsing fever

scarlet fever

smallpox

tetanus

typhoid fever

typhus

viral haemorrhagic fever

whooping cough

yellow fever

This list can be extended if considered necessary, and the law also has powers to stop a person with certain infections from working and therefore spreading infection.

• The police may detain patients in hospital. For example, if a person taking part in an armed robbery is injured during the ensuing chase and capture, the police will remain with him throughout his stay in hospital. The hospital authority does not have to take the responsibility.

The example at the start of this section illustrates a different situation in that it is the nurse who has to take action here. In fact, the law accepts that some patients who are light-headed or delirious might not be allowed to leave as they do not know what they are doing. The term used is that 'his right mind is not in him', and this would clearly apply to Mrs Biggs. On the whole, this use of the law should be restricted to short-term problems of detention only and very great care must be taken in detaining any patient without statutory authority. An action by the patient for unlawful detention can result in very heavy damages.

## Self-discharge

If a patient not included in any of the above categories wishes to discharge himself, he has the right to do so, but the nurses should ensure that certain procedures are followed to avoid later legal problems.

First, the patient should be warned of possible adverse effects of leaving hospital before treatment has been completed. Attempts should be made to change his mind. If the patient first communicates his intention to a junior nurse, she should quickly inform the senior nurse who will speak to the patient. If the patient is adamant, she will ask the doctor to come to the ward to see the patient and explain the risks.

# Health District

## DISCHARGE AGAINST MEDICAL ADVICE

I, ............................................................................................................................................

of ............................................................................................................................................

am discharging myself from.................................................................................Hospital. I do this
at my own risk and realise that it is against the advice of the medical staff.

       Signed:      Patient   .............................................................................

       Witnessed by: Sister  .............................................................................

               House Officer  .............................................................................

Date :.................................................................

15 132 0025

**Figure 5.6**   Sample self-discharge form.

Finally, the patient is required to sign the appropriate self-discharge form (Figure 5.6).

The circumstances surrounding a patient's self-discharge are often very emotional, and it is not unusual for a patient to refuse either to stay and see the doctor or to sign the self-discharge form. The nurses involved must record what has happened and two nurses who were present should sign the appropriate form, witnessing that the patient has discharged himself.

Some nurses feel somewhat irritated when a self-discharged patient has, shortly afterwards, to be readmitted, but no hospital can morally turn away a patient on the grounds that he chose to discharge himself. It is also worth bearing in mind that a lack of awareness on the nurses' part of how angry and unhappy the patient was feeling may have contributed to his leaving. (See also section 5.6 regarding complaints.)

## Questions and concluding comments on 5.4

*Question:* A 30-year-old man had to be admitted as an inpatient because of a nose bleed that failed to respond to treatment. Three procedures and one operation later, the nose was still bleeding and the patient was becoming very agitated and abusive to the medical and nursing staff. Finally, he threatened to discharge himself. What should the nurse in this situation do?

*Comments:* Somewhat understandably, the patient was feeling disenchanted by the failure of treatment to stop his nose bleed. The nurse had at all costs to remain calm herself and persuade the patient to remain in bed while she fetched the ward sister. The ward sister was unable to reassure the patient that treatment would eventually work, so she contacted the doctor who came to the ward as quickly as possible. The relevant self-discharge form was kept available.

As a postscript to this story, the patient was persuaded to stay although he was very reluctant to do so. After yet another operation, the bleeding finally stopped!

*Question:* A 50-year-old man has been admitted to hospital for investigations into rectal bleeding. However, when these investigations are arranged he refuses to participate. The ward sister suggests to him that there is not much point in him remaining in hospital but he does not respond to this suggestion. What action is available in this situation?

*Comments:* Consent to treatment is to some extent implied by the patient agreeing to come into hospital. Therefore, if the patient thereafter refuses to consent to suggested treatment, the consultant has every right to discharge that patient even if he is unwilling to leave.

## 5.5  BIRTHS AND DEATHS

One of the happiest events with which the nurse may be involved is birth, and one of the most upsetting is death. These two emotional events also have their legal requirements.

## Births

In law, anyone present at a birth may be required to register the event. This responsibility is usually undertaken by the parents or next of kin, but if for some reason this is not possible, the duty falls on 'every other qualified informant', for example, someone present at the birth or any occupier of the premises where the birth took place. Thus, the midwife may very occasionally have to register a birth.

However, the midwife is more likely to be involved in the case of a stillbirth. The registrar for births and deaths will require a certificate signed by or a declaration made by the midwife or medical practitioner present at the time. The midwife will declare that she has examined the body and the baby was not born alive.

There is a further requirement of notification of a birth within 36 hours. This must be done to the local medical officer of health by any person in attendance on a woman in childbirth or during the six hours afterwards. The health authority is likely to have regulations for its midwives to follow in order to comply with the law.

Mistakes in identification of newly-born babies in hospital are possible and have occurred with most traumatic after-effects when the mistakes have been discovered. The obstetric nurse must be extremely careful in following hospital procedure in labelling newborn infants. This should take place as soon as possible after the birth.

## Deaths

The hospital nurse is more likely to be present at the death of a patient than the nurse in the community. When a patient appears to have died, the nurse has a duty to inform the doctor. He is the only person who can certify death. The nurse, of course, will become used to recognising the signs of death. Legally the actual time of death is not so easy to pinpoint. A dictionary definition of death is the total stoppage of the circulation of the blood, and the cessation of the animal and vital functions of the body, such as respiration and pulsation. There is a continuing debate on the usefulness of this definition, and the problems involved are discussed further in Part IV.

As with births, deaths have to be registered, and the same regulations apply. Thus, the nurse will rarely be involved in this. The doctor who has been treating the patient will issue a death certificate and, although he must have seen the deceased prior to death, there is no legal requirement that the doctor should view the body after death. However, if there are any doubtful circumstances, the doctor will report the death to the coroner, and the certificate is marked to this effect (see page 11). In addition, the registrar is required to report to the coroner where the deceased was not attended by a doctor in his last illness and where he was not seen by the doctor after death or in the 14 days preceding death.

A final point needs to be made concerning the identification of the dead person in hospital. As with newly-born babies, great care must be taken to avoid mistakes. It is insufficient to mark only the outside of the shroud. Preferably the body itself must be clearly labelled, for example by leaving the hospital identity bracelet in place or attaching a label around the ankles.

# 5.6  COMPLAINTS

Mr Hughes went to the local accident and emergency department after dropping a heavy chest on his foot. The department was busy with other, more urgent accident cases with the result that he had to wait for three hours, in considerable pain, before being examined. He had to wait a further one and a half hours for the X-ray to be seen and treatment instigated. By this time he was feeling considerably upset and complained to the staff nurse on duty.

Nurses will need to know how to deal with complaints by patients and relatives, and the legal framework in existence.

## Dealing with complaints at a local level

In a service that cares for people who are unwell and anxious, it is perhaps inevitable that complaints and criticisms will be made. Nurses must accept that in many cases a person's tolerance under stress is likely to be reduced so that even seemingly small complaints can loom large. A nurse can play an important role at this initial stage. Maintaining good communication and giving appropriate information when it is needed will often prevent complaints. If a patient becomes aggrieved, the nurse must remain receptive and make attempts to resolve any minor complaint, and in many cases this will prevent escalation into formal complaints procedure.

However, if the complaint appears to have a sound foundation and cannot quickly be resolved, the nurse should inform someone more senior, for example the nursing officer. She will need to decide whether the complaint concerns clinical judgement, in which case it must be referred to the doctor in charge of the patient, or whether it can be dealt with by the complaints procedure as required by the Hospital Complaints Procedure Act (1985). It is advisable that the clinical nurse, as well as the manager, has some idea of the requirements of this Act so that she can advise the patient or his relatives accordingly.

A complaints procedure must include the following components.

First, complaints should be investigated thoroughly, fairly and speedily. They should also be handled at a sufficiently senior level to command the confidence of patients, the co-operation of staff concerned and to enable recommendations to be followed through. All involved should be kept fully informed as to the progress of the investigation and any staff implicated should be given the opportunity to reply. In addition the complaints procedure should be adequately publicised and readily accessible to patients.

Health Authorities are directed to implement a complaints procedure in the following way. There should be a designated officer to receive complaints (this could be the Unit General Manager). Where the patient is dead or unable to act for himself, the complaint can be made by his personal representative, a member of his family or a body or individual suitable to represent him (for example a member of the Community Health Council). Complaints must be made in writing and should normally be within six months of the incident but this time may be extended in some circumstances.

The Hospital Complaints Procedure Act (1985) covers in-patients, out-patients and accident and emergency cases. However, at present there is no legislation concerning complaints about community health services, though some health authorities may well extend their provisions to this area.

In Mr Hughes' case, if the above procedure were to be followed, it may well highlight that his long delay in the accident and emergency department was not an isolated incident. The health authority would then have sufficient evidence on which to act, for example by improving staffing levels. The nurse must take the view that complaints are one means whereby care can be improved, rather than feeling threatened or annoyed by them.

The position of a private patient is rather different to the National Health Service patient just described. The private patient has a contract with the hospital to supply the services required (see page 29), and can therefore sue under the Supply of Goods and Services Act (1982) if there is a failure in this provision. The National Health Service patient cannot take such action.

## The Health Service Commissioner

If a complainant is not satisfied with the conduct or outcome of the health authority's own investigations, he can take his complaint to the Health Service Commissioner (Commissioner for Complaints in N. Ireland).

The Health Service Commissioner is an independent office, established by Act of Parliament, to carry out investigations into complaints concerned with hospitals and other health services. The commissioner has to investigate complaints from the public where they have suffered injustice or hardship as a result of failure to provide a required or adequate service or because of maladministration by the health authorities. The commissioner cannot take action where the complaint is already being dealt with in a court of law or could be dealt with in this way, or where the complaint concerns clinical judgement, staff appointments or disciplinary procedures.

The nurse must always advise the patient to complain first to the responsible authority, as the commissioner cannot investigate until this authority has had sufficient chance to reply. The only exception to this is if a person is unable to act for himself and a member of the health authority staff submits the complaint on the patient's behalf. As with the civil courts, there is a time limit. Complaints must normally reach the commissioner within one year of their occurrence though he has power to waive the ruling if necessary.

The written complaint sent to the commissioner should give full details of the name and address of the complainant, the authority concerned and the location involved. It is also helpful to include copies of any correspondence with the health authority together with a full description of the circumstances.

On receipt of the complaint, the commissioner first has to decide whether the matter is within his jurisdiction. If it is, an investigation will be held in private. A report of the findings is sent to the individual concerned, the authority complained against and any other appropriate bodies.

## Question and concluding comments on 5.6

*Question:* Miss Martin's mother had to be admitted to hospital following a stroke with resultant hemiplegia and dysphasia. During the following weeks, Mrs Martin made little progress and was transferred to a geriatric ward. Over the next few months, Miss Martin became increasingly worried about the treatment her mother was receiving. She often found her in soiled clothing with her hair unkempt and her dentures uncleaned and left in the locker. She finally decided she must do something when she found bruises on her mother's upper arms. What advice could be given to Miss Martin?

*Comments:* Miss Martin should try to discuss the situation with the ward staff but if she feels that nothing positive results, she must put her complaints in writing to the health authority administrator.

After allowing several months for the situation to be improved, Miss Martin could, if there appears to be no reasonable outcome, take her complaint further. It is unlikely that there could be any redress in the courts as Mrs Martin has not clearly suffered damage. Therefore, the best course of action would be to complain to the Health Service Commissioner. Miss Martin can complain on her mother's behalf as her mother is unable to do so herself on account of her disabilities.

# REFERENCES

British Medical Association (1981). *Handbook of Medical Ethics*, BMA, London.

Court Training Services (1986). *Record Keeping and Giving Evidence in Court*, Court Training Services, London.

Cowan, V. (1987). Documentation, *Nursing* (Oxford), Vol. 3 (14), p. 527.

Department of Health and Social Security (1980). *Family Planning Service Memorandum of Guidance—Revised Section G, The Young*, Appendix HN 80 46, DHSS, London.

Department of Health and Social Security (1986). *Hospital Complaints Procedure Act (1985)*, DA 86 14, DHSS, London.

Farndale, W. A. J. and Larman, E. C. (1973). *Legal Liability for Claims Arising from Hospital Treatment*, Ravenswood, Beckenham, Kent.

Finch, J. A. (1981). A Complicated Case—Whitehouse *v.* Jordan, *Nursing Mirror*, 8 Jan., Vol. 152, p. 7.

Hargreaves, M. (1979). *Practical Law for Nurses*, Pitman Medical, Tunbridge Wells, Kent.

Lavin, J. (1987). The Jasmine Beckford inquiry, *Nursing* (Oxford), Vol. 3 (14), p. 521.

Marsh, G. (1984). The Ombudsman, functions and jurisdiction, *Nursing Times*, Vol. 80, p. 47.

Medical Defence Union (1986). *Consent to Treatment*, Medical Defence Union, London.

Medical Defence Union and Royal College of Nursing (1978). *Safeguards against Failure to Remove Swabs and Instruments from Patients*, Medical Defence Union, London.

Medical Defence Union and Royal College of Nursing (1983). *Safeguards against Wrong Operations*, Medical Defence Union, London.

Medical Defence Union, Royal College of Nursing, National Association of Theatre Nurses (1986). *Theatre Safeguards*, Medical Defence Union, London.

National Consumer Council (1983). *Patients' Rights: a Guide for NHS Patients and Doctors*, HMSO, London.

Skegg, P. D. G. (1984). *Law, Ethics and Medicine*, Clarendon Press, Oxford.

Tingle, J. H. (1988). Nurses and the Law, *Senior Nurse*, Vol. 8 (1), p. 8.

Tingle, J. H. (1988). Negligence and Wilsher, *Solicitors' Journal*, Vol. 132 (25), p. 910.

# 6. Mentally Disordered Patients

The nurse plays a role in caring for mentally disordered patients in a number of different ways. The mental nurse works in this area, either in hospital, or more recently in the community where she also needs to support the family and educate the community. The general nurse may have to care for patients with some mental disorder in addition to a physical condition that has required admission to a general hospital or care at home.

This chapter will look at how law affects the mentally disordered patient within the framework of the Mental Health Acts for England and Wales and Scotland. Section 6.8 will indicate the differences found in N. Ireland as the 1961 Act has yet to be updated. Acts and cases involved are as follows:

Homicide Act (1957)
Mental Health Act (N. Ireland) (1961)
Criminal Procedure (Insanity) Act (1964)
Criminal Procedure (Scotland) Act (1975)
Mental Health Act (1983)
Mental Health (Scotland) Amendment Act (1983)
Bolam *v.* Friern Hospital Management Committee (1957)

## 6.1 DEFINITIONS

Mental disorder is a wide-ranging term that refers to all categories of mental disability ranging from mental handicap to psychoses, neuroses and personality disorders. Conventionally, the term 'mental illness' has been used to describe the psychoses and neuroses, but the Mental Health Act (1983) does not define this term, considering that its usage is a matter of clinical rather than legal judgement.

The Act makes the following definitions:

- Mental disorder means mental illness, arrested or incomplete development of mind, psychopathic disorder and any other disorder or disability of mind.
- Severe mental impairment means a state of arrested or incomplete development of mind which includes severe impairment of intelligence and social functioning and is associated with abnormally aggressive or seriously irresponsible conduct.
- Mental impairment means a state of arrested or incomplete development of mind (not amounting to severe mental impairment) which includes significant impairment of intelligence and social functioning and is associated with abnormally aggressive or seriously irresponsible conduct.
- Psychopathic disorder means a persistent disorder or disability of mind (whether or not including significant impairment of intelligence) which results in abnormally aggressive or seriously irresponsible conduct.

Aggressive or irresponsible behaviour is emphasised in these definitions but this does not mean that individuals who are mentally impaired are likely to be aggressive or irresponsible. What is ensured by the Act is that mentally handicapped people who are not aggressive or seriously irresponsible cannot be admitted compulsorily to hospital. Similarly the psychopath cannot be admitted unless abnormally aggressive or irresponsible, and being repeatedly unreliable in his dealings with others would be insufficient reason. Interestingly, the 1983 Act omits any mention of psychopathic disorder requiring or being susceptible to medical treatment as in the previous 1959 Act. This is in line with current psychiatric views that this condition is untreatable, and alleviating or preventing a deterioration is all that is possible.

Sexual deviancy in any of its facets, or dependence on alcohol or drugs are not in themselves recognised under the Act.

Finally, the Mental Health Act uses the term 'medical treatment' to include nursing care, habilitation and rehabilitation under medical supervision.

## Question and comments on 6.1

*Question:* Mary Hodgson, now 18 years old, had meningitis as a baby and this left her with a mental age of approximately a 4 year old and impaired hearing. As she got older she became more boisterous, frequently throwing temper tantrums. Her mother was only a small woman and became increasingly concerned at her ability to care for Mary. Mrs Hodgson discussed the situation with her doctor. On what grounds could Mary's behaviour be seen as falling within the remit of the Mental Health Act (1983)?

*Comments:* The grounds for defining Mary's condition as being severe mental impairment or mental impairment are that her behaviour is abnormally aggressive. Her temper tantrums may well be sufficiently severe to warrant this if she caused damage to herself, her mother or her surroundings at these times.

## 6.2 ADMISSION TO HOSPITAL (see Figure 6.11, p.163, for summary)
### Informal admissions

The main bulk of patients entering psychiatric hospitals or units do so informally. This means that anyone over the age of 16 years can choose to be admitted, in the same way as a patient entering a general hospital.

Section 131 of the Mental Health Act (1983) is the only part of the Act relating to informal admissions, and states:

> 'Nothing in this Act shall be construed as preventing a patient who requires treatment for mental disorder from being admitted to any hospital or mental nursing home in pursuance of arrangements made in that behalf and without any application, order or direction rendering him liable to be detained under this Act, or from remaining in any hospital or mental nursing home in pursuance of such arrangements after he has ceased to be so liable to be detained.'

In practice the patient can actively seek or agree to admission, but even if this is not the case, the patient can still be admitted informally as long as he does not specifically refuse. Some mentally ill people become very apathetic due to their illness and those concerned in their care have to make assumptions as to their co-operation. This is not really any different from how a number of patients reach the general hospital, as their physical illness makes them feel too ill to react one way or another to the assumption that hospital admission is necessary.

# Compulsory admission

Occasionally, compulsory admission of a patient may be necessary for his own sake or that of his family or the general public. In this situation, it is important that the patient is told of his rights and that this is followed up in writing (see pages 148–54 for sample forms, Figures 6.1– 6.5). The sections concerned (except those to do with criminal offenders) arc as follows.

### Section 2 Admission to hospital for assessment (or for assessment followed by treatment)
This detention is valid for 28 days and the grounds are that:

- The patient is suffering from a mental disorder of a nature or degree which warrants the detention of the patient in a hospital for assessment (or assessment followed by treatment) for at least a period.
- The patient ought to be so detained in the interests of his own health or safety or with the view to the protection of other persons.

Application for admission can be made by the nearest relative or an approved social worker, preferably the latter because of the likely emotional involvement of the relative with the patient. The application must be supported by the recommendation, in writing, of two registered medical practitioners, one of whom must have special experience in the diagnosis or treatment of mental disorder. These two doctors can examine the patient separately, but not more than five days must have elapsed between the two examinations, and the later one must have taken place within the period of 14 days prior to admission. If practicable, one of the doctors should have had previous acquaintance with the patient. (See pages 155–59 for sample forms, Figures 6.6, 6.7 and 6.8).

Admission under this Section probably forms a fairly large proportion of civil compulsory admissions. The patient may stay in hospital at the end of 28 days as an informal patient.

### Section 3 Admission to hospital for treatment
The duration of this order is for six months but it can be extended by a further six months and thereafter for periods of one year at a time. The grounds are that (continued on page 160):

Mental Health Act 1983 Leaflet 6
Section 2

Name _____

Your hospital doctor is _____

Date of admission _____

# Your rights under the Mental Health Act 1983

**Why you are being held**

You are being held in this hospital/mental nursing home on the advice of two doctors. You can be kept here for up to 28 days (4 weeks) so that doctors can find out what is wrong and how they can help. You may also be given any treatment you may need while you are kept here. You must not leave before the end of the 28 days unless a doctor tells you that you can. If you try to leave before then the staff can stop you, and if you do leave you can be brought back. You can be held in this way because of Section 2 of the Mental Health Act 1983. These notes are to tell you what that means.

After 28 days you can only be kept in hospital if your doctor thinks you need to stay longer and makes new arrangements (under Section 3 of the Mental Health Act). If your doctor is thinking of doing this he will talk to you about it towards the end of the 28 days, and you will be given a further leaflet to explain your rights.

**If you want to leave**

The doctor will tell you when he thinks you are well enough to leave hospital. If you want to go before the end of the 28 days and before he says you are ready, you will have to get the agreement of either

1

– the hospital managers; or
– the Mental Health Review Tribunal

If you think you should be allowed to leave hospital you should talk to your doctor. If he thinks you should stay, but you still want to leave, you can ask the hospital managers to let you go. You should write to them to ask them to do this. Their address is _____

**The Tribunal**

You can also ask the Mental Health Review Tribunal to decide if you can leave hospital. You can ask the Tribunal to look at your case by writing to them or sending them a form which the hospital can give you. The Tribunal's address is _____

You must write to the Tribunal in the first 14 days (2 weeks) of your stay in hospital. If you need help writing the letter or filling in the form your social worker or the hospital staff will help you.

There are usually three people on the Tribunal – a lawyer, a psychiatrist (doctor) and a third person who is not a doctor. All these people will come from outside the hospital.

If you ask the Tribunal to look at your case they will probably ask to see you and your doctor. If the Tribunal see you, they will be able to make sure that they have full details of your case, and you will be able to tell them yourself why you want to leave hospital. You may not have to see the Tribunal if you do not want to but you can insist on seeing them if you want. The doctor from the Tribunal will want to talk to you in any case. The Tribunal will listen to what you and your doctor say, and to what everyone else says, and then decide if you can leave hospital.

2

**Figure 6.1** Patient's right under Section 2.

You can also ask someone, including a solicitor if you wish, to help you to ask the Tribunal to look at your case and help you put your views to the Tribunal. Because of the legal advice and assistance scheme this solicitor's help may be free or it may only cost you a little. The Tribunal office or social worker will tell you how to find a solicitor or other help if you ask them.

### Your treatment

You are being kept in hospital to make sure that you get the medical treatment you need. Your doctor will talk to you about any treatment he thinks you need. In most cases you will have to accept his advice except in the case of certain treatments.

— If your doctor wants you to have certain very specialised and rare treatments he *must* have your agreement and he must get another doctor's opinion on the treatment that he wants you to have. You can withdraw your agreement at any time. The other doctor will have to talk to other staff who are involved in your case, including a nurse. The law protects you in other ways too. If your doctor wants you to have one of these treatments he will explain all this to you.

— If your doctor feels that you need to have ECT (electro convulsive therapy, sometimes called electric or shock treatment) and you agree, he can go ahead with the treatment. But if you do not agree, unless it is an emergency, he must first ask a doctor from outside the hospital to see you. This other doctor will talk to you and to other staff who are involved in your case, including a nurse, about the treatment and decide whether you need it. If the second doctor says you should have this treatment you will be given it.

— If at first you agree that your doctor may give you ECT but later you change your mind you should tell your doctor that you no longer agree to this treatment. He will then have to ask a doctor from outside the hospital to see you to decide whether you need to go on having it. Again, he will talk to other staff.

### If you have any questions or complaints

If you want to ask something, or to complain about something, talk to the doctor, nurse or social worker. If you are not happy with the answer you may write to the

3

hospital managers. If you are still not happy with the reply you are given you can ask the Mental Health Act Commission to help you. You can also write to the Commission even after you have left hospital.

### The Mental Health Act Commission

The Commission was set up specially to make sure that the mental health law is used properly and that patients are cared for properly while they are kept in hospital. You can ask them to help you by writing to them at

_____

_____

_____

### Your letters

Any letters sent to you will be given to you. You can send letters to anyone except a person who has said that he does not want to get letters from you. Letters to these people will be stopped by the hospital.

### Your nearest relative

A copy of these notes will be sent to your nearest relative who we have been told is

_____

If you do not want this to happen please tell the nurse in charge of your ward or a doctor. Your nearest relative can write to the hospital managers to ask them to let you leave. The managers will need at least 72 hours (3 full days) to consider such a request, so that your doctor can consider whether you should leave or not.

**If there is anything in this leaflet you do not understand, the doctor or a nurse or social worker will help you. If you need help in writing a letter you should ask one of them, or a relative or friend.**

Printed in UK for HMSO D881 6310 1083 8831

4

Mental Health Act 1983 Leaflet 7
Section 3

Name _____

Your hospital doctor is _____

Date of admission _____

# Your rights under the Mental Health Act 1983

## Why you are being held

You are being held in this hospital/mental nursing home on the advice of two doctors. You can be kept here for up to 6 months so that you can be given the treatment and care that you need. You can only be kept in hospital for longer than 6 months if your doctor thinks you need to stay. If your doctor thinks you should stay longer he will talk to you about this towards the end of the 6 months.

You must not leave unless a doctor tells you that you can. If you try to leave before then the staff can stop you, and if you do leave you can be brought back. You can be held in this way because of Section 3 of the Mental Health Act 1983. These notes are to tell you what that means.

## If you want to leave

The doctor will tell you when he thinks you are well enough to leave hospital. If you want to go before the end of the 6 months, or before he says you are ready, you will have to get the agreement of either

– the hospital managers; or

– the Mental Health Review Tribunal

If you think you should be allowed to leave hospital you should talk to your doctor. If he thinks you should stay, but you still want to leave, you can ask the hospital managers to let you go. You should write to them to ask them to do this. Their address is

1

## The Tribunal

You can also ask the Mental Health Review Tribunal to decide if you can leave hospital. You can ask the Tribunal to look at your case by writing to them or sending them a form which the hospital can give you. The Tribunal's address is

_____

You can apply to the Tribunal any time in the next 6 months and if you withdraw your application you can apply again. If you need help writing the letter or filling in the form your social worker or the hospital staff will help you.

There are usually three people on the Tribunal – a lawyer, a psychiatrist (doctor) and a third person who is not a doctor. All these people will come from outside the hospital.

If you ask the Tribunal to look at your case they will probably ask to see you and your doctor. If the Tribunal see you, they will be able to make sure that they have full details of your case, and you will be able to tell them yourself why you want to leave hospital. You may not have to see the Tribunal if you do not want to but you can insist on seeing them if you want. The doctor from the Tribunal will want to talk to you in any case. The Tribunal will listen to what you and your doctor say, and to what everyone else says, and then decide if you can leave hospital.

You can also ask someone, including a solicitor if you wish, to help you to ask the Tribunal to look at your case and help you put your views to the Tribunal. Because of the legal advice and assistance scheme this solicitor's help may be free or it may only cost you a little. The Tribunal office or social worker will tell you how to find a solicitor or other help if you ask them.

If you have not applied after 6 months, the hospital managers will apply for you. If your doctor advises that you need to stay in hospital for a further 6 months you will be able to apply again. After that you can apply every year you are still kept in hospital under the Mental Health Act.

## Your treatment

You are being kept in hospital to make sure that you get the medical treatment you need. Your doctor will talk to you about any treatment he thinks you need. In most cases you will have to accept his advice except in the case of certain treatments.

2

**Figure 6.2** Patient's rights under Section 3.

— If your doctor wants you to have certain very specialised and rare treatments he *must* have your agreement and he must get another doctor's opinion on the treatment that he wants you to have. You can withdraw your agreement at any time. The other doctor will have to talk to other staff who are involved in your case, including a nurse. The law protects you in other ways too. If your doctor wants you to have one of these treatments he will explain all this to you.

— If your doctor feels that you need to have ECT (electro convulsive therapy, sometimes called electric or shock treatment) and you agree, he can go ahead with the treatment. But if you do not agree, unless it is an emergency, he must first ask a doctor from outside the hospital to see you. This other doctor will talk to you and to other staff who are involved in your case, including a nurse, about the treatment and decide whether you need it. If the second doctor says you should have this treatment you will be given it.

— If at first you agree that your doctor may give you ECT but later you change your mind, you should tell your doctor that you no longer agree to this treatment. He will then have to ask a doctor from outside the hospital, to see you to decide whether you need to go on having it. Again, he will talk to other staff.

— Your doctor will talk to you about any medicine or drug treatment he thinks you need. You must accept the treatment for the first 3 months that you are kept in hospital under the Mental Health Act. (If you are not given any medicines or drugs at first, the 3 months only begins when your doctor starts to give you them.) If after 3 months your doctor wants you to carry on having any drug treatment or medicine he must, except in an emergency, get your agreement first. If you agree he can continue the treatment. But if you do not agree, he must ask a doctor from outside the hospital to see you. This other doctor will talk to you and to other staff who are involved in your case, including a nurse, about the treatment and decide whether you need it. If the second doctor says you should have this treatment, you will continue to be given it.

— If when the 3 months is up at first agree that your doctor can carry on giving you any medicine or drug treatment but later you change your mind, you should tell your doctor. He will then have to ask a doctor from outside the hospital to see you and decide whether you need to go on having it. Again, he will talk to other staff.

3

## If you have any questions or complaints

If you want to ask something, or to complain about something, talk to the doctor, nurse or social worker. If you are not happy with the answer you may write to the hospital managers. If you are still not happy with the reply you are given you can ask the Mental Health Act Commission to help you. You can also write to the Commission even after you have left hospital.

## The Mental Health Act Commission

The Commission was set up specially to make sure that the mental health law is used properly and that patients are cared for properly while they are kept in hospital. You can ask them to help you by writing to them at

_____

_____

_____

## Your letters

Any letters sent to you will be given to you. You can send letters to anyone except a person who has said that he does not want to get letters from you. Letters to these people will be stopped by the hospital.

## Your nearest relative

A copy of these notes will be sent to your nearest relative who we have been told is

If you do not want this to happen please tell the nurse in charge of your ward or a doctor. Your nearest relative can write to the hospital managers to ask them to let you leave. The managers will need at least 72 hours (3 full days) to consider such a request, so that they can get a report from your doctor. Only one request will be considered in any one period of 6 months. If your doctor reports that you should not leave, your nearest relative can ask for a Tribunal to look at your case.

**If there is anything in this leaflet you do not understand, the doctor or a nurse or social worker will help you. If you need help in writing a letter you should ask one of them, or a relative or friend.**

Printed in UK for HMSO Dd8916311 10/83 8832

4

Mental Health Act 1983 Leaflet 2
Section 4

Name _____

Your hospital doctor is _____

Date of admission _____ Time of admission _____

# Your rights under the Mental Health Act 1983

## Why you are being held

You are being held in this hospital/mental nursing home on the advice of a doctor who thinks it is urgently necessary for you to be here, so that doctors can find out what is wrong and how they can help you. You can be kept here for up to 72 hours (3 full days) so that you can be seen by another doctor. You must not leave during this time unless a doctor tells you that you can. If you try to leave before then the staff can stop you, and if you do leave you can be brought back. You can be held in this way because of Section 4 of the Mental Health Act 1983. These notes are to tell you what that means.

When the second doctor sees you he may say that you must stay in hospital for a longer time. If so he, or your own hospital doctor, will tell you why and for how long it is likely to be, and you will be given another leaflet to explain your rights. If he decides that you do not need to stay, your doctor or social worker will talk to you about what other help you should have. If you are not seen by a second doctor by the end of 72 hours, you may leave or you can stay as a voluntary patient, but if you want to leave please discuss this with your doctor first.

## Your treatment

The doctor will tell you about any treatment he thinks you need. Only in very exceptional circumstances, which would be explained to you, can you be given treatment you do not want.

## If you have any questions or complaints

If you want to ask something, or to complain about something, talk to the doctor, nurse or social worker. If you are not happy with the answer you may write to the hospital managers. You may do this even after the 72 hours is over.

If you are still not happy with the reply you are given you can ask the Mental Health Act Commission to help you. You can also write to the Commission even after you have left hospital.

## The Mental Health Act Commission

The Commission was set up specially to make sure that the mental health law is used properly and that patients are cared for properly while they are kept in hospital. You can ask them to help you by writing to them at

## Your letters

Any letters sent to you will be given to you. You can send letters to anyone except a person who has said that he does not want to get letters from you. Letters to these people will be stopped by the hospital.

## Your nearest relative

A copy of these notes will be sent to your nearest relative who we have been told is your

If you do not want this to happen please tell the nurse in charge of your ward or a doctor.

**If there is anything in this leaflet you do not understand, the doctor or a nurse or social worker will help you. If you need help in writing a letter you should ask one of them, or a relative or friend.**

Printed in UK for HMSO Dd8816307 10/83 8828

2

**Figure 6.3** Patient's rights under Section 4.

Mental Health Act 1983 Leaflet 3
Section 5(2)

Name _____

Your hospital doctor is _____

His nominated deputy is _____

Date of compulsory admission _____ Time of compulsory admission _____

# Your rights under the Mental Health Act 1983

## Why you are being held

You are being held in this hospital/mental nursing home on the advice of a doctor, so that doctors can find out what is wrong and how they can help you. You can be kept here for up to 72 hours (3 full days) so that you can be seen by two doctors. You must not leave during this time unless a doctor tells you that you can. If you try to leave before then the staff can stop you, and if you do leave you can be brought back. You can be held in this way because of Section 5(2) of the Mental Health Act 1983. These notes are to tell you what that means.

When the second doctor sees you he may say that you must stay in hospital for a longer time. If so he, or your own hospital doctor, will tell you why, and for how long it is likely to be, and you will be given another leaflet to explain your rights. If he decides that you do not need to stay, your doctor or social worker will talk to you about what other help you should have. If you are not seen by a second doctor by the end of 72 hours, you may leave or you can stay as a voluntary patient, but if you want to leave please discuss this with your doctor first.

## Your treatment

The doctor will tell you about any treatment he thinks you need. Only in very exceptional circumstances, which would be explained to you, can you be given treatment you do not want.

1

## If you have any questions or complaints

If you want to ask something or to complain about something, talk to the doctor, nurse or social worker. If you are not happy with the answer you may write to the hospital managers. You may do this even after the 72 hours is over. Their address is _____

If you are still not happy with the reply you are given you can ask the Mental Health Act Commission to help you. You can also write to the Commission even after you have left hospital.

## The Mental Health Act Commission

The Commission was set up specially to make sure that the mental health law is used properly and that patients are cared for properly while they are kept in hospital. You can ask them to help you by writing to them at

## Your letters

Any letters sent to you will be given to you. You can send letters to anyone except a person who has said that he does not want to get letters from you. Letters to these people will be stopped by the hospital.

## Your nearest relative

A copy of these notes will be sent to your nearest relative who we have been told is

_____ you do not want this to happen please tell the nurse in charge of your ward or a doctor.

**If there is anything in this leaflet you do not understand, the doctor or a nurse or social worker will help you. If you need help in writing a letter you should ask one of them, or a relative or friend.**

Dd881012 50000 1/84

2

**Figure 6.4** Patient's rights under Section 5(2).

Mental Health Act 1983 Leaflet 1
Section 5(4)

Name _____

Your hospital doctor is _____

His nominated deputy is _____

Date _____ Time when holding power started _____

# Your rights under the Mental Health Act 1983

## Why you are being held

You are being held in this hospital/mental nursing home for up to six hours so that you can be seen by a doctor. You must not leave during this time unless a doctor or nurse tells you that you can. If you try to leave before then the staff can stop you, and if you do leave you can be brought back. You can be held in this way because of Section 5(4) of the Mental Health Act 1983. These notes are to tell you what that means.

If the doctor does not see you within these six hours you will be free to go, but if you want to go, please talk to a nurse first. When the doctor sees you he may say that you need to stay in hospital for a longer time. If he does, he will tell you why, and for how long it is likely to be, and you will be given a further leaflet to explain your rights. If he decides you do not need to stay he will talk to you about what other help you should have.

## If you have any questions or complaints

If you want to ask something, or to complain about something, talk to the doctor, nurse or social worker. If you are not happy with the answer you may write to the

hospital managers. You may do this even after the six hours is over. Their address is

_____

If you are still not happy with the reply you are given you can ask the Mental Health Act Commission to help you. You can also write to the Commission even after you have left hospital.

### The Mental Health Act Commission

The Commission was set up specially to make sure that the mental health law is used properly and that patients are cared for properly while they are kept in hospital. You can ask them to help you by writing to them at

_____

### Your nearest relative

A copy of these notes will be sent to your nearest relative who we have been told is

_____

If you do not want this to happen please tell the nurse in charge of your ward or a doctor.

**If there is anything in this leaflet you do not understand, the doctor or a nurse or social worker will help you. If you need help in writing a letter you should ask one of them, or a relative or friend.**

Printed in UK for HMSO D8816306 10/83 8827

2

1

**Figure 6.5** Patient's rights under Section 5(4).

Form 1

# Application by nearest relative
# for admission for assessment

Mental Health Act 1983
Section 2

To the Managers of

(name and address of
hospital or mental
nursing home)

(your full name)   I

(your address)   of

hereby apply for the admission of

(full name of patient)

(address of patient)   of

for assessment in accordance with Part II of the Mental Health Act 1983.

*Complete (a) or (b)*

(a) To the best of my knowledge and belief I am the patient's nearest relative within the meaning of the Act. I am the patient's

(state relationship)

(b) I have been authorised to exercise the functions under the Act of the patient's nearest relative by

delete the phrase
which does not
apply

a county court

the patient's nearest relative.

A copy of the authority is attached to this application.

(date)   I last saw the patient on

This application is founded on two medical recommendations in the prescribed form.

If neither of the medical practitioners knew the patient before making their recommendations, please explain why you could not get a recommendation from a medical practitioner who did know the patient:-

Signed _____    Date _____

Printed in the UK for HMSO Dd8826256 3/84 100m 21169

**Figure 6.6**   Application by nearest relative for admission for assessment.

**Figure 6.7**  Application by an approved social worker for admission for assessment.

Form 2

## Application by an approved social worker for admission for assessment

Mental Health Act 1983
Section 2

To the Managers of

(name and address of hospital or mental nursing home)

(your full name)  I

(your office address)  of

hereby apply for the admission of

(full name of patient)

(address of patient)  of

for assessment in accordance with Part II of the Mental Health Act 1983.

(name of local social services authority)  I am an officer of

appointed to act as an approved social worker for the purposes of the Act.

*Complete the following section if nearest relative known*

(a) To the best of my knowledge and belief

(name and address)

is the patient's nearest relative within the meaning of the Act.
OR
(b) I understand that

(name and address)

has been authorised by

delete the phrase which    a county court
does not apply            the patient's nearest relative

to exercise the functions under the Act of the patient's nearest relative.

delete the phrase which    I have
does not apply            I have not yet

informed that person that this application is to be made and of his power to order the discharge of the patient.

*Complete the following section if nearest relative not known*

(a) I have been unable to ascertain who is this patient's nearest relative within in meaning of the Act.

delete the phrase
which does not
apply

OR

(b) To the best of my knowledge and belief this patient has no nearest relative within the meaning of the Act.

*The following section must be completed in all cases*

(date)   I last saw the patient on

I have interviewed the patient and I am satisfied that detention in a hospital is in all the circumstances of the case the most appropriate way of providing the care and medical treatment of which the patient stands in need.

This application is founded on two medical recommendations in the prescribed form.

If neither of the medical practitioners knew the patient before making their recommendations, please explain why you could not get a recommendation from a medical practitioner who did know the patient:-

_____

_____

_____

_____

_____

_____

Signed  _____    Date  _____

Printed in the UK for HMSO Dd ******* 11/83 80m 20355

**Figure 6.8** Joint medical recommendation for admission for assessment.

Form 3

# Joint medical recommendation for admission for assessment

Mental Health Act 1983
Section 2

(full names and addresses of both medical practitioners)

We ☐

registered medical practitioners, recommend that

(name and address of patient)

be admitted to a hospital for assessment in accordance with Part II of the Mental Health Act 1983.

(name of first practitioner)

I ☐

(date)

last examined this patient on ☐

*Delete if not applicable

*I had previous acquaintance with the patient before I conducted that examination.

*I have been approved by the Secretary of State under section 12 of the Act as having special experience in the diagnosis or treatment of mental disorder.

(name of second practitioner)

I ☐

(date)

last examined this patient on ☐

*Delete if not applicable

*I had previous acquaintance with the patient before I conducted that examination.

*I have been approved by the Secretary of State under section 12 of the Act as having special experience in the diagnosis or treatment of mental disorder.

We are of the opinion

(a) that this patient is suffering from mental disorder of a nature or degree which warrants the detention of the patient in a hospital for assessment

AND

(b) that this patient ought to be so detained
    (i) in the interests of the patient's own health or safety

    (ii) with a view to the protection of other persons
Delete (i) or (ii) unless both apply

AND

(c) that informal admission is not appropriate in the circumstances of this case for the following reasons:-

(Reasons should state why informal admission is not appropriate)

_____

_____

_____

_____

_____

_____

Signed _____ Date _____

Signed _____ Date _____

Printed in the UK for HMSO Dd8884916 3/85 40m 23018

- The patient is suffering from mental illness, severe mental impairment, psychopathic disorder or mental impairment and his mental disorder is of a nature or degree which makes it appropriate for him to receive treatment in hospital.
- In the case of psychopathic disorder or mental impairment, such treatment is likely to alleviate or prevent deterioration of the condition.
- It is necessary for the health or safety of the patient or for the protection of other persons that he should receive such treatment, and it cannot be provided unless the patient is detained under this Section.

Application can be made as in Section 2 with one difference, that the socal worker cannot make the application if the nearest relative objects. It is occasionally possible to overcome this objection by applying to the county court to have another person appointed as the nearest relative. This person could be another relative, a person with whom the patient is residing or even an approved social worker.

Medical recommendations are as for Section 2 with the addition that reasons for diagnosis must be given.

At the end of six months, either the patient is released, or becomes an informal patient, or the order is extended by the responsible medical officer (usually the patient's consultant psychiatrist).

## Section 4 Admission to hospital for assessment in cases of emergency

The duration of this order is 72 hours and the grounds are an urgent necessity that the patient should be admitted and detained for assessment, and the compliance with the normal procedure would involve undesirable delay.

Application is as for Section 2 but the applicant must have seen the patient within the previous 24 hours prior to the date of application. The medical recommendation differs from Section 2 and 3 in that only one medical practitioner is required. The recommendation should clarify the circumstances of the emergency and the doctor must have seen the patient within the 24 hours prior to admission.

An example of a patient needing to be admitted under this Section would be a patient who has threatened suicide and is likely to carry out this threat or has actually attempted suicide and is likely to attempt suicide again.

Form 13

# Record for the purposes of
# Mental Health Act 1983 section 5(4)

Mental Health Act 1983
Section 5 (4)

To the Managers of

(name and address of
hospital or mental
nursing home)

(full name of the patient)

It appears to me –

(a) that this patient, who is receiving treatment for mental disorder as an in-patient of this hospital, is suffering from mental disorder to such a degree that it is necessary for the patient's health or safety or for the protection of others for that patient to be immediately restrained from leaving the hospital;

AND

(b) that it is not practicable to secure the immediate attendance of a registered medical practitioner for the purpose of furnishing a report under section 5(2) of the Mental Health Act 1983.

(full name of nurse)   I am

a nurse registered –

delete the phrase
which does not
apply

(a) in Part 3 (first level nurse trained in nursing persons suffering from mental illness);
OR
(b) in Part 5 (first level nurse trained in the nursing of persons suffering from mental handicap)

of the professional register.

Signed _____   Date _____

Time _____

Printed in the UK for HMSO Dd.8405913 6/83 (11037)

**Figure 6.9**   Record for the purposes of Mental Health Act (1983), Section 5(4).

Form 12

# Report on hospital in-patient

Mental Health Act 1983
Section 5 (2)

(name of hospital or
mental nursing home
in which the patient is)

To the Managers of

I                              am

delete the phrase
which does not
apply

the registered medical practitioner

the nominee of the registered medical practitioner

in charge of the treatment of

(full name of patient)

who is an in-patient in this hospital and not at present liable to be detained under the Mental
Health Act 1983. I hereby report, for the purposes of section 5(2) of the Act, that it appears
to me that an application ought to be made under Part II of the Act for this patient's
admission to hospital for the following reasons:-

(Reasons should indicate why informal treatment is no longer appropriate)

Signed ——————————————————— Date ——————————

Time ——————————

Printed in the UK for HMSO Dd.8816357 11/83 50m 20355

**Figure 6.10**   Report on hospital in-patient.

## CIVIL ADMISSIONS

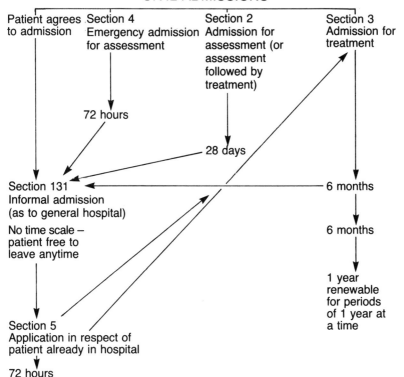

Patient agrees to admission

Section 4 Emergency admission for assessment

Section 2 Admission for assessment (or assessment followed by treatment)

Section 3 Admission for treatment

72 hours

28 days

Section 131 Informal admission (as to general hospital)

No time scale – patient free to leave anytime

6 months

6 months

1 year renewable for periods of 1 year at a time

Section 5 Application in respect of patient already in hospital

72 hours

## CRIMINAL ADMISSIONS

Admissions where criminal proceedings are involved

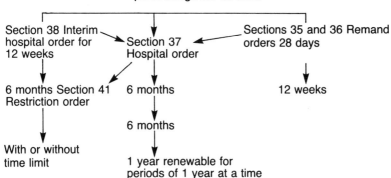

Section 38 Interim hospital order for 12 weeks

Section 37 Hospital order

Sections 35 and 36 Remand orders 28 days

6 months Section 41 Restriction order

6 months

12 weeks

6 months

With or without time limit

1 year renewable for periods of 1 year at a time

**Figure 6.11**  Admission procedure of the mentally disordered patient to hospital.

## Section 5 Application in respect of a patient already in hospital

Sometimes a patient who was originally admitted informally wishes to discharge himself but those caring for the patient are of the opinion that this is strongly inadvisable. The duration, grounds and medical recommendations are identical with those of Section 4. The responsible medical officer however may nominate another medical practitioner to act for him. Application is by the registered nurse and further details of the nurse's role under this Section are given later in this chapter (see page 175). In addition, samples of the two forms concerned are shown on pages 161–2.

## Section 136 Mentally disordered persons found in public places (police admissions)

This detention order is valid for 72 hours, and can be invoked when a police constable finds a person in a public place who appears to be suffering from a mental disorder and in immediate need of care or control. The police constable can take this person to a place of safety, defined under the Act as a police station, psychiatric hospital, a mental nursing home or local-authority residential accommodation for mentally disordered persons. It may not always be easy for the police constable to decide whether the person is mentally ill, drunk or under the influence of drugs, so a fairly common practice would be for the police constable to call on the police surgeon to examine the person at the police station prior to further action.

As well as being examined by a medical practitioner during the 72 hours of detention, an interview with an approved social worker may also be arranged.

# Question and comments on 6.2

*Question:* Mr Menzies had a history of manic-depressive illness. He had been well for about six months, but Mrs Menzies noticed as the weeks went by that he was becoming more and more overactive. He decided that the house was not large enough and planned an extension at the back. He even started digging the foundations for this himself. He continually criticised his wife for failing to help him, woke her up repeatedly during each night for her assistance in a number of other schemes and disturbed the neighbours by repeatedly telling them what they should be doing. Finally, Mrs Menzies reached the end of her tether and the general practitioner decided that further action was needed to admit Mr Menzies to hospital. How could this be done?

*Comments:* It is unlikely that Mr Menzies would see the need for hospital admission. The likely action would be for his doctor to contact the family's approved social worker if they have one or the duty social worker who would visit Mr Menzies and if she agreed that admission was advisable, would make the formal application. The GP would consult a colleague specialising in mental disorders (probably Mr Menzies' consultant psychiatrist) who would jointly with the GP make medical recommendation for compulsory admission, probably using Section 2 Admission for Assessment (see page 147).

# 6.3 PATIENTS INVOLVED IN CRIMINAL PROCEEDINGS OR UNDER SENTENCE

People who commit crimes when they are mentally ill require special consideration by the state for a number of reasons. At one end of the spectrum is the person who kills another but whose mental state may lead to the concept of diminished responsibility being used and the charge altered from murder to a lesser charge. Some people, due to their illness, may not even be fit to face trial and require immediate admission to hospital. Others are found unfit to plead at the time of the trial, but with proper treatment they may at a later stage be found fit to plead. The Mental Health Act (1983) provides a framework for a number of these complexities.

## Sections 35, 36 and 38 Remand to hospital

Section 35 makes it possible for a Magistrate's Court or Crown Court to remand an accused person to hospital for a report on his mental condition. This applies when the offence is punishable by imprisonment and can be while the person is awaiting trial or before sentence is passed. The period of remand is 28 days renewable up to a total of 12 weeks.

Section 36 only applies to the Crown Court and remands an accused person for treatment. This may make it possible for someone who was unfit to stand trial or to plead, to later be able to do so. The period is the same as Section 35.

Section 38 is an interim hospital order concerning convicted criminals where the offence can be punished by imprisonment. Both the Magistrate's Court and the Crown Court can make this order which has a time span of 12 weeks renewable by periods of 28 days up to a total of six months. This section therefore makes it possible for a convicted individual to be fully assessed and treated before a final decision is made by the courts about the disposal of the case.

Remand will to a large extent be to regional secure units.

## Section 37 Hospital order—powers of court to order hospital admission or guardianship

This section is usually used after conviction in a Magistrate's Court or Crown Court for an offence punishable by imprisonment, but the magistrate may use this order if certain that the person did act in the way charged. The mental disorder from which the person is suffering must be of a nature and degree which makes detention in a hospital for treatment appropriate, or in the case of psychopathic disorder or mental impairment that treatment is likely to alleviate or prevent deterioration of his condition. The order may put the offender into guardianship rather than hospital and the court will take into account all relevant circumstances.

The duration of the order is for six months with an initial extension of six months and thereafter for one year at a time.

As under previous sections, admission will usually be to regional secure units.

## Section 41 Restriction order—power of higher courts to restrict discharge from hospital

For an individual dealt with under Section 37 with admission to hospital, a crown court can place a restriction on his release, for example if this is considered necessary for the protection of the public. In addition the court has to consider the nature of the offence, the antecedents of the offender and the risk of his committing further offences if discharged. This restriction order can be made with or without limit of time and the only person who can lift it is the Home Secretary.

Care of this individual may take place in a special hospital.

# Question and concluding comments on 6.3

*Question:* William Harris, a 59-year-old single man, lived in a bedsitting room. One evening, another tenant discovered him attempting to set light to some of his landlady's clothing. He was charged by the police with arson. It quickly became apparent that Mr Harris was suffering from mental illness, most likely paranoid delusions. How could the courts deal with Mr Harris?

*Comments:* The most likely action would be for the court to use Section 37 for hospital admission. Mr Harris could then be given the treatment he needed.

# 6.4 DISCHARGE AND LEAVE

## Discharge from hospital

Informal patients can be discharged or discharge themselves as in a general hospital. The only exception to this is if the doctors and nurses decide it is appropriate to take action under Section 5. One weakness of this system is that there is no statutory review process if the patient fails to ask to be discharged. There is therefore the possibility that some informal patients may stay in hospital longer than is really necessary.

Specific consideration is necessary for compulsorily detained patients. First, their situation is exactly the same as for the informal patient once the order has reached the end of its time limit, i.e. they are free to discharge themselves unless they wish to become informal patients. Secondly, if discharge is wanted prior to expiry of the order, special procedures must be followed.

There are several discharge procedures applying to Sections 2 and 3. The patient can be discharged by:

- The responsible medical officer.
- Three members of the district health authority as long as they first inform the nearest relative unless either the patient or the relative has asked for this information not to be conveyed.
- The nearest relative, provided the doctor does not think the patient is a danger to himself or others, in which case the doctor will issue a barring certificate. The relative must give at least 72 hours' notice.
- The Mental Health Review Tribunal. The Tribunal will set a date in the future to allow time for preparation of the patient (see page 178 for further details of the Tribunal).

In addition a patient who is absent without leave will automatically be discharged if a Section 2 order expires during this period of leave, or if under Section 3 he is absent without leave for 28 days or continuously absent with leave for six months.

The discharge of patients involved with criminal proceedings is sometimes subject to greater restrictions. Discharge from Section 37 is similar to Section 3 but Section 41 orders must involve the Home Secretary.

# Leave

Informal patients can be given leave at any time and patients under Sections 2 and 3 can be granted leave by the medical officer conditionally or otherwise. It can be for a defined period or not, and the period may be extended for some patients. One condition that is sometimes laid down is that the patient should remain in the custody of some specified officer of the hospital or some other authorised person.

Leave of absence can be cut short if it is in the best interests of the patient or others to do this, for example for their protection. The exception to this is if the patient has been on leave continuously for six months (Section 3) or if the order detaining the patient has expired during the leave. Leave for patients involved in criminal proceedings is very limited.

A problem may arise when patients on leave damage property or cause injury. A claim could be made against the health authority but, if the hospital had taken reasonable care in giving the patient leave, it is unlikely that any damages would be awarded.

# Absence without leave

The Mental Health Act lays down certain rules regarding absence without leave.

Under Section 18, if a patient under detention is absent without leave or breaks a condition of leave, he can be brought back to the hospital by an approved social worker, a member of the hospital staff or a policeman. Normally patients can only be brought back in these circumstances within 28 days of the first day of absence.

Finally, the Act states plainly that it is an offence to assist a patient to be absent without leave, by inducing him to do so, knowingly harbouring him, hindering his return to hospital or by any other way.

## Question and concluding comments on 6.4

*Question:* Amanda Wilson had been admitted to hospital under Section 4 as an emergency after having attempted suicide on discovering that her husband was having an affair with another woman. On expiry of this order at the end of 72 hours she asked to stay in hospital as she still felt very depressed and unable to cope with the home situation. During the following week she agreed to see her husband who made it clear to Amanda that he very much wanted to salvage the marriage. What regulations regarding leave and discharge now apply to Amanda?

*Comments:* Amanda can request leave and is free to discharge herself whenever she wishes as she is no longer being compulsorily detained. As she is beginning to make progress in the relationship with her husband, it is unlikely that she will attempt suicide again and there is no need to invoke Section 5 to keep her in hospital.

In fact, Amanda went home for a weekend leave and two weeks later was discharged home to her husband.

# 6.5  PATIENTS' RIGHTS REGARDING CONSENT, CORRESPONDENCE AND PROPERTY

It is important that mentally ill patients know their rights on admission and thereafter. In particular, hospital managers must ensure that every detained patient understands the implications of the section under which he is being held as well as rights concerning appeals, consent to treatment, correspondence and discharge. This statement of rights should be in written form as well as an explanation being given orally (see pages 148–54 for sample forms given to patients).

## Consent

Informal patients are in the same position as any physically ill patient regarding consent to treatment (see Chapter 5, Section 5.1, pages 102–7). Two points are worth mentioning here. The first is that agreement to come into hospital implies consent to assessment and treatment procedures, but verbal or written consent is still required for all but the most minor of interventions. Failure to co-operate as mentioned on page 137 is grounds for the consultant psychiatrist to discharge that patient from hospital. Secondly, if a patient fails to consent to treatment and the doctor and nurse feel that it is urgently necessary for his own and others' safety to undergo treatment, then Section 5 can be invoked, followed by Section 2 or Section 3 as appropriate. Urgent treatment can then be given as below.

In certain circumstances urgent treatment can be given to the patient without his consent if that treatment is immediately necessary:

- To save the patient's life.
- To prevent a serious deterioration of his condition (the treatment not being irreversible).
- To alleviate serious suffering by the patient (the treatment not being irreversible or hazardous).
- And represents the minimum interference necessary to prevent the patient from behaving violently or being a danger to himself or others (the treatment not being irreversible or hazardous).

A treatment is considered irreversible if it has unfavourable irreversible physical or psychological consequences, and hazardous if it entails significant physical hazards, and this is decided by the responsible doctor.

The Act does not define what timespan is covered by this urgent treatment but another section of the Act does specify that a detained patient may not be given any form of drug or other specified treatment for more than three months without his consent. If at the end of this time, the patient still does not consent, then the responsible medical officer must contact the Mental Health Act Commission (MHAC), and a doctor appointed by the MHAC must certify that the treatment must none the less be given having first consulted the medical officer, the nurse and one other involved professional.

Specific requirements regarding consent are required for the carrying out of psychosurgery and electroconvulsive treatment (ECT).

No form of brain surgery may be given unless:

- The patient has consented to it; and a doctor appointed by the MHAC and two other appointed members of the Commission (may be non-medical members) have certified in writing that the patient is capable of understanding the nature, purpose and likely effects of the treatment; and
- the appointed doctor after consulting the patient's doctor, nurse and

one other involved professional (neither a doctor nor a nurse) has certified in writing that the treatment should be given.

If the patient does not consent or is not considered to be capable of giving a legal consent, the treatment cannot be given.

For ECT or other treatment (e.g. certain drugs) specified in the Act, either the patient must consent and the doctor must certify in writing that the patient is capable of understanding its nature, purpose or likely effects, or if the patient does not consent then a doctor appointed by the MHAC must certify that the treatment must be given after consultation as for psychosurgery.

Where consent has been accepted, the patient can at any time withdraw this consent and the procedure must be reviewed, as appropriate.

For any treatment, the nearest relative no longer has the authority, under the Mental Health Act (1983), to give consent on the patient's behalf.

## Correspondence

The formally detained patient has certain rights and restrictions concerning correspondence. He can write to the Secretary of State, any Member of Parliament, any officer of the Court of Protection, the managers of the hospital, the health authority, the Ombudsman, the social or probation service, community health councils, his solicitor, any authority having power of discharge, the Mental Health Review Tribunal, the European Commission of Human Rights, or the European Court of Human Rights.

However, there are some possible restrictions on formal patients' correspondence. The medical officer may withhold correspondence to patients if it is likely to interfere with treatment or cause him unnecessary distress. If possible, the letter concerned should be returned to the sender. Letters from patients may be stopped if the recipient of them has given notice in writing that he wishes the letters to be withheld, or if it is believed that letters are unnecessarily offensive or defamatory (excluding hospital staff) or would prejudice the interests of the patient. The nurse, however, has no right to read a patient's letters without his consent, and a record must be made of any mail withheld.

## Voting rights

All informal patients have the vote, whether they have an address at home, at a psychiatric hospital or at a general hospital. Often postal votes are required as patients can only vote in the constituency from which they were admitted.

## Property

People should always be encouraged to look after their own affairs even when mentally ill. However, there are a few mentally ill and mentally handicapped people who need help in dealing with their property. This can be provided by power of attorney or the Court of Protection.

Power of attorney can be granted by any adult to someone else who is then able to act on his behalf. However the person must understand the nature and extent of his property, be aware of others who have claims on him, be able to judge the relative strength of these claims and not be abnormally suggestible. On the whole, the use of power of attorney is limited for the mentally ill as, if they are able to understand the requirements for this, they are probably able to manage their affairs themselves. However, some patients may wish to be rid of the trouble of sorting out their finances and this would be a possible solution.

When someone becomes incapable of managing his affairs, the usual procedure is to apply to the Court of Protection. The Mental Health Act gives the court jurisdiction when medical evidence shows that a person is incapable of managing his affairs by reason of mental disorder. A relative, friend, solicitor or creditor may apply to the court for the appointment of a receiver who could be the nearest relative, a solicitor, an accountant or the local authority.

Unfortunately where a patient's income is small, e.g. a pension, often no action is taken to ensure that he receives some benefit from this money, but even small sums will accumulate to a reasonable amount over a period of time. Often there is no relative to consider the patient's interests and the only route to take is via the Court of Protection. In practice this rarely happens, and possibly some simpler way of dealing with these cases is needed.

## Question and concluding comments on 6.5

*Question:* Julie Ahmed, an 18-year-old student, was admitted to hospital in a very depressed and withdrawn state. On admission she repeatedly muttered that she was going to 'end it all'. The nurses admitting Julie were concerned that she might attempt suicide and decided that it was necessary to go through her belongings without her permission and remove anything that Julie could use to harm herself. They found and removed into safe keeping a penknife, a scarf and a belt. Were the nurses within their rights to act in this way?

*Comments:* The law on negligence is clear that if the nurses had not taken this action and Julie had killed or harmed herself, they could have been sued for not taking the proper care of Julie, knowing her frame of mind (see page 121). In other cases where the risk of patients harming themselves or others is unlikely, the nurses would not have been justified in invading the patient's privacy in this way. As in all situations where the patient is not fit or unwilling to check the property with a nurse, two nurses must check and record together what property the patient has and what is removed into safe keeping.

# 6.6   ROLES OF THE NEAREST RELATIVE, GUARDIAN AND HEALTH CARE WORKERS

The roles of these people have already been mentioned under the previous sections but are here summarised for easier access to this information.

## Role of the nearest relative

Whereas for the general patient the identity of the next of kin has limited legal repercussions except where children are concerned, the role of this person for the mentally disordered patient has much greater significance. The Act lays down a list of nearest relatives; if the first name is not available, then the second name is taken and so on. The nearest relative is the one with whom the patient 'ordinarily resides' or from whom he receives care. The list names the nearest relative as husband or wife (including a partner to whom the patient is not married but with whom the patient has been living for at least five years), son or daughter (including adopted or illegitimate children), father or mother, brother or sister, grandparent, grandchild, uncle or aunt, nephew or niece. For a child in care the local authority takes on the function of the nearest relative. An acting nearest relative can be appointed by the court if there is no other nearest relative as described by the Act, or if the nearest relative is unwilling to take on this role or is acting without due regard to the welfare of the patient.

The nearest relative can make an application for formal admission of the patient to the hospital managers (see page 155). In addition, he or she can direct the local social services department to consider making an application. The nearest relative also has a role to play at the end of the patient's stay in hospital, having the authority to discharge him from all civil sections provided the doctor does not think he is a danger to himself or others. The care of a patient's property may also come under the control of the nearest relative either through power of attorney or as a receiver appointed by the Court of Protection.

## Role of the guardian

The guardian's powers defined under the Mental Health Act are as follows:

- To require the patient's residence at a specified place.
- To require his attendance at specified places and times for medical treatment, occupation, education or training.
- To require access to the patient to be given to a doctor, approved social worker or other person so specified.

A guardianship order is made in a similar way to Section 3 for compulsory admission to hospital but instead of the patient entering hospital he stays in the community while receiving treatment. Either the local social services authority or any other adult named by the local authority can be appointed as guardian. The time span of the order is six months in the first instance, renewable for a further six months and then yearly as in Section 3. These orders can only be used for patients over 16 years old.

There may be difficulties in finding individuals who are willing to take on this responsibility. Guardianship orders are used more extensively with the mentally handicapped than the mentally ill.

## Role of the doctor under the Act

The doctor's duties regarding admission of patients are clearly defined.

Section 2 and Section 3 admissions must be supported by two doctors, one of whom knows the patient if practicable, and one who knows about mental disorder (see page 147). In an emergency, the recommendation of one doctor who has seen the patient within 24 hours of the application for admission is sufficient under Section 4.

Once the patient is admitted to hospital informally, his doctor may detain him for up to 72 hours under Section 5 (see page 164). The doctor may nominate one other medical practitioner on the staff of that hospital to act for him in his absence.

Admissions from the courts will have to be on the recommendations of two doctors.

A code of practice prepared by the Mental Health Act Commission for the Secretary of State gives guidance to doctors regarding admission and consent for treatment.

## Role of the approved social worker

An approved social worker is appointed after he has undergone special training in mental disorder and has achieved the necessary competence. This approved social worker can make an application for admission of a patient to the hospital managers (see page 156). Prior to doing so, he is instructed by statute to interview the patient in a suitable manner and satisfy himself that detention in a hospital is in view of all the circumstances the most appropriate way of providing the care and treatment needed. If the nearest relative has asked for an application to be made and the social worker decides not to follow this up, then he must inform the nearest relative of the reasons, in writing.

If the patient has been detained because of the nearest relative's application, the local social services department must be informed by the hospital managers and a social worker will interview the patient and report to the hospital managers on the relevant social circumstances.

The local social services department has a duty to provide aftercare services for certain discharged patients (see above).

## Role of the nurse

The Mental Health Act mentions a specific role for the nurse in two instances. The first is that the patient's nurse must be consulted before psychosurgery is given, and will need to be consulted before ECT is carried out if the patient has not given his consent.

The second role is in relation to holding an informal patient under

Section 5 of the Act. A registered mental nurse or a registered nurse for the mentally subnormal may detain an inpatient for six hours if:

- The patient is suffering from a mental disorder to such a degree that it is necessary for his health or safety or for the protection of others for him to be immediately restrained from leaving hospital.
- It is not practicable to secure the immediate attendance of a practitioner for the purpose of furnishing a report under Section 5.

Certain procedures must be followed. First, the holding power starts after the nurse has recorded her opinion on the prescribed form (No. 13) (see page 161) and this must then be delivered to the hospital managers as soon as possible. Finally, the nurse should let the hospital managers know as soon as the holding power has lapsed on the prescribed form (No. 16). However, the Act gives no further guidance as to how this holding power should be exercised. Most psychiatric hospitals have drawn up their own guidelines to which nurse employees should adhere, and the Royal College of Nursing has issued a document on *Seclusion and Restraint in Hospitals and Units for the Mentally Disordered*.

## Seclusion

Seclusion involves isolation of a patient in a room, the door of which is fastened so that he is prevented from leaving the room. In an emergency, a patient, whether formal or informal, can be secluded by the nurses, but only as a last resort, and the duty medical officer and nursing officer should be informed as soon as possible. If necessary, the nurse can invoke the appropriate part of Section 5 and as soon as is practicable the doctor can arrange the appropriate detention order. In other circumstances, seclusion should only be carried out on doctor's orders. In any case, the doctor should attend as soon as possible.

Once a patient is secluded, indirect observation should take place not less than every 15 minutes. A full nursing review should occur not less than once every two hours, and a review involving the medical officer not less than once every four hours. It is important that proper records are kept, detailing the reason for the seclusion and the total number of hours the patient was secluded. The Royal College of Nursing guidelines also suggest that all patients entering a psychiatric hospital should be informed of the need occasionally to segregate individual patients.

# Restraint

Restraint can be manual or mechanical and should only be used where absolutely necessary, otherwise hospital staff could be accused of assault and battery. Manual restraint should only be used for the protection of the patient or others. The nursing officer and duty doctor, if not already present, should be informed immediately of restraint. Mechanical restraint involves restricting the patient's free movements by means of equipment, furniture, furnishings, linen or clothing. It should not be used under any circumstances unless ordered by the medical officer. Any occasions involving the use of restraint should be recorded.

# Protection of the staff

Because of the particular problems involved in caring for the mentally disordered, the Act includes protective clauses for staff concerned. It states that no criminal proceedings shall be brought against any person acting in pursuance of his duties without reference to the Director of Public Prosecutions.

The problem of a mentally disordered patient attacking and injuring a nurse has been discussed on page 71.

# Question and concluding comments on 6.6

*Question:* Rebecca Duke, a 42-year-old with a long-term history of schizophrenia, was admitted on this occasion as a voluntary patient. Over the next 24 hours she became increasingly aggressive and on one occasion grabbed a fork from the table and threatened to stab the staff nurse with it. Following this, the staff observed her closely but in spite of this Rebecca grabbed a student nurse round the neck and tried to strangle her. The student got away with the help of a staff nurse. What action can the nurses now take?

*Comments:* Two nurses, one of whom should be a registered mental nurse, should restrain the patient, if necessary invoking their holding power under Section 5. The on-call doctor and nursing officer should be called. In this case it is likely that the doctor would sedate the patient, compulsorily detain her under Section 5 and arrange for her transfer to a secure unit. The registered mental nurse will need to complete the necessary documentation.

## 6.7 MENTAL HEALTH REVIEW TRIBUNALS AND MENTAL HEALTH ACT COMMISSION

### The Mental Health Review Tribunal

The Mental Health Review Tribunal consists of legal, medical and lay members with a lawyer as chairman. A panel consists of at least one member from each of the three groups. Its role is to hear appeals concerning discharge from patients, patients' relatives and guardians, and the hospital managers on behalf of patients.

Appeals can be made at certain times and briefly these are as follows:

- Within the first 14 days of detention under Section 2.
- Twice within the first year of detention under Section 3 and annually thereafter.
- If the patient or nearest relative does not appeal, then the tribunal will hear the patient's case after six months and thereafter every three years.

For further details, see Table 6.1.

The right of appeal is very important as has been seen in the operation of other parts of the Mental Health Act. It is particularly vital for the mentally disordered patient, in case decisions have been arrived at in rushed circumstances and in a way less than fair to all concerned.

In summary, the actions taken by the tribunal may be one of the following:

- Directing the patient to be discharged.
- Directing the patient to be discharged at a future date.
- Recommending that the patient be granted leave of absence.
- Recommending transfer to another hospital or into guardianship.

For tribunal appeals, some financial help is available for travelling expenses, subsistence and loss of earnings for the applicant and witnesses where applicable.

### The Mental Health Act Commission

The Mental Health Act Commission (MHAC) was established under the Mental Health Act (1983). It is multidisciplinary and exercises the Secretary of State's new powers to protect detained patients. The

**Table 6.1** *Applications to the Mental Health Review Tribunal.*

| Circumstances | When patient may apply for review | When nearest relative may apply for review |
|---|---|---|
| Detained Section 2 | In first 14 days | |
| Detained Section 3 | In first six months | |
| Received into guardianship | In first six months | |
| Transferred to hospital from guardianship | In first six months of detention in hospital | |
| Detention or guardianship is renewed | At any time in period for which detention is renewed | |
| Responsible medical officer bars relative's discharge | | In first 28 days from being notified |
| Nearest relative barred from acting as such | | In first 12 months, then every 12 months |
| Hospital order Section 37 | After six months, then every 12 months | As for patient |
| Hospital order with restriction Section 41 | After six months, then every 12 months | |

MHAC appoints the doctors and others who provide a second opinion on treatments which are covered by the new Act. On the direction of the Secretary of State it may also keep under review the care and treatment in hospitals and mental nursing homes of patients who are not liable to be detained.

The MHAC may investigate any complaint of a detained patient unless it considers it inappropriate to do so. Any records relating to the detention or treatment of a detained patient may be inspected and patients interviewed in private. It will publish and present to Parliament a report every other year. The MHAC will draw up for the Secretary of State two codes of practice, one on admissions, the other on medical treatment.

# 6.8 MENTAL HEALTH ACT (NORTHERN IRELAND) (1961)

The Mental Health Act (Northern Ireland) will eventually be revised on lines similar to the Mental Health Acts for England and Wales and Scotland.

## Definitions

Psychopathy is not mentioned, so people suffering from this condition cannot be compulsorily detained. The mentally handicapped patient is known as a special care case as the services for the mentally handicapped are called special care services. The Act contains powers compelling children who are special care cases to attend training centres, and lays down penalties on the parent or guardian who fails to ensure the child's attendance.

## Admission to hospital

Informal admissions can be made in the same way as for England and Wales.

Compulsory admission works slightly differently. Section 12 *Admission to hospital* is valid for 21 days and the grounds are as follows:

- The patient is suffering from mental illness or he requires special care.
- The mental disorder from which he is suffering is of a nature or degree which warrants his detention in hospital.
- It is necessary that he should be so detained in the interests of his own health or safety or for the protection of other persons.

Application is similar to the 1983 Act but the social worker is usually known as the welfare officer. Only one medical recommendation is needed from a doctor who knows the patient and a special knowledge of psychiatry is not needed.

Emergency admission takes place under Section 15. A statement must be included that because the situation is so urgent, compliance with all the provisions of Section 12 would cause too much delay. This order runs for seven days.

Section 19 most closely equates with Section 3 of the 1983 Act. This can come into force after admission of the patient under Section 12 or Section 15. Medical recommendation is made by a doctor approved by the hospital authority that the patient should be detained for a longer period.

Section 16 *Detention of informal patients* equates with Section 5 and Section 106 *Mentally disordered persons found in public places* is almost identical to Section 136 of the 1983 Act.

## Patients involved in criminal proceedings

There are a number of differences here as the N. Ireland Act equates more closely with the previous 1959 Act for England and Wales.

However, Section 48 is broadly similar to Section 37 *Hospital Order* of the 1983 Act. Section 53 *Restriction Order* is similar to Section 41 and the patient can only be discharged, transferred to another hospital or given privileges on an order from the Minister of Home Affairs, known as 'the Minister' in the Act. Under Sections 48 and 53 the patient can make an appeal in the same way as appeal against conviction.

## Patients' rights

In N. Ireland it is often assumed that a detained patient can be forced to undergo treatment even if he does not give consent, as long as the nearest relative has been consulted if possible. However, this assumption is probably false as Section 26 refers to the use of compulsion only in detaining the patient, not to the giving of treatment. Therefore, it is probably wiser to approach the question of consent in accordance with the comments earlier in this chapter (see page 169), but the N. Ireland Act does not spell out the procedures to be followed when psychotherapy, ECT or other specified treatments are proposed.

There are similar legal controls to correspondence as in the 1983 Act. Correspondence to certain individuals must be forwarded unopened, i.e. Lord Chief Justice, the Minister of Health and Local Government, any Member of Parliament, the Review Tribunal, the Ministry, the Registrar of the Department of the Affairs of Mental Patients and the patient's nearest relative.

## Roles of those associated with the patient

These roles are very similar except for the following points:

- Application of guardianship is made in a similar way but the role of the guardian differs in that it is less specific. The guardian is given the same powers as a parent of a child under 14 years old.
- The doctor's role is similar but there is a difference regarding the numbers and specialisation of doctors required for compulsory admission.
- The role and functioning of the Mental Health Review Tribunals is very similiar. In any other facets of the legislation concerning the mentally disordered that have not been mentioned here, the N. Ireland Act is broadly in line with the Acts for England and Wales and Scotland.

## REFERENCES

National Consumer Council (1983). *Patients' Rights, a Guide for NHS Patients and Doctors*, HMSO, London.
Royal College of Nursing (1979). *Seclusion and Restraint in Hospitals and Units for the Mentally Disordered*, RCN, London.
Skegg, P. D. G. (1984). *Law Ethics and Medicine*, Clarendon Press, Oxford.
Squibb Ltd (1986). *Mental Health Act (1983)*, E. R. Squibb & Sons, Hounslow, Middlesex.
Whitehead, T. (1983). *Mental Illness and the Law*, Blackwell, Oxford.

# 7. The Nurse and Visitors

The nurse is inevitably concerned with the patient's relatives and friends as well as with the patient himself. In the hospital and health centre the nurse needs to know the law in relation to these visitors. She may also have to deal with trespassers. In the community, the nurse becomes the visitor and needs to be aware that the patient in his own home has certain responsibilities towards others.

The law involved is the law of torts—trespass, negligence and occupiers' liability.

*Acts*
　Occupiers Liability Act (1957)
　Occupiers Liability Act (1984)

## 7.1  INJURIES TO VISITORS

Mr Poole was walking along the hospital corridor on his way to visit his wife, a patient in one of the wards. Suddenly he was struck a violent blow on the head. A sign suspended above the corridor had fallen just as Mr Poole passed underneath. He required treatment for a severe scalp wound and was so shaken that he was unable to go to work for several days. Mrs Poole was very upset and the worry about her husband led her to discharge herself against medical advice.

The health authority has to take responsibility for some injuries to patients and staff, and visitors who are lawfully on health service premises must also be protected against any negligence on the part of that health authority. In the example above, Mr Poole should have been able to walk safely through the hospital premises without fear of such an accident, and hospital employees had clearly failed to secure or maintain the sign adequately.

Other examples of injuries to visitors commonly involve slipping on wet floors or mats, or falling down worn stairs. The nurse will also be involved when a visitor suffers injury because of some hazard on the ward, such as tripping over wires and slipping on wet floors. As with patients, the nurse owes some duty of care to visitors, although this is to a much lesser extent. Thus, all that has already been said about these accidents in section 5.2 applies to visitors as well as patients. The nurse has a duty to remove hazards, to report those that cannot be dealt with immediately and make sure that warning notices are displayed nearby.

A report must be made of any accident to a visitor in exactly the same way as that to a patient (see page 116).

## Question and concluding comments on 7.1

*Question:* At 23.00, a man was making his way down some stairs in a hospital when he slipped, fell and broke his leg. He was treated in the accident and emergency department. Here, he threatened to sue the hospital for damages, saying that the stairway had been inadequately lit. However, on questioning him as to what he was doing in the hospital, he became evasive and it was eventually ascertained that he was not, in fact, authorised to be there at that time of night. Would he have any grounds for suing the hospital?

*Comments:* It appears that this man was trespassing in the hospital and as he was not known to be present until the accident occurred, the health authority cannot be held to have the same duty of care towards him as towards an authorised visitor. However, the health authority still has some responsibility towards any person on their property and should ensure that places not open to the public are clearly labelled to that effect and any areas where people may inadvertently go are safe. Thus, this man may have some grounds for complaint. (See sections 7.3 and 7.4.)

## 7.2 ANSWERING ENQUIRIES

Miss Logan had had a major operation the previous day and was slowly recovering. Sister Blake was on duty during the morning when a junior nurse informed her that Miss Logan's employer was on the telephone enquiring after her. Sister felt that it would be wise for her to take the call and, after ascertaining the name of the caller, informed him that Miss Logan was making satisfactory progress. The employer then asked what operation had been done and how long Miss Logan was likely to be in hospital. Sister Blake said she was not in the position to be able to tell him.

Answering enquiries of relatives, friends and others about a patient's condition is an everyday occurrence for the nurse. It does involve the area of patient confidentiality which is discussed further in Part IV. On the whole, there appears to be no harm in answering the queries of close relatives unless the patient has forbidden this or the nature of the condition indicates otherwise, for example if the patient has venereal disease or is having an abortion. However, information should only be given to other people with the patient's permission. In the example above, to give to the employer facts of the patient's illness and amount of time off work could lead to the person losing his job if the condition was serious, disabling or involving a lengthy convalescence. The same care needs to be taken where the press are concerned. Most hospitals have rules for answering such enquiries and these usually involve referring the press to someone senior who will either give them a prepared statement only or have the authority to refuse to give them any information at all.

Telephone enquiries pose a further problem as they could be fraudulent. For example, a person could enquire after his wife, but in fact not be that woman's husband, and it is difficult to be sure until the patient's relatives have been seen and spoken to face to face. Thus, unless the nurse is quite certain of the enquirer's identity, the amount of information given over the telephone should be limited, and if necessary, an arrangement should be made to see the enquirer when he comes to visit.

Occasionally, the nurse is asked for information by the police. The nurse is under no legal compulsion to supply this (see page 20). However, there are occasions where it may be advisable to give the required information if this is clearly in the best interests of the public or the patient. The nurse should always be wary of this situation and not be over willing to disclose too many details. Again, a sensible rule is for the ward staff to refer the enquiry to a more senior member of staff.

## Question and concluding comments on 7.2

*Question:* The ward sister of a gynaecological ward received a telephone call from the police asking for information about one of her patients.

The police informed the sister that they believed that one of her patients, Miss Godfrey, had been admitted in the process of having an abortion. Was this a spontaneous abortion or were there grounds for suspecting it to be a criminal abortion, they asked. How could the ward sister best deal with this type of enquiry?

*Comments:* The ward sister need not give them an answer if she felt it were breaking patient confidentiality. She could refer the police to the appropriate medical officer for him to decide on the answer. However, nursing staff should try to co-operate with the police where possible. If, as far as the ward sister knows, the patient's abortion has been spontaneous, then she would probably be saving the patient and the police a lot of time and trouble if she told them this without elaborating on the facts.

## 7.3 TRESPASSERS

Hospitals are very open places. It is very easy for unauthorised individuals to walk around without being accosted. As these trespassers are usually there for criminal purposes, it is important that nurses are aware of the law relating to them and the practical procedures to follow to procure their removal.

A trespasser is anyone who is on health service premises without the express or implied consent of the health authority. An off-duty nurse going into a ward to check her duties, a nurse's husband waiting in the corridor for his wife to come off duty, a son visiting his sick father out of visiting hours as his shift work does not allow him to visit in the evening—all these people can imply the consent of the authority as they are on the premises for authorised reasons.

In a small hospital, the porters at the reception desk become used to regular authorised visitors and can accost those who are not familiar. This plays a big part in deterring trespassers. However, in a large establishment this is practically impossible. Thus, the nurse in the hospital ward or health centre clinic must observe who is coming into the ward or room and make efforts to check on strangers. She can do this quite politely so that no offence is given where the visitor is genuine. An enquiry of 'Can I help you?' can be followed up by escorting the person in the required direction. Some trespassers can seem very plausible and ask after a fictitious patient which is why it is necessary to follow the enquiry through. The nurse should even be suspicious of a white-coated individual. A trespasser may work on the assumption that a white coat is an acceptable hospital garment worn by numerous professional workers and that he will therefore not be questioned. Nurses should also be suspicious of an individual who claims to be a television maintenance worker required to take the ward television for overhaul. Many televisions have been lost from hospitals in this way!

When a nurse suspects that an individual is a trespasser, she should order him to leave. If he refuses, reasonable force may then be used to remove him. The nurse will require physical reinforcements for this and should contact the senior nursing and security staff for assistance. If necessary, the police can be called in.

An individual who has been authorised to be on health service premises can become a trespasser if, on being requested to leave, he refuses to do so.

## Question and concluding comments on 7.3

*Question:* At the end of visiting hours, a patient's boyfriend remained on the ward. As it was clear that the patient was wanting him to go, the staff nurse asked him to leave. He refused to do so. What should the staff nurse do?

*Comments:* The boyfriend is now technically a trespasser and has no right to stay on the ward. The staff nurse should contact her immediate superior who will come to the ward and tell the man to leave. If he still refuses, this nurse should contact the security staff on call for assistance to remove this trespasser. A report should be made to the health authority.

## 7.4  THE NURSE AS VISITOR OR TRESPASSER

Mrs Parsons was severely disabled with multiple sclerosis, unable to walk and with limited movement in her arms. Her husband cared for her at home with some help from the community nurse. A hoist had been fitted to lift Mrs Parsons, who was rather overweight, into the bath. One day when the nurse arrived to bath Mrs Parsons, Mr Parsons refused to allow the nurse to use the hoist, saying his wife was frightened of it, but he offered to help the nurse lift Mrs Parsons into the bath. The nurse refused to bath the patient without the hoist because of the risk of injury to her back and she reported the incident to her nursing officer.

As the health authority has certain responsibilities towards visitors on its property, so the occupier of a private dwelling has similar responsibilities. If the nurse feels that the risks of entering and working on someone else's property constitute a danger, then she may refuse to give the care required. If harm did befall her, she may have grounds for suing the occupier. For example, the property could be in a dangerous condition with rotten floorboards or inadequate lighting. There could be dangers present such as fierce dogs allowed loose around the property. Threats of violence from other inmates of the property constitute a very unpleasant danger and need careful handling (see page 71). A refusal by a patient or relative to co-operate in a safe system of working as in the example above also constitutes a serious risk.

The community nurse may inadvertently become a trespasser. A patient may want to give the nurse a key to the front door, leave the key with a neighbour or on a piece of string hanging inside the letterbox. The nurse should obviously advise the patient against such practices because of the risk of thieves and possible accusations against herself. If the patient insists, leaving the key with a neighbour is probably the safest practice. In these circumstances the nurse could be accused of trespass if the patient were not at home. In other circumstances the nurse may become so concerned at the failure of a patient to answer the door that she decides to investigate, possibly by entering the back garden and trying the back door. It would be wiser to report her concern and if necessary contact the police.

As in the hospital setting, the occupier has some duties towards the trespasser as well as to the visitor. Under the Occupiers Liability Act (1984), the occupier may reasonably be expected to offer the trespasser some protection against a danger on the premises that he, the occupier, is aware of. This protection should be in the form of some warning or discouragement. For example, if fierce dogs are on the premises there should be a clear warning 'Beware of the dog' and the dogs should be restricted in their movements.

## Question and concluding comments on 7.4

*Question:* The community nurse, concerned at there being no answer when she rang the doorbell and knowing that her patient was old and frail, decided to investigate round the back of the house. She entered the back garden through an unlocked, unmarked gate. Once in the garden she was suddenly attacked by a large Alsatian dog and severely bitten before she managed to escape. What was her legal position?

*Comments:* Legally she was trespassing but the occupier should have placed some warning in a permanent and visible place that a dog was loose and the gate should have been locked to discourage trespassers. However, the nurse, if wise, should have avoided placing herself in such a situation at all.

# REFERENCES

Speller, S. R. (1978). *Law Relating to Hospitals and Kindred Institutions*, Lewis, London.
Whincup, M. (1982). *Legal Aspects of Medical and Nursing Service*, 3rd edn, Ravenswood, Beckenham, Kent.

# 8. The Nurse, Drugs and Radiation

A knowledge of drug and radiation controls is essential to the safety of the nurse.

Acts and Regulations involved

Radioactive Substances Act (1948), (1960)
Medicines Acts (1968) and (1971)
The Misuse of Drugs Act (1971)
The Misuse of Drugs Act (1971) (Modification), Order 1985
The Poisons Act (1972)
The Misuse of Drugs Regulations (1973)
The Misuse of Drugs (Notification of and Supply to Addicts) Regulations (1973)
The Misuse of Drugs (Safe Custody) Regulations (1973)
The Misuse of Drugs (Amendment) Regulations (1974), (1975)
The Misuse of Drugs (Safe Custody) (Amendment) Regulations (1974), (1975)
Health and Safety at Work Act (1974)
The Misuse of Drugs Regulations (1985)
The Misuse of Drugs (Safe Custody) (Amendment) Regulations (1985)

## 8.1 DRUGS

An important part of the nurse's job is the administration of medicines. As already discussed, the nurse may be guilty of negligence in their administration (see section 5.2) or subject to disciplinary action if she does not abide by the required professional standards (see section 4.5). There is also a statutory framework controlling drugs and some aspects of these Acts of Parliament are applicable to the nurse, although other parts mainly concern the manufacturer, supplier, pharmacist and medical practitioner.

The following paragraphs aim to clarify those sections of the law of interest and use to the nurse.

## Some definitions

The Medicines Acts (1968) and (1971) control the manufacture, sale and supply of medical products, and these are defined as:

> 'any substance or article (not being an instrument, apparatus or appliance) which is manufactured, sold, supplied, imported or exported, wholly or mainly for use
> (a) By being administered to one or more human beings or animals for a medicinal purpose
> (b) As an ingredient in the preparation of a substance or article which is to be administered to one or more human beings or animals for medical purpose.'

The Acts proceed to define medical purpose as one of the following:

> '(a) Treating or preventing disease
> (b) Diagnosing disease or ascertaining the existence, degree or extent of a physiological condition
> (c) Contraception
> (d) Inducing anaesthesia
> (e) Otherwise preventing or interfering with the normal operation of a physiological function, whether permanently or temporarily, and whether by way of terminating, rendering or postponing or increasing or accelerating, the operation of that function, or in any other way.'

Certain products are excluded and the list of these can be added to by delegated legislation. At present, the list concerns substances used in dental surgery for filling cavities, and bandages and surgical dressings, where no medication with a curative function is included. The Acts do not sanction the use of medical products in tests in a laboratory or research establishment.

The nurse is concerned with the categorisation of drugs and poisons, and this legislation is contained in the Misuse of Drugs Act (1971) and the Poisons Act (1972).

The Poisons List in the latter Act contains two parts. Part I consists of those substances prohibited from being sold except by a person lawfully conducting a retail pharmacy business. Part II consists of poisons prohibited from being sold except by a person as above *or* by a person whose name is entered on a special list. Thus Part II can permit certain poisons, such as weed killers, to be reasonably available. This Act controls the supply, packaging, storage, transport and sale of non-medicinal poisons as well as medicinal poisons.

The Misuse of Drugs Act is of greater relevance to the nurse. There are various groups of regulations; the main ones concern the classification of drugs into schedules, of which there are five.

*Schedule 2.* This is the most important schedule in practical terms. Over 100 drugs and their derivatives are listed. The best known to the nurse are cocaine above certain concentrations, diamorphine, dihydrocodeine in injection form, methadone, morphine, opium in certain preparations, papaveretum and pethidine. In addition, the stringent controls of Schedule 2 drugs are also applied to amphetamine, dexamphetamine, methylamphetamine, methaqualone, methylphenidate, glutetimide, lefetamine and phenmetrazine.

*Schedule 5.* This has to be considered in conjunction with Schedule 2 as it is an exempting schedule for some preparations. Certain substances that are included in Schedule 2 when administered by injection are exempted from these strict controls if given orally, for example dihydrocodeine. Others are exempted as they were not included under the old Dangerous Drugs Act and the new Act does not aim to control these preparations more strictly, for example Dover's powder which contains opium. However, if an additional controlled drug is added to the preparation exempted, the exemption is lost, for example the addition of dexamphetamine to a tablet containing codeine.

*Schedule 3.* Only 12 drugs are named in this schedule, none of them of wide clinical use in this country. They are benzphetamine, chlorphentermine, ethchlorvynol, ethinamate, mazindol, mephentermine, meprobamate, methprylone, pentazocine, phendimetrazine, phentermine and pipradol.

*Schedule 1.* This schedule contains the most strictly controlled drugs. Some are not used as medicines at all. They include cannabis and lysergide, with their derivatives, raw opium and a variety of hallucinogens. A licence from the Home Secretary is required to possess, produce, supply or administer any of these drugs.

*Schedule 4.* Benzodiazepine drugs.

## Storage and supply of drugs

In a hospital or similar institution, controlled drugs are kept in the care of the pharmacist and he may supply these drugs in accordance with fixed regulations. If there is no pharmacist, and where the hospital or nursing home is mainly maintained by a public authority out of public funds or by a charity or voluntary subscriptions, the matron or acting matron can take charge of these drugs. She may supply drugs from Schedules 2 and 3 to those authorised to receive them.

A requisition is required from the sister in charge of a ward, department or theatre for the supply of stock controlled drugs. This must be in writing and signed by the recipient specifying the total quantity of drug supplied. Once this has been complied with, the requisition should be marked to denote this. A messenger can be empowered to collect these drugs from the pharmacy on the recipient's behalf if he produces a statement in writing. However, in the hospital, it is not clear if this is necessary where the messenger is delegated this task regularly, or whether the controlled drugs need to be kept in a locked receptacle while in transit.

At ward level, stocks of drugs are in the charge of the sister or acting sister. She is authorised to possess Schedule 2 and Schedule 3 drugs lawfully supplied to her for administration to patients in that area as directed by the doctor.

In the community, a certified midwife has certain rights under the Act. She may possess and administer pethidine as is necessary for the practice of her profession. Her supplies must be obtained on a midwife's supply order signed by the appropriate medical officer. In the hospital or nursing home, the midwife must revert to the usual practice of the drug only being administered on the doctor's instructions.

The hospital or community nurse needs not only to take charge of drugs, but to keep them safe. The Safe Custody Regulations (1973) apply to controlled drugs but the nurse must ensure that all drugs are locked up securely. The regulations mentioned require controlled drugs to be kept in a locked safe, cabinet, room or receptacle. This last enables community nurses to take controlled drugs with them in the performance of their work. In fact, hospitals usually ensure extra security by keeping controlled drugs in a locked cupboard within a locked room or cupboard.

Finally, a patient may possess a controlled drug for his own use as long as it has been properly prescribed.

## Administration of drugs

All hospitals have their own rules for the administration of drugs, in order to safeguard the patient, and these must be strictly followed. In addition the UKCC published an advisory paper in 1986 on the administration of medicines. This is a framework to assist the individual and help in the development of local policies and guidelines. It supports the view that nurses whose names are on the first-level parts of the register are competent to administer medicines on their own, although a second person may well be involved in a learning role. Guidance is also given on the position of the enrolled nurse regarding the administration of medicines, the UKCC opposing the use of the second-level practitioner in this role unless under the direction of the first-level nurse. However, most health authorities would find this restriction difficult to implement in many areas. A way around this is to treat the administration of drugs as an extension of the enrolled nurse's role and follow the requirements as described on page 230.

Legislation also covers details of prescriptions and registers for controlled drugs.

The prescription for a controlled drug must be written in ink by the doctor, be signed by him and be dated, although the date need not be in handwriting. In addition, to minimise the risk of forgery, the following details must also be given in the doctor's own writing:

- Name and address of the patient.
- Dose to be taken, the form of the preparation, for example, tablets, capsules, and the strength of the preparation if appropriate.
- The total quantity to be supplied written in words and figures.

In the hospital where ward stocks of certain drugs are held, these details are not required, but if a drug has to be dispensed for a particular patient, then the requirements should be followed.

Registers must be kept for drugs in Schedules 2 and 1. The pharmacist has a register for the supply of drugs, and a further register of drugs administered must also be kept. The register does not have to be printed, but must be bound and not loose leaf. Any entries must be in ink and may not be cancelled, obliterated or altered. Any correction must be included in the margin or at the foot of the page and be dated. The register is kept for a period of two years from the date of last entry. Records of the administration of other drugs must also be kept carefully, although not a statutory requirement, in case of possible legal action concerning negligence.

The nurse is at risk from drug abuse because of ease of access, not just to controlled drugs but to other drugs as well, such as sedatives and hypnotics. The pharmacist and ward sister are usually required by the hospital authority to carry out regular checks on drugs. These are a local requirement rather than a statutory one. The nurse should also remember that taking any drugs from the ward is theft and she would face criminal charges as well as disciplinary action.

# Drug addicts

It would be unusual for a nurse never to be involved with a drug addict although the mental nurse's knowledge of this situation needs to be greater than that of the general nurse. It is useful to know the legal framework as drug addicts can be manipulative of the less experienced nurse.

As already seen, the drugs of addiction are included in Schedule 2 of the Misuse of Drugs Act, and therefore subject to stringent controls. In addition, the Misuse of Drugs (Notification of and Supply to Addicts) Regulations (1973) aim to control drug addiction. Doctors are required to notify the Chief Medical Officer at the Home Office of persons considered or suspected to be addicted to certain controlled drugs. The regulations lay down the criteria for this: a person is regarded as an addict if he has as a result of repeated administration become so dependent on a drug that he has an overwhelming desire for the administration of it to be continued. The regulations include a list of drugs where notification is required.

Notification is not required if the drug is being used for the treatment of organic disease or injury, or if notification has already been made within the previous twelve months by another doctor. Thus, the patient who is receiving diamorphine in the control of terminal cancer pain, even if becoming addicted, will not be considered for notification.

The regulations also cover the supply of diamorphine and cocaine to addicts. No doctor can supply these drugs to an addict unless he is licensed to do so by the Home Secretary. Usually a condition of a doctor's licence is that he supplies drugs to the addict only at a hospital or nursing home named in the licence. The exemption to this is if the drugs have to be administered for treatment of the addict for organic disease or injury.

The nurse administering the above controlled drugs to addicts can assume that the law is being followed unless she suspects otherwise. If she is concerned that all is not well, she should refuse to administer the drugs until the situation has been clarified.

## Questions and concluding comments on 8.1

*Question:* A staff nurse and a second-year student nurse were preparing to give an injection of 20 mg of morphine to a patient. As the student nurse went to break the ampoule, she accidentally crushed the glass and the drug was wasted. What would the nurses do in this situation?

*Comments:* The drug has not been administered to the patient and another ampoule will have to be used. However, as morphine is a controlled drug where the quantities of ward stocks are rigidly controlled, the wastage of 20 mg of morphine must be recorded on the appropriate page in the register and witnessed by both nurses.

*Question:* The two nurses above then drew up 20 mg of morphine for the patient and the staff nurse went to administer the drug to the patient. The student stayed by the drug cupboard to tidy up. Half an hour later, the patient asked the student for her injection. The student expressed surprise as the patient said she had never received the injection. What should the student nurse do about this?

*Comments:* Both nurses may have been negligent here. Both should sign the register to witness that the drug is given to the patient, but the student nurse failed to go with the staff nurse to do so. No nurse should ever be distracted from this duty. It is now impossible to find out exactly what happened. Did the staff nurse negligently give the drug to the wrong patient? Or is the situation possibly even more serious with the staff nurse being guilty of stealing the drug for her own or another's use? Or is the patient lying or very forgetful? The situation would have to be reported to the senior nurse as well as the appropriate medical staff. Both nurses would be required to make statements, and all the nurses on the ward would be reminded of their duties in connection with controlled drugs.

## 8.2   RADIATION

Nurse Thomas, a 22-year-old enrolled nurse working in the paediatric area, was often asked to take the babies and toddlers for their X-rays and was expected to assist the radiographer by holding them still in the required positions. It was not until she heard a doctor discussing the dangers of too many X-rays for patients that she realised that she may have been exposing herself to unnecessary risks.

Nurses in hospital, by the nature of their work, are the members of the medical team who spend most time with their patients. Therefore, there is always the possibility of nurses being exposed to unnecessarily high doses of radiation, either from a radioactive source being used in the treatment, for example of cancer of the uterus, or from X-rays being used for diagnostic or treatment purposes. All hospitals have local rules for nurses to follow, but the legal framework is a *Code of Practice for the Protection of Persons against Ionising Radiations Arising from Medical and Dental Use* (DHSS, 1972), backed up by the Health and Safety at Work (etc.) Act (1974).

## Definitions

Radiation is classifed into several types. The nurse will hear of X-rays, beta (β) rays and gamma (γ) rays. X-Rays are generated in an electrical machine, while β- and γ-rays are emitted from radioactive substances. X-Rays and γ-rays have the greatest powers of penetration into the human body.

The nurse is likely to be in contact with X-rays for their diagnostic use. A patient receiving radiotherapy treatment will also be exposed to X-rays or some other form of radiation. In this case, because of the intensity generated, the patient receives his treatment in a sealed room, and a nurse working in the radiotherapy department or accompanying a patient will remain outside and observe the patient through a special observation window.

The nurse on the ward will meet two other sources of radiation. Sealed sources of radiation consist of radioactive material permanently enclosed in solid containers. For example, radium needles are used in the treatment of carcinoma of cervix and radiogold grains for carcinoma of bladder. These sources remain radioactive for a very long time, described by the half-life of the substance. (The half-life of a radioactive substance is the time it takes for one half of the mass of a particular

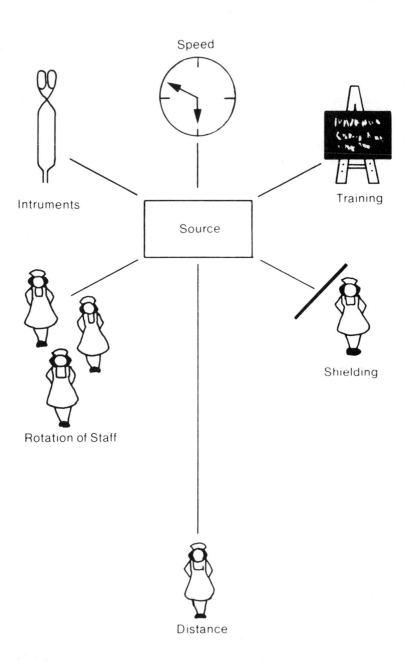

**Figure 8.1** Principles of safe use when working with ionising radiation.

substance to decay.) The half-life of radium is 1600 years. Thus the nurse must always regard the source as radioactive, although it remains localised.

She will also meet unsealed sources which are radioactive materials in liquid form, used either for treatment or diagnosis. For example, radio-iodine is concentrated by the thyroid gland and can be used in the treatment of malignancy here. However, as the substance is in liquid form, it will pass through the body and be excreted in body fluids such as urine. Thus there is always the risk of contamination, although the risk is reduced because the half-life of radio-iodine is only eight days.

# Principles of safe use

The code of practice lists a number of basic principles to be followed to ensure safety of all those working with ionising radiations (Figure 8.1).

## 1. Distance
The dose of radiation decreases markedly with distance. Therefore the nurse should move as far as possible from the source, for example when accompanying a patient to X-ray.

## 2. Shielding
A thick and dense protective material such as concrete or lead absorbs a large amount of radiation. The patient receiving radiotherapy is contained in a specially screened room. A patient being treated by a sealed source can have some movable barriers placed around his bed, and before and after the source is put in place it should be kept in a sealed protective container. A nurse who has to support a patient or hold a baby for X-rays (as Nurse Thomas had to do) should wear protective lead apron and gloves.

## 3. Speed
The shorter the time spent near a radioactive source, the less radiation is received. Therefore the nurse must work as rapidly as is efficiently possible in the care of a patient with a radioactive source.

## 4. Instruments
Radioactive sources must never be handled and instruments will enable staff to remain at a distance and behind barriers.

## 5. Training
All nurses should have some basic training and those working in areas where the risks are especially high should receive extra tuition. Patients can also play an important part if they are taught how to co-operate with the required precautions.

## 6. Rotation of staff
Rotation of staff will apply particularly in the nursing of patients with radioactive sources, and the senior staff on the ward should plan patients' care with this in mind. Even accompanying patients to X-ray, nurses must be rotated, as Nurse Thomas should have been. If rotation is impossible, for example for the nurse working in an X-ray department, she should be regarded as a designated person where extra controls are employed, and the amount of radiation received by her should be monitored by a film badge.

# Question and concluding comments on 8.2

*Question:* A patient who had been given radioactive iodine is incontinent of urine the following night. What precautions should the nurse take?

*Comments:* The nurse should work quickly and efficiently because of the radiation present. The sheets will have become contaminated with radioactivity and therefore must be placed in a special container. The nurse should work with gloved hands and apron or gown to prevent contamination of clothing and skin.

# REFERENCES

Department of Health and Social Security (1972). *Code of Practice for the Protection of Persons Against Ionising Radiation Arising from Medical and Dental Use*, 3rd edn, HMSO, London.
Department of Health and Social Security (1977). *Guide to the Misuse of Drugs Act (1971) and to Certain Regulations Made Under the Act*, DHSS, London.
Department of Health and Social Security (1986). *Letter*, CNO 86 3, DHSS, London.
Radioactive Substances Advisory Committee (1965). *The Safe Use of Ionizing Radiation, a Handbook for Nurses*, Dd 1630501, HMSO, London.

# PART IV
## Legal and Moral Problems

# 9. The Nurse and Ethics

This chapter sets the scene for a further look at the interaction between law and ethics.

## 9.1 THE NATURE OF ETHICS

Staff Nurse King was giving Pupil Nurse Allerton some instructions about her work. 'You will be responsible for Mrs Brown's care this morning. There is nothing that urgently needs to be done for her, but you ought to check that she has had a wash. It would be a good idea to find her some occupation and you should encourage her to talk to the other patients.'

Nurse Allerton is left with a set of instructions involving her with a fair amount of judgement and personal decision making. Such is typical of the nature of ethical statements. Wherever the words should, ought, prefer, desire, responsible, good, bad, right and wrong are heard or seen, a whole set of moral reactions is called into play. As they are so deeply engrained in the nursing profession, it is worth exploring them more fully.

### The ethical basis of behaviour

A practical definition of ethics as 'moral rules governing behaviour' is sufficient to the nurse for most purposes. However, a deeper study of ethics may well help her to appreciate that we all make underlying moral assumptions when dealing with problematic situations. Theoretically, there are three basic codes on which these moral assumptions are built.

- *The code of duty (deontologist code).* This is based on the principle that duty is absolute in nature, for example that we have an inherent duty to care for those who cannot care for themselves.
- *The utilitarian code.* The principle of utility works on the basis that actions can only be judged by their consequences and are decided on the basis of the greatest good of the greatest number. This code would help us to decide how to use the limited resources in the health service by considering the largest number who would benefit.
- *The 'rights of man' ethic.* This code has arisen more recently and is based on the notion of social contract. For example, government and governed have a contract involving rights and responsibilities on both sides, with consent being an implicit part of this contract.

For the nurse, many ethical considerations will influence her in her work. For example, the way she treats herself and others, the way she both exercises authority and accepts discipline, and the manner in which she makes those value judgements already mentioned at the start of this section, are all coloured by her moral code and will therefore affect the care the patient receives.

## Links between law and ethics

A quick glance at the contents of this book will bring to mind a number of ethical areas that are also the concern of the law. Most notably, negligence reflects the ethical concern with duty, in its expectation that the individual must anticipate the results of his actions and act in such a way as to safeguard those who may be affected by such actions (see page 27). In fact, the whole area of civil law with its root in common law grew out of people's appreciation of their having responsibilities towards each other.

More recently, a major concern of employment legislation is to protect the employee and ensure fair treatment from his employer. The development of codes of practice to assist in the interpretation of these Acts is one way that a bridge is built between law and ethics (page 63).

## 9.2 A CODE OF CONDUCT FOR NURSES

One of the hallmarks of a profession is the codification of a set of moral principles into its structure. Doctors, lawyers and nurses all have their

Each registered nurse, midwife and health visitor shall act, at all times, in such a manner as to justify public trust and confidence, to uphold and enhance the good standing and reputation of the profession, to serve the interests of society, and above all to safeguard the interests of individual patients and clients.

Each registered nurse, midwife and health visitor is accountable for his or her practice, and, in the exercise of professional accountability shall:

1 Act always in such a way as to promote and safeguard the well being and interests of patients/clients.

2 Ensure that no action or omission on his/her part or within his/her sphere of influence is detrimental to the condition or safety of patients/clients.

3 Take every reasonable opportunity to maintain and improve professional knowledge and competence.

4 Acknowledge any limitations of competence and refuse in such cases to accept delegated functions without first having received instruction in regard to those functions and having been assessed as competent.

5 Work in a collaborative and co-operative manner with other health care professionals and recognise and respect their particular contributions within the health care team.

6 Take account of the customs, values and spirtual beliefs of patients/clients.

7 Make known to an appropriate person or authority any conscientious objection which may be relevant to professional practice.

8 Avoid any abuse of the privileged relationship which exists with patients/clients and of the privileged access allowed to their property, residence or workplace.

9 Respect confidential information obtained in the course of professional practice and refrain from disclosing such information without the consent of the patient/client, or a person entitled to act on his/her behalf, except where disclosure is required by law or by the order of a court or is necessary in the public interest.

10 Have regard to the environment of care and its physical, psychological and social effect on patients/clients, and also to the adequacy of resources, and make known to appropriate persons or authorities any circumstances which could place patients/clients in jeopardy or which militate against safe standards of practice.

11 Have regard to the workload of and the pressures on professional colleagues and subordinates and take appropriate action if these are seen to be such as to constitute abuse of the individual practitioner and/or to jeopardise safe standards of practice.

12 In the context of the individual's own knowledge, experience, and sphere of authority, assist peers and subordinates to develop professional competence in accordance with their needs.

13 Refuse to accept any gift, favour or hospitality which might be interpreted as seeking to exert undue influence to obtain preferential consideration.

14 Avoid the use of professional qualifications in the promotion of commercial products in order not to compromise the independence of professional judgement on which patients/clients rely.

**Figure 9.1.** UKCC Code of Professional Conduct for the nurse, midwife and health visitor.

own ethics which are learnt subconsciously to some extent by the participants during their training. This aspect of the nursing profession has been considered so important that codes have been drawn up at both national and international level. The International Council of Nurses originally drew up a Code of Ethics for Nurses in July 1953 and has revised this on a number of occasions since. For the UK nurse, the UKCC produced the second edition of a code of

Professional Conduct for the Nurse, Midwife and Health Visitor in 1984 (see Figure 9.1).

The status of this code demonstrates a further interesting link between law and ethics. The UKCC has legal status and authority under the Nurses, Midwives and Health Visitors Act (1979) to prepare rules that carry the weight of law. However, the code of conduct is issued for 'guidance and advice', laying a moral responsibility rather than a statutory duty on members of the profession. A marked failure to abide by the code could, in turn, lead to the UKCC using its disciplinary function, with legal implications of removal of the nurse's name from the register.

The code of conduct is reproduced in full on page 205, and the comments below indicate some of the legal implications of different parts of this document. Many of these have been taken up in more detail elsewhere in this book.

A number of the statements in the code are linked with the law relating to negligence. Number 2 is very similar to the legal definition given on page 27. Numbers 1, 3, 4, 10, 11 and 12 all overlap with the law of negligence.

Number 1 has perhaps created many difficulties of interpretation. Safeguarding the well-being of an individual does appear to go further than merely avoiding negligence. The nurse must be wary that although this may involve acting as the patient's advocate, she does not place herself outside other sections of the law, for example, by refusing to co-operate with treatment that the doctor has prescribed for the patient on the basis that she disagrees with it.

Numbers 3 and 4 emphasise the importance of competence and this has been discussed on page 112. Number 4 also involves the extension of the nurse's role into areas normally under the responsibility of the doctor. On no account can the nurse legally take on extra duties unless certain conditions are met (see page 230).

The law regarding health and safety at work has an input into statement Number 10 (see page 65) but the mention of safe standards of practice in both Numbers 10 and 11 again relates to the law of negligence. In this case it may be negligence of the Health Authority through the actions or omissions of its nurse managers once the clinical nurse has informed her superiors of her concern (see page 112).

Number 12 relates to the importance of careful delegation both to trained nurses and to students (see page 112). However, rather than merely preventing harm, the code does emphasise the positive side of this role.

The remaining statements have some links with other parts of the law. A failure to work in a collaborative manner with other professionals (Statement No. 5) may lead to being disciplined, and in a number of places in this book the roles of these colleagues have been defined, for example the roles of the doctor and social worker in relation to the mentally disordered patient (page 174). Conscientious objection (No. 7) is enshrined in the Abortion Act (1967) (page 208). The legal and moral problems relating to confidentiality (No. 9) are explored in Chapter 11 (page 238). The nurse's legal situation regarding gifts is described on page 132.

Thus, there are clear legal implications to the Code of Professional Conduct and the nurse must always bear in mind that when behaving in accordance with this code she does so in such a way that she always remains within the law.

# REFERENCES

Faulder, C. (1985). *Whose Body is it?* Virago, London.
International Council for Nurses (1973). *Code for Nurses: Ethical Concepts Applied to Nursing*, ICN, Geneva.
Kennedy, I. (1981). *The Unmasking of Medicine*, Allen and Unwin, London.
Mackenzie, N. (1971). *The Professional Ethic and the Hospital Service*, English University Press, London.
United Kingdom Council for Nurses (1984). *Code of Professional Conduct for the Nurse, Midwife and Health Visitor*, 2nd edn, UKCC, London.

# 10. Major Areas of Dispute

The overlap of law and ethics is clear in some areas of the nurse's work. Arguments on abortion, sterilisation, euthanasia, resuscitation and experimentation will continue to occupy medical and nursing staff for many years yet, and the following pages do not aim to present all the possible facets, only the most usual problems.

As well as criminal and civil law, some of the Acts mentioned in Part III also apply in Part IV.

*Additional Acts and Cases*
  Anatomy Act (1832)
  Infant Life (Preservation) Act (1929)
  Human Tissues Act (1961)
  Abortion Act (1967)
  Anatomy Act (1984)
  Consumer Protection Act (1987)

  D. (a minor) (Wardship Sterilisation) (1976)
  B. (a minor) (Wardship Medical Treatment) (1981)
  R. *v*. Leonard John Henry Arthur (1981)

## 10.1 ABORTION

Student Nurse Watkins was allocated to a gynaecological ward for 10 weeks. On starting on the ward, she spoke to the ward sister about her feelings regarding abortions. She realised that some abortions were being carried out on the ward while others were being performed in the theatre. As she was a practising Roman Catholic, she was concerned about her involvement with these patients, as she felt strongly that abortion was taking life and therefore wrong.

## Conscientious objection

The learner nurse is in a predicament in that she cannot choose where to nurse, whereas the trained nurse does have this choice. Thus, Nurse Watkins' concern is not unusual.

The Abortion Act (1967) gives some guidance on this problem. It provides for conscientious objection on the part of the nurse or doctor. The nurse may refuse to assist in an abortion unless the treatment is necessary to save life or prevent grave permanent injury to the physical or mental health of the pregnant woman.

This statement does not answer all the problems. First, what constitutes 'grave'? A patient with a serious heart defect who had accidentally become pregnant and required an abortion as a life-saving measure would raise few ethical conflicts in the nurse assisting. However, a patient with a history of depressive mental illness may be as severely at risk, but it is often more difficult for the general nurse to appreciate this. The other problem is what is involved in assisting in an abortion. The nurse has no right to opt out of caring for any patient admitted for an abortion either before or after the event, only from the actual abortion. Where this is carried out in the operating theatre, the ward nurse has no difficulty. However, more and more abortions are now carried out on the ward. Does the conscientious objector refuse to help the patient who is vomiting as a result of the drugs being given to bring about the abortion? It seems unlikely that any nurse would see her role in this way, although she may more justifiably refuse to monitor the progress of the abortion or clear up the fetus afterwards.

A practical solution would be to have the ward-based abortions only carried out in a special unit where learners are not required to work. As already mentioned, trained staff have choice as to where they work and would not take such a job if they had strong views against abortions.

## The Abortion Act (1967)

This Act applies to England and Wales and Scotland. There is no such Act in Northern Ireland, where abortion is illegal. The main terms of the Abortion Act are as follows. Save in an emergency, a pregnancy may be terminated before the 28th week only by a registered medical practitioner in a National Health Service hospital or other place approved by the Secretary of State for the purpose, and only if two medical practitioners have given certificates in a prescribed form that the abortion is necessary on one of the grounds below:

- That the continuance of the pregnancy would involve risk to the life of the pregnant woman, or of injury to the physical or mental health of the pregnant woman, or of any existing children of her family, greater than if the pregnancy were terminated.
- That there is a substantial risk that if the child were born, it would suffer from such physical or mental abnormalities as to be seriously handicapped.

The nurse can usually assume that the law is being followed unless she has reason to think otherwise. She will not be committing any offence unless she knowingly assists in an illegal abortion.

However, the nurse may come across different interpretations of the Act. The wording is vague and open to different interpretations, particularly the words 'greater than if the pregnancy were terminated'. The accessibility of abortion to the patient is therefore variable and may depend on which doctor the person approaches. Availability is also known to vary quite markedly in different parts of the country. This is scarcely an ideal situation and can lead to confusion and suffering to the prospective patient.

The nurse can do little in this situation but abide by the doctor's decision. If a person approaches her for advice about an abortion, she may feel that she can direct this person towards a doctor or agency known to be fairly liberal in the interpretation of the law. However, this must be a personal decision on the nurse's part.

## The Infant Life Preservation Act (1929)

As medical technology has advanced, the seemingly impossible becomes increasingly likely. It is now not unusual for a fetus of between 24 and 28 weeks to survive, and occasionally fetuses even younger. Fortunately, from a practical viewpoint, very few therapeutic abortions take place so late and it is still only a small proportion that occur after 18 weeks (4 per cent in 1986).

The doctor and the nurse have a legal duty to take action if a fetus is born alive and is viable. The Abortion Act (1967) did not affect the provisions of the Infant Life (Preservation) Act (1929) which stated that it was child destruction if there was the intent to destroy the life of a child capable of being born and remaining alive. The law on homicide may also become relevant but this does not apply to the destruction of a viable fetus before or during birth, only to death after birth. However, for late abortion to be a crime under either of these statutes, there would have to be proved the necessary intention.

In practice, where it is unlikely that a viable fetus will be born but where it may well be still clearly alive, the doctor will usually ensure that the fetus dies *in utero*, for example by injecting saline. In a unit where late abortions may take place, it is usual to have special facilities ready in case the fetus is born alive and can be transferred to a paediatric intensive-care unit.

## Further ethical viewpoints

The Christian Church, on the whole, frowns on abortion, and therefore if any nurse with strong religious beliefs is being interviewed for a job in an area where abortions are being carried out, she should be asked about her personal stance in the matter. The Roman Catholic Church has the strictest views, although not all Roman Catholic nurses feel that they need to be conscientious objectors.

Abortion is a subject that creates very strong emotional reactions from most people. There are organisations for the furtherance of opposite viewpoints, for example the Society for the Protection of the Unborn Child, and the feminist movement claiming that women should have full control over their lives and bodies.

It is unusual for nurses to take extreme views once they have been involved in caring for patients having abortions. The individual problems of their patients tend to emphasise the need for tolerance. The nurse is likely to feel particularly sympathetic to the woman having an abortion after she has been raped, to the young girl of 12 years old, or to the woman having to make a decision because of the likelihood of severe fetal abnormality. The 20-year-old girl having her third abortion is in need of help rather than condemnation.

## 10.2  STERILISATION

Mrs O'Connor, a Roman Catholic and mother of seven children, had been admitted with a spontaneous abortion and needed to go to theatre for an evacuation of the retained products of conception. The doctor suggested that she had a sterilisation operation carried out at the same time, as it was clear she was not physically well enough to have any more children. Mrs O'Connor was prepared to agree but Mr O'Connor was very strongly against this.

## Voluntary sterilisation

As discussed briefly in Part III, a woman can legally consent to any procedure concerning her own body. Therefore in the example given above Mrs O'Connor could consent to sterilisation without her husband's agreement, and the surgeon would legally be able to proceed with the operation.

However, the ethical position may be somewhat different.

The Roman Catholic Church considers sterilisation to be a mutilation of the body and immoral conduct unless there is a serious threat to life or health in not carrying it out. Mr O'Connor may be persuaded to see the seriousness of not performing a sterilisation on his wife, and calling in a priest to discuss it further may help him to reach a conclusion. The wife, although legally able to give consent herself in this situation, would be likely to feel that morally she must have her husband's consent and support before allowing the surgeon to proceed.

A single person having a sterilisation does not face these complications. It is worth bearing in mind, though, that should this person marry without telling his or her prospective partner, this non-disclosure could at a later date become grounds for annulling the marriage.

The nurse is less likely to face the problems of conscientious objection in the case of sterilisation than with abortion, as many of these procedures, particularly vasectomies, are undertaken in special clinics where nurses have a choice of working or, for the female, in the operating theatre. Legally, unlike with abortion, the nurse has no statutory right to refuse to participate in the care of a patient undergoing sterilisation.

## Compulsory sterilisation

At present there are no legal grounds for compulsory sterilisation in this country. For a number of reasons, the nurse is likely to be drawn into the debate on the rights and wrongs of having some kind of legislation in certain circumstances.

Theological views are mixed on this subject. One quotation, 'Not everyone, simply by being, has the right to propagate', will particularly appeal to nurses who have seen the affected offspring of parents with certain genetically transmitted diseases. The woman whose father died of Huntington's Chorea deciding to have children when she herself has a 50 per cent chance of developing this disabling condition and transmitting it to her children is only counselled at present against her decision. Those working with the severely subnormal adult can do little to prevent pregnancies apart from attempting to supervise their charges as closely as possible.

The opposite argument puts the freedom of the individual above other considerations. Certainly there is the risk, if legal intervention is allowed, of the power of the state being gradually extended to control procreation on a scale reminiscent of Germany under Hitler.

It is as well for nurses to consider their ethical position in case legislation is suggested at some future date.

In 1987, the legal position of sterilising a child of under 18 years went through the English courts. In this case a severely subnormal 17-year-old girl was in the care of the local authority, and her parents with whom she lived were extremely concerned that the girl's sexual behaviour would lead to pregnancy. Sterilisation was suggested and the local authority in the position of guardian gave their consent as the girl was a minor and unable to understand the implications of the procedure. The courts upheld this decision as the girl would never have had the mental powers to make a decision herself, though a previous case had failed as it was held that the girl might at some future date be able to have the necessary understanding to give or withhold consent. However, it is only possible to carry out sterilisation in these circumstances prior to the age of 18 years and in no way alters the position that compulsory sterilisation of an adult is illegal.

## 10.3 EUTHANASIA

Mr Charles had carcinoma of the tongue. He was a well built, 41-year-old man, married with two young children. The diagnosis was made too late for any treatment. He was finally admitted to the ward for terminal care, one of his main problems being the severe pain he was suffering. Diamorphine was commenced to control this. Initially, the usual dose of 5 to 10 mg four hourly was given with some success. After several weeks this dose was insufficient and it had to be gradually increased. The patient remained mobile and alert during this time. Finally, the pain reached a point at which it was no longer being controlled by the drug and his condition was deteriorating fairly rapidly. The dose of diamorphine was increased still further to 400 mg, and this controlled the pain for the next 48 hours. The following day the dose was increased to 600 mg to control pain, the patient by this time fluctuating between consciousness and semiconsciousness. A final dose of 800 mg was given and the patient died shortly afterwards.

It was debatable whether Mr Charles had died from his carcinoma or from the dose of diamorphine administered.

## The legal situation

Euthanasia means happy death and has come to be associated with the control that man can exercise over the time and manner of his or another's death, usually in the situation of that death being expected within some limited space of time.

The law gives no consent for euthanasia. The most recent attempt at changing the law, The Incurable Patient's Bill (1975), was defeated in Parliament. The main clauses in this bill were that a patient would be entitled to take steps that could cause his death and that he may make a written request that, in the event of brain damage, he wished to refuse further treatment. However, the problem of how that individual's consent to euthanasia is obtained presents insuperable legal problems. It is difficult to ensure by legislation that relatives do not exert undue pressure on the patient.

However, in other areas, the law is vague and broadly defined. At present any euthanasia would involve intent and therefore the person ordering or administering some drug or treatment leading to death could be guilty of murder. But if the drug or treatment is required for the relief of suffering, the doctor or nurse involved would not be guilty of either murder or manslaughter if their patient died, as their intention was to save the patient pain. Thus, in the case of Mr Charles, there would have been no illegality even if his death had been due to drug overdose as it was clearly necessary to increase the drug dose to control the pain.

On the whole, the nurse can safely follow the doctor's instructions regarding the administration of drugs. If, in the above example, the dose of diamorphine had suddenly been increased from 50 mg to 800 mg, the nurse would find herself in a somewhat different situation. It would be difficult for her to reconcile this increase as being necessary merely for the relief of suffering and she would be wise to refuse to give such a dose as the doctor's intentions may be tending towards euthanasia.

The law is involved not only with the performance of certain procedures on patients with terminal conditions, but also with the omission of certain treatments or care.

A baby was born with a severe spina bifida and, as an inevitable result, this became infected shortly after birth. The doctor prescribed antibiotics which the nurse administered. The situation occurred twice more within a short space of time and antibiotics were given to keep the baby alive. On the next occasion of infection, the doctor did not prescribe any drugs on the grounds that the treatment was useless, and the baby died.

The law clearly expects that doctors and nurses have a duty of care to preserve life, but where the patient is expected to die in spite of any treatment administered, the law is less clear. In the above example, the baby would probably have only survived for a limited amount of time and the doctor is justified in witholding treatment on the grounds that it was useless after having attempted it on several occasions with scant success. However, a nurse failing to report a patient's pyrexia and chesty cough on the grounds that the patient was likely to die shortly from carcinoma could be grossly negligent and therefore possibly guilty of manslaughter if the patient died first from this chest infection. She could not answer that treatment was useless as a chest infection could probably be dealt with by antibiotics regardless of the patient's underlying condition. (For the special problems of cardiac resuscitation and turning off ventilators, see section 10.4.)

The law has a useful contribution to make regarding the omission of treatments. The patient is required to consent to any treatment and he is within his rights to refuse treatment that does not seem to him to be useful in any way, even if this leads directly to his death. For example, a patient with carcinoma of the breast has already had a mastectomy. As the secondary deposits develop, the patient is persuaded to have both ovaries removed. Finally, as even this operation fails to control the spread of the disease, a hypophysectomy is suggested. The patient refuses consent for this operation and dies seven days later. Similarly, a patient could refuse further investigations, radiotherapy or drugs.

If the patient is a baby and therefore unable to consent or otherwise, the situation may depend on a number of factors.

One factor is the degree of handicap suffered by the child. In one court case regarding a baby with Down's syndrome who also had an intestinal blockage, the court decision to operate was based on 'whether the life of the child is demonstrably going to be so awful that in effect the child must be condemned to die, or whether the life of the child is still so imponderable that it would be wrong for her to be condemned to die'.

This baby was a ward of court so it was up to the court to consent or otherwise. Another factor is a failure of parental consent to give care to a handicapped child. The doctor's primary obligation must be to the child, although this degree of obligation may be less for a newly born baby than for an older child. The Dr Arthur case involved a newly born baby with Down's syndrome. The doctor wrote, 'Parents do not wish baby to survive', and he prescribed dihydrocodeine and nursing care only, with only water being given. He was acquitted of murder or attempted murder, and the overall conclusion to be drawn is that the omission of treatment to a severely handicapped baby is unlikely to lead to a conviction of homicide.

Therefore, as with the giving of treatment that may possibly lead to the patient's death, it seems that the nurse can also safely follow the doctor's instructions regarding omission of treatment.

## Some ethical viewpoints

An important part of the ethical code of both doctors and nurses is the preservation of human life. Nurses are reminded of the need to consider the dignity of each individual and the nurse's role in the alleviation of suffering. The ethical standpoint therefore leaves it open to the individual to decide on the right balance between prolonging life even if the patient's comfort and ease is ignored, and considering the patient's dignity in being allowed to die without further medical intervention. It is a balance that will vary from person to person. Nurses tend to be particularly conscious of maintaining the patient's dignity without subjecting him to further traumatic treatments. On the other hand, the doctor may have the slightly different knowledge to appreciate that intervention may in the long run lead to a better death than leaving the patient's condition to follow its usual course. It is important that discussion of the ethical problems involved in any course of action is undertaken by all the people concerned with the care of the patient. Unfortunately this does not always take place.

As mentioned above, the law accepts that the patient can refuse his consent to treatment. An ethical problem also arises here in that a patient's consent or refusal may depend on what information is given to him (see page 103). As pointed out in Part III, any consent should be a properly gained consent. Therefore, both legally and ethically, the patient should receive clear information as to the possible outcomes of any treatment, both regarding prognosis and side effects. If a treatment is only palliative, he should not be led to believe it to be curative. If there are side effects of nausea and hair loss as a result of cytotoxic therapy, the patient should be told, as well as explaining the benefits. (See section 11.5 for further discussion.)

Overlying much of the above discussion is the unfortunate fact that death is still considered a 'taboo' subject. If we could learn to accept death as being a natural part of life, perhaps the problem of how patients, doctors and nurses cope with the inevitable accompaniments could be conducted in a more open atmosphere.

## 10.4 THE PROCESS OF DEATH

In the preceding section, some of the problems in the period leading up to death were explored. Further legal/ethical problems arising at the time of death are now considered. These are particularly associated with turning off life-support systems and cardiac resuscitation.

### A definition of death

A definition of death that has been used satisfactorily for years, and is still adequate in most cases, is the total stoppage of circulation of the blood and cessation of the animal and vital functions of the body such as respiration and pulsation.

However, there are times when this definition is inadequate. A patient on a ventilator may be dead although his respirations and heart beat are being maintained. A patient who has had a cardiac arrest will have no pulse nor be breathing, but may still be alive and able to be resuscitated.

The concept of brain-stem death has therefore been developed as the brain stem contains the vital centres for maintaining life. Certain tests have been developed to ascertain brain death. These are as follows:

- Tests of respiration:
  Arterial blood analysis of $pCO_2$.
  Absence of any spontaneous ventilation on disconnecting ventilator within five minutes (ten minutes if $pCO_2$ not carried out).

- Brain-stem reflexes:

  No pupil reactions.

  No nystagmus present when each ear is syringed with ice-cold water for one minute.

  No response when each cornea is touched.

  No movement in head or neck either spontaneously or in response to any stimulus.

  No gag reflex or reflex response to bronchial stimulation when a suction catheter is passed down the trachea.

- Body temperature:

  Core (rectal) temperature below 35 °C.

  Ideally, when brain death is suspected, the patient should be nursed on a heated water mattress and covered with a heat-reflecting blanket to maintain a core temperature above 35 °C in order for the tests for brain death to be carried out. However, if primary hypothermia has been excluded, a core temperature of less than 35 °C is indicative of brain death.

- Drugs and certain causes of coma:

  For the tests of brain death to be reliable certain drugs affecting consciousness or ventilation should not be given within the previous twelve hours, for example neuromuscular blocking drugs and benzodiazepine.

  Metabolic or endocrine causes of coma must be ruled out. The necessary blood tests should therefore be done prior to carrying out brain-death tests.

In addition, certain practices are advised regarding the frequency and timing of tests, and who carries out the tests.

It is usual for the tests to be performed twice, but the two tests could be separated by as little as ten minutes or up to 24 hours. Two doctors carry out the tests and a health authority will have guidelines as to which doctors. It is usual for one to be a consultant and one should be experienced in intensive-care work.

A further difficulty is that all the definitions that are acceptable legally assume that death takes place at some point in time. The reality is usually that death is not a fixed point but a process over time; hence the title of this section.

## Turning off 'the machine'

Mary, an 18-year-old girl, had a subarachnoid haemorrhage. She survived the first bleed, but haemorrhaged again prior to surgery and became unconscious. As her condition deteriorated, she was linked to a respirator. After 24 hours, the decision was made by the doctors in conjunction with Mary's parents to turn off the machine as there was no brain response, and it was apparent that Mary had died.

Once the criteria of what constitutes death have been clarified, there should not be a legal problem when to switch off life-support systems. Ethically, there are many problems which can have a strong influence on what occurs.

Who makes the decision is one problem area. In this country, the medical staff have the responsibility, but it is usual for the decision to be seen as being made by the team of doctors caring for the patient, rather than just one doctor. Such a burden of responsibility is better shared. The influence of other staff and the patient's relatives may also make the decision more difficult to take in an objective legal manner. Nursing staff who have repeatedly resuscitated a patient may find it difficult to accept the doctors decision that the patient is, in fact, dead. The relatives will inevitably affect the situation where they refuse to accept that there is no longer any hope. This particularly arises where the patient has been linked to life-support systems for a long period of time. For example, if a four-year-old child who has had viral meningitis and has been on a ventilator for two months eventually satisfies the criteria of death, the parents may become so distressed at the thought of the machine being switched off, that the doctors delay the moment in the hopes that the parents can start accepting the situation. The other factor that may affect the moment the ventilator is disconnected is if any organs are required for transplantation. Turning off the machine may be delayed until the prospective recipient is available and ready (see section 10.6). The legal and ethical considerations here are somewhat hazy.

The nurse's involvement is two-fold. First, she will have to come to terms with her own emotions at this final statement of the death of one of her patients. This, not surprisingly, can be more difficult than a patient dying in more usual circumstances. Second, she may be involved in explaining what has happened to relatives. She must, therefore, be quite clear in her own mind that switching off the machine is not synonymous with the death of the patient which has, in fact, occurred prior to this moment.

## Cardiac resuscitation

Mrs Edna Tully had been admitted eight weeks previously having had a serious cerebrovascular accident. Although she partially regained consciousness, she remained completely paralysed down one side of her body and quite unresponsive to the nurses. She was expected to remain on the ward for long-term care. Unexpectedly one morning after being sat out of bed, she was found by the staff nurse to have had a cardiac arrest. There were no instructions in the Kardex that this patient was not for resuscitation, but the nurse did not call the cardiac arrest team. Instead she bleeped the doctor in charge of the patient. The doctor concurred with the nurse's decision and certified the patient dead.

The subject of cardiac resuscitation is one that arouses a great deal of controversy. The legal implications are not entirely clear. Nurses and doctors, as seen in the previous section, have a special duty of care to preserve life and therefore cannot often justify doing nothing if a patient has a cardiac arrest. If the patient dies as a result of a failure to carry out resuscitation, the nursing and medical staff are negligent and guilty of manslaughter. In practice, it would be difficult to be sure that death had occurred as a result of this omission to act or that death would have resulted from the patient's condition anyway. It is also debatable if the nurse or doctor has the same duty to act if the patient is likely to die or be severely incapacitated, even if temporarily resuscitated.

The duty of care expected of the nurse or doctor is to 'avoid acts or omissions that one can reasonably foresee as being likely to injure one's neighbour' (see page 28). The nurse and doctor could argue legally that in their judgement it would have been more of an injury to attempt resuscitation than to let the patient be. The staff nurse who discovered Mrs Tully might state that she did not know how long it was since the patient arrested and therefore what further brain damage may have already occurred. It would in her judgement have been a greater wrong to attempt resuscitation. In this area of the law, there are very few guidelines due to a paucity of court cases to draw on. On the whole, the professional judgement of the nurse or doctor, if seriously arrived at, is upheld in the courts.

## The nurse's involvement

Technically, it is the doctor's decision as to which patients to try to resuscitate. In practice, it is very often left to the nurse who is present when a cardiac arrest occurs.

Most hospitals have some method of dealing with this problem, for example, some system of recording in the Kardex which patients are for resuscitation, and which are not. How this is done would depend on the nature of the ward. An acute surgical ward would only mark the few patients not for resuscitation, whereas a long-stay geriatric ward may use different criteria. Where no instructions are given, the nurse can usually assume that resuscitative measures must be taken. Thus, in theory, the medical staff can consider each patient individually and apply their appropriate criteria.

In practice, the Kardex is often not kept up to date. The turnover of patients is rapid, new admissions, even if terminally ill, may have no note made on their records, or the condition of patients in the ward may change. The result is that the nurse, on a number of occasions, is left with the decision.

## Some ethical constraints

The safest legal pathway for the nurse to follow would be to attempt to resuscitate all patients if there are no medical instructions to the contrary. For the inexperienced nurse, this is probably the best rule to follow.

For the more experienced nurse, various ethical constraints will influence her decision. In the example of Mrs Tully, the nurse would have felt that it would have been morally wrong to have attempted resuscitation on a patient with such severe brain damage from her stroke. She would also have been morally constrained by not knowing how long it had been from the time of the cardiac arrest to its discovery. Although the law could be made to support these views, they are decisions which are dictated principally by ethical considerations rather than by legal requirements.

Most doctors and nurses feel that any unexpected cardiac arrest should be dealt with by initiating resuscitation. This is a useful guide-line, although one that some nurses may query if the patient is very old. For example, an 86-year-old severely arthritic lady was admitted to hospital to enable her married daughter who normally looked after her to go on holiday with her family. Five days later, the old lady was getting herself out of bed when she collapsed and was found to have had a cardiac arrest. Resuscitation was attempted although unsuccessful, as the arrest was unexpected. Some nurses present at the time felt saddened that the old lady had been subjected to this final indignity. On the other hand, if she had recovered, she may have lived happily for several more years.

Nurses are aware of their role in helping patients to a peaceful death.

Some junior doctors are unfortunately less willing to accept the inevitability of a patient's death, perhaps as their training has geared them towards thinking of death as some kind of failure on their part. It would be encouraging if decisions on resuscitation of patients could be made after discussion between doctors and nurses who have their own slightly different perspectives. In some areas, this does take place. Perhaps one day it will be unusual to find that this is not so.

At present, it is also unusual for decisions to be made after consultation with the patient and his relatives. It may be that the patient with a severe, chronic and disabling illness may not wish to be resuscitated should cardiac arrest occur. If he has made these wishes clearly known, legally the medical and nursing staff could abide by these wishes as long as the quality of life the patient could expect after resuscitation was very limited. As has been stated elsewhere, relatives cannot make decisions for the patient, but for practical reasons it may also be useful to listen to their views.

# 10.5   EXPERIMENTATION AND RESEARCH

Mr May was admitted to hospital for treatment of his Parkinsonism. The doctor responsible for his care told him that there was a new drug being tried out for this condition and asked whether he would be prepared to receive it. He agreed to this and the nurses administering the trial drug were asked to make certain observations for any useful or harmful effects.

The nurse becomes involved in experimentation particularly in relation to drug trials, although the theatre and X-ray nurse may also come across experimental surgical techniques or investigations. Other more controversial experiments for example, concerning human embryos, are unlikely to be of practical concern to the nurse and this area is likely to be clarified by legislation in due course following the 1984 Warnock Report.

## The legal situation

The law is not clearly defined in this area. If experimentation resulted in harm to the patient, the doctor may find himself facing professional charges of malpractice and civil charges of negligence. However, it has very rarely been argued in the courts.

The doctor is left in a predicament. He has a duty to promote advancement of knowledge in his profession at the same time as acting in a manner to safeguard his patient's wellbeing. It appears that some experimentation has to be accepted—over 90 per cent of drugs used today have been developed since 1950. On the whole, the law accepts that a doctor will perform his duties with due skill and learning even in the realm of new and little tried treatments.

Most nurses accept this need for experimentation and should be able to follow the doctor's instructions in the administration of trial drugs with legal safety. However, the area of the law of most concern to the nurse is to gain the patient's consent for any experimental work, as she may be involved in expanding the doctor's explanation.

This consent is central to any legal argument on the validity of an experiment on a patient. The Nuremberg Code (1948) states that 'voluntary consent of the human subject is absolutely essential'. The later Declaration of Helsinki (1975) drew up twelve principles that should be applied in these situations. Concerning consent it stated that 'each potential subject must be adequately informed of the aims, methods, anticipated benefits and potential hazards of the study and the discomfort it may entail. He should be informed that he is at liberty to abstain from participation in the study or to withdraw consent to participation at any time'. Unfortunately these codes are not legally binding, although what they suggest provides a sound basis on which to work. However, some doctors are of the opinion that to give too much information to a patient may reduce the effectiveness of the research programme, and they therefore choose to give less than full information. As with gaining consent in other situations, in this country the doctor has the legal right to make decisions regarding what information to give (see page 103). The form in which consent is given can be variable. A written consent would be safest, but very often a verbal consent is thought sufficient. It would be legally dubious to assume the patient's consent through his being in hospital.

The inclusion of a release clause in the consent form is occasionally mt in relation to experimentation. This exonerates the medical staff and hospital authority from any untoward incident or damage resulting from the experiment. Such a waiver would be unlikely to stand up in court.

Drug experimentation is also a major concern of the manufacturers. A patient suffering damage from a new drug can always sue the manufacturer for negligence in not having tested the drug sufficiently to know of its harmful effects. This is extremely difficult to prove. The

Consumer Protection Act which is in operation from 1989 may make it easier for the patient to get some financial recompense for damage as he will not have to prove negligence, just that the drug caused the damage.

## Other methods of research

Apart from experiments, research projects involving other methodology may well be undertaken. These may include questionnaires, interviews, and observation, with variable use made of video and tape recordings.

The gaining of the subject's consent should be considered in a similar way to experimentation. As stated in the Helsinki Declaration, 'concern for the interests of the subject must always prevail over the interests of science and society'.

## Ethical considerations

Most health authorities have set up ethical committees that screen any form of research being undertaken within that authority and give a decision on whether it may proceed or not. However, this type of committee is usually medically orientated and it may not always have lay members whose concern will be towards the patients.

The nurse may sometimes have reservations about the experiments and other research she encounters. This concern may be particularly associated with how the patient's consent is gained. Many patients are overawed by the establishment and will agree to any form of treatment, especially if it is not made absolutely clear to them that they have a choice. This problem appears to be particularly critical in a teaching hospital where staff may feel that patients admitted must expect to be involved in experimental work, as well as for teaching purposes. It is within this framework that the patient's consent may be assumed rather than gained in the proper manner. Ethically this undermines the concept of individual choice. Because patients cannot often choose *not* to be treated in a teaching hospital, this should not restrict their freedom in other directions.

The nurse working in a teaching hospital may also feel concern at some experimental treatments being carried out on patients whose prognosis is poor. In some cases, a new untried treatment being used as a last resort is morally acceptable as being the only possible way to try to help the patient. In a few cases, the nurse may suspect that the patient is being used merely for the trial without enough regard as to what is best for that individual. The nurse can have no direct responsibility here although she may feel it her duty to query what is being done. (See section 11.3, page 237, for further discussion.)

## 10.6  TRANSPLANTS

Transplantation is an acceptable form of treatment in a number of instances, although still experimental for some organs.

Renal transplants are carried out widely and successfully. However, many more transplants could be carried out if more donor kidneys were available. A small but important reason for this shortage is the legal framework controlling the removal of organs for transplantation. Heart, lung and liver transplants are also becoming accepted treatments although the numbers involved are small. Speed of removal and transplantation becomes increasingly important for these organs and the law may at times seem slow and unwieldy in these circumstances.

The legal and ethical problems involved can be divided into those affecting transplants from dead donors and those from living donors. The former includes kidneys, hearts, lungs, livers and corneas, and the latter kidneys and bone marrow.

### Transplants from dead donors

One of the main legal problems here has already been covered in section 10.4. With clear criteria of brain death now in existence and local regulations laid down concerning the seniority and experience of the doctors carrying out the required tests, there should be little anxiety from potential donors and relatives that death has not occurred prior to removal of organs.

The other major issue relates to who can give consent for the removal of an organ for transplantation. The lack of clarity in the law can potentially lead to delay in gaining consent and loss of organs.

The Human Tissue Act (1961) is the enabling legislation stating that parts of the human body can be removed after death 'for therapeutic purposes or for purposes of medical education and research'. Removal of organs can be authorised if:

- The deceased person has made a declaration in writing (or orally in the presence of two witnesses) expressing a wish that his organs be used for this purpose; or

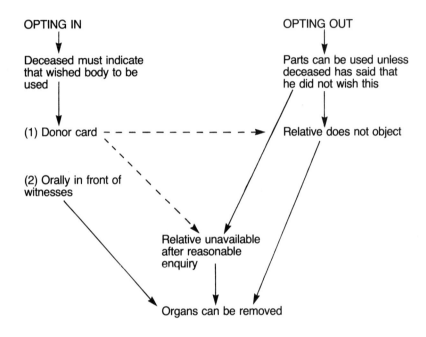

**Figure 10.1** Grounds for removal of organs from deceased.

- After making reasonable enquiry, there is no reason to believe that the deceased had objected to this use of his body and that the surviving relative does not object (see Figure 10.1).

Authorisation is given by the person lawfully in possession of the body and this is where legal difficulties may arise. A corpse cannot be treated under property law but a number of people have rights regarding possession. These are certain close relatives, the occupier of the premises where the deceased died or where the deceased now lies, and, if an inquest or post-mortem is required, the coroner. The right to

**Figure 10.2**  Sample donor card.

dispose of the body is usually seen to belong to the close relatives and although the other categories of people have rights of possession, they must make the body available after a reasonable time. In reality there is nearly always a gap in time after death until the body is claimed for disposal.

The law seems to support the view that the hospital authority is legally in possession until the body is claimed and during this time certain persons can be designated to remove parts of the body for therapeutic purposes. This action is supported by the Anatomy Act (1984), particularly if the deceased has made a declaration. However, under common law, the individual has limited power over the disposal of his own remains, and the next of kin are entitled to possession of the body in the same condition as when death occurred.

In practice, decisions have to be made rapidly. Where a declaration exists, for example a donor card (Figure 10.2), the health authority has fairly sound justification in proceeding with the removal of organs. However, even in these circumstances the authority will usually try to contact the relatives for their consent as well. If there is no declaration, the relatives' consent should be gained. The law at this stage produces another dubious area. The hospital authority is only expected to make reasonable enquiry to gain consent. Because of the speed required, the doctors involved may interpret 'reasonable' somewhat differently from the relatives, for example the decision may be made to proceed if the relatives are not immediately available.

Nurses have an important and specialist role to play in the area of organ transplantation. Many regions now employ transplant co-ordinators whose legal and practical knowledge is used to educate and advise people regarding making their organs available after death. Clearly, to advise the individual to make a written declaration which he carries with him all the time would be to save a number of people a great deal of time and trouble.

## Transplants from living donors

The legal problems with transplants from living donors are few, though the moral problems are significant. Legally, as long as consent is gained in the proper manner, the operation to remove the required part can proceed.

Morally, there may be considerable pressure on a relative to give a kidney to a person suffering from severe renal failure. The medical and nursing staff should be aware of this and attempt to put forward all the options of treatment in as objective a way as possible. For example, renal dialysis is a feasible medical alternative, even in the long term. There is also the possibility of a fairly well-matched kidney from a dead donor if all concerned are prepared to be patient. On the other hand, the relative who could usefully give some of his bone marrow is at little medical risk and there should be few ethical problems.

## A major ethical concern

Most nurses at some stage of their careers will be brought up short by the financial restraints in treating patients. It seems morally wrong that the treatment received by patients should depend on how much money is available, but this fact has been made only too apparent to both staff and public recently.

Transplant surgery is costly and the more that is spent in this area, the less there is for work with, for example the elderly and mentally ill. Most nurses will happily accept the worthwhile nature of renal transplants, but query the ethics of a liver transplant where success is, at present, limited.

The arguments will rage on for a long time yet, and are certainly well outside the scope of this book!

# REFERENCES

Bliss, B. P. and Johnson, A. G. (1975). *Aims and Motives in Clinical Medicine*, Pitman Medical, London.

Faulder, C. (1985). *Whose Body Is It?*, Virago, London.

Karanja, E. and Moran, A. (1981). The criteria for brain death in England—1, *Nursing Times*, Vol. 77, p. 1495.

Karanja, E. and Moran, A. (1981). The criteria for brain death in England—2, *Nursing Times*, Vol. 77, p. 1554.

Kuhse, H. (1984). A modern myth: That letting die is not the intentional causation of death: some reflections on the trial and acquittal of Dr Leonard Henry, *Journal of Applied Philosophy*, Vol. 1 (1), pp. 21–38.

Meyers, D. W. (1970). *The Human Body and the Law*, Edinburgh University Press, Edinburgh.

National Consumer Council (1983). *Patients' Rights, a Guide for NHS Patients and Doctors*, HMSO, London.

Skegg, P. D. G. (1984). *Law, Ethics and Medicine*, Clarendon Press, London.

Tate, B. L. (1977). The Nurse's Dilemma—Ethical Considerations in Nursing Practice, ICN, Geneva.

Veatch, R. M. (1977). *Case Studies in Medical Ethics*, Harvard University Press, Boston.

Warnock, M. (1984). *Report of the Committee of Inquiry into Human Fertilisation and Embryology*, HMSO, London.

# 11. Less Clearly Defined Areas

This final chapter discusses some areas of legal and ethical overlap impinging very closely on the nurse. In some of these, the legal implications are rarely considered by nurses, although present with the moral ones. As before, all that can be presented is a discussion of some common situations rather than an exhaustive overview. Areas of the law involved again include criminal and civil law.

*Additional Acts*

Data Protection Act (1984)

## 11.1 THE NURSE'S EXTENDING ROLE

A doctor attending a patient in the intensive care unit drew up a drug for intravenous injection and gave it to Staff Nurse Harty to administer. This she did. The patient died as a result as the dose given was wrong and the nurse had not checked the drug with the doctor nor had she any special expertise in the administration of drugs intravenously.

The role of the nurse is continually developing and new skills are being added to the nurse's normal range of duties. However, some definition of the nurse's basic role has to be laid down in order to protect the public and the nurse herself. The International Council of Nurses states that 'a nurse is a person who has completed a programme of basic nursing education and is qualified and authorised in her country to practise nursing'. Thus, decisions have to be made on what to incorporate in basic training and for what the trained nurse can legally be held responsible.

Problems arise where there is an overlap of medical and nursing functions. Conventionally, the nurse has undertaken a caring role and the doctor, a diagnostic and curative function. However, the nurse's role has been extended in response to emergency situations and by delegation from doctors. Extension by delegation poses particular legal problems.

## Common areas involving extension of the nurse's role

Specialist areas are susceptible to the pressures leading to an extension of the nurse's role. As shown in the example above, the nurse and doctor work in very close collaboration in the care of very ill patients in an intensive care unit, and a similar situation is liable to arise in renal and other specialist units where staff are highly trained to cope with particular problems. Often it seems only a very small step for the nurse to take over some of the doctor's functions.

More drugs are now being given intravenously and where drug administration is normally seen as part of the nurse's role, it may seem a logical extension for intravenous drugs also to be given by the nurse rather than frequently having to contact the doctor. Taking blood samples and carrying out suturing are other extensions.

In the community, immunisations given by the nurse rather than by the doctor may often be a practical alternative where time is at a premium. In highly specialised situations, a nurse may even modify drug therapy originally prescribed by the doctor, for example insulin dosages for the diabetic. Again, these are extensions of her role.

The above examples have mainly involved giving certain treatments. The nurse's role can also be extended in the realm of diagnosis. This usually occurs where a doctor is not readily available. The district nurse or midwife already takes some responsibility in the area of diagnosis by making decisions on when referral is necessary. In a number of Accident and Emergency Departments, a nurse may undertake the initial screening of patients and may even be asked to make decisions on whether a patient should be seen by a doctor as an emergency or be asked to return to a later clinic and his general practitioner. Thus, there are marked possibilities of extension outside the nurse's normally accepted role. This is occurring in other countries, for example in Canada or the

USA where distances are so vast that the nurse may not have ready access to medical back-up.

## Legal consequences

If a patient suffers damage, the nurse may be liable if she has failed to perform the skills expected of her, *or* if she has undertaken tasks that she was not competent to perform (see page 112). Thus, Nurse Harty laid herself wide open to legal action by performing a task that she was not competent to perform. Giving intravenous drugs is not included as part of basic training. In addition, the doctor was negligent in delegation.

There is an additional legal problem for the nurse who is asked to undertake initial screening, for example in the Accident and Emergency Department. The DHSS expect hospitals with Casualty Departments not to turn away patients without a doctor seeing them. Failing to do this may lay a doctor open to an action for negligence if the patient suffers as a result, and a nurse must be quite clear as to her responsibilities if she is asked to do this initial screening.

There are ways around these dilemmas. As seen from the examples given above, it is sometimes more practical for nurses to carry out certain tasks rather than doctors. In fact, the nurse's role can be legally extended, but only in the following circumstances:

- The nurse has been specifically and adequately trained for the performance of the new task and she agrees to undertake it.
- This training has been recognised as satisfactory by the employing authority.
- The new task has been recognised by the professions and by the employing authority as a task which may be properly delegated to a nurse.
- The delegating doctor has been assured of the competence of the individual nurse concerned.

In practice, this requires careful consultation for drawing up a training programme and some method of checking the nurse's competence after training, for example by a set period of supervised practice.

## Ethical problems

The pressure on nurses to carry out certain procedures because requested by the doctor can be severe. Particularly where the patient is seriously ill, the nurse may feel that it would be wrong to refuse to perform some job for the doctor if it appeared to her that the patient would suffer by her refusal. What she should seriously bear in mind is that the patient may suffer more harm through her incompetence.

The nurse can also be put in a difficult moral situation where a delegated procedure is to be taught to nurses. The Department of Health's guidelines quoted above state that, as well as the nurse receiving adequate training, she must also agree to undertake it. She may feel strongly that she should concentrate on her normally accepted role in caring for her patients and that to accept more responsibilities would give her less time to carry out her other duties to a high standard. However, the pressure on her to undertake further training may be difficult to resist. The health authority concerned should make sure that a real choice is given to each nurse.

## Further considerations

Extensions are not always in areas encroaching on the doctor's role. As nursing changes, the nurse's role extends quite naturally and rightly. Some of the nurse's professional colleagues may feel anxious or threatened by some of these extensions. For example, the format of the nursing process with its 'diagnosis' of nursing problems may at first sight seem to encroach on the medical function. Education of all concerned should enable colleagues to understand and make use of these changes.

At the other end of the scale, nurses are often concerned by restrictions of their role. The ward sister no longer has the responsibility for the cleanliness of the ward or the supervision of many of her patients' meals. The domestic supervisor has relieved nursing staff of a number of onerous duties, but some nurses are concerned that these tasks on the periphery of nursing have been removed to the detriment of the patients' care. Good relationships with domestic staff as well as other colleagues are obviously essential.

## 11.2 THE ADMINISTRATION OF DRUGS AND TREATMENTS

The administration of drugs and treatments to unwilling patients is an area that merits discussion.

## Administration of treatments to confused patients

Miss Connolly was admitted with severe congestive cardiac failure. She was semiconscious and drugs were initially administered intravenously. She improved slightly but remained confused. Drugs were altered to oral administration. When the nurses came to give her her tablets, she pushed the nurses away and turned her face aside. After several attempts, the nurses, on the pretext of giving her a drink managed to put the tablets in her mouth prior to her taking some water. However, the patient spat them out. In desperation, the nurses then physically restrained her while the tablets were put in her mouth and enough water given so that the patient had to swallow.

It is on occasions such as these that the consent of the patient to treatment is in doubt. Miss Connolly, by her gestures, made it quite clear that she did not want the tablets. Did the nurses therefore act wrongly in proceeding with the administration of the drugs?

### Legal considerations
The patient could be expressing a reluctance to swallow the tablets rather than an overall refusal of treatment, but this scarcely condones the nurses proceeding as they did.

Legally, there are several arguments that seem to support the giving of treatment to a confused patient without his consent.

First, as with the unconscious patient, doctor and nurse are entitled to proceed without consent with procedures necessary to save life or prevent serious damage to health (see page 107). However, this defence of necessity only allows for treatment in the short term. Of course, the longer the postponement of less urgent treatment due to lack of consent, the greater the necessity for this treatment as time goes by, and therefore the doctor could possibly extend the legal argument of necessity in this way.

Where there is time to plan, it would be wiser to take another legal route. It is common for medical and nursing staff to consult the next of kin, though rightfully it is only a legal guardian (appointed by a court) who can give consent for another adult.

A third legal option for the nurse in treating the patient who is confused and therefore unable to give consent over a period of time is to use the powers of the Mental Health Act. However, this is a big step to take and potentially upsetting for the relatives.

Thus, in relation to the nurses treating Miss Connolly, they probably acted in a legally acceptable manner due to the necessity and urgency of the situation.

### Ethical considerations
To administer drugs and other treatments to confused and unwilling patients does seem to be a dubious practice on ethical grounds.

From one point of view, the nurse needs to do her best to promote the health of her patient, but she also needs to respect his dignity. In many situations, the nurse should therefore attempt to find a way around the problem which will combine both of these ethical considerations. This is often possible with a little thought. For example, Miss Connolly need not have been put through the experience described if the nurses had asked the doctor to prescribe either liquid preparations of the oral drugs that the patient could swallow easily, or intramuscular injections until the patient was well enough to understand the significance of her treatment.

### The use of restraint
Where confused patients are unwilling to co-operate with treatment, the use of restraint sometimes seems to be the only possibility.

A patient admitted following a serious road accident was confused and shocked. An intravenous infusion was set up, but the patient continually attempted to pull it out. The nurse put 'mitts' over his hands to deter him, but he still struggled to remove the infusion. The patient was then physically restrained by the nurses but, as the ward was short staffed, after five minutes they loosely tied his hands to the cot sides on his bed and left him.

The nurses appear to have been guilty of assault and battery to the patient. Where a treatment seems to be so clearly necessary to the patient's recovery, it is difficult for the nurses to know how to proceed, in spite of such obvious guidelines. The legal defence of necessity when a patient is confused may, as seen above, be some kind of justification depending on the particular circumstances of the case.

The nurses in a general hospital would, however, be wise to follow similar guidelines to those issued to nurses caring for mentally disordered patients (see page 177). They should only use any kind of restraint with the doctor's knowledge and permission.

# Administration of treatments to weak and unwilling patients

In the first example given, Miss Connolly may not have been confused, merely very weak. When severely ill, some patients feel too exhausted to communicate orally and can only let their wishes and feelings be known by gestures. Thus nurses must consider carefully what construction to put on a patient's actions as the legal situations can be markedly different.

If a patient who is very weak refuses treatment, the nurse must accept the patient's lack of consent and not proceed with the administration of drugs or other treatments. It is tempting for nurses to override the weak and very ill patient as they want to help that patient to recover. It is also fairly easy to do so physically. Neither legally nor ethically does the nurse have grounds for any such action. Nurses should remind themselves regularly that patients do have choice and that nurses themselves are not infallible in knowing what is best for their patients. A very good rule to bear in mind is, if the patient in the same circumstances had given his consent, would that consent have been regarded as valid? If so, then the refusal of consent must also be valid.

## Lack of consent in other special circumstances

Two difficulties arise in the Accident and Emergency Department. First, a patient may not be in a fit state to understand and therefore consent to treatment due to the effect of drugs or alcohol. As with the patient confused for other reasons, the doctor and nurse can proceed without consent if it is urgent in order to save life or prevent serious damage.

A second problem is the patient who has attempted suicide but on being brought to the Casualty Department refuses any medical intervention. One legal consideration must be of the mental state of the patient. If the patient is depressed to such an extent that he could be considered mentally ill, then the appropriate section of the Mental Health Act could be invoked and the necessary treatment given. If the patient is fully aware of his actions and cannot be considered mentally ill, then his refusal is legally valid, but it is difficult to imagine how any doctor or nurse could stand by in these circumstances and watch a patient die. To proceed without consent could theoretically lead to a later legal action. However, either the patient will be so determined to end his life that he will ensure that his next attempt is successful, or he will in retrospect be so relieved that his life was saved, that suing the hospital staff for ignoring his wishes at the time will be totally inappropriate.

The unconscious patient may in special circumstances be able to refuse consent if the situation has been foreseen. For example a patient who is to undergo an operation but because of his beliefs (for example one of the Jehovah's Witnesses) will not accept a blood transfusion, should have these wishes honoured as long as the situation remains controlled and does not change to an emergency. Some health authorities may ask the patient to put his refusal to consent to a blood transfusion in writing.

# 11.3 CARRYING OUT PROCEDURES ON DYING PATIENTS

The question of administering or omitting treatments to the dying patient has been discussed at some length in section 10.3. The nurse can also come across legal and ethical difficulties in the performance of purely nursing procedures on these patients.

Mrs Forster was dying of carcinomatosis. She was gradually lapsing into unconsciousness and the nurses found it increasingly difficult to get her to take any fluids or nourishment orally. The ward sister made the decision to pass a nasogastric tube and for the next 48 hours, until Mrs Forster died, she was tube fed. Some nurses felt that this had been an unnecessary procedure on a patient so near death and could have caused her added discomfort at the time.

## Legal and ethical considerations

As already explained, nurses have a clear duty of care to preserve life, and in law that means not carrying out or omitting procedures that may hasten death. The only excuse is if these procedures are being performed for maintaining the patient's comfort, as in the administration of pain-killing drugs, or being omitted as treatment has been shown to be of no use, as in the omission of certain drugs. Legally, the nurse can have no excuse for not maintaining the patient's nutrition to the end unless the doctor took the responsibility of prescribing water only (see page 215).

Ethically, the nurse needs to consider the possible outcome of the omission of nursing procedures. Although death may be hastened, the patient may die in greater discomfort than if all usual procedures had been followed.

Another common example that can cause nurses distress is the continuation of care for the prevention of pressure sores by two-hourly turning even when each movement causes the patient extreme discomfort. Again, some nurses would argue the necessity of carrying out this procedure when the patient is dying.

Legally, it is unlikely that the nurse would face a charge of negligence if a patient developed pressure sores in the last few days of life. However, the development of sores would be likely to cause the patient increased discomfort and ethically the nurse would not be doing her best to alleviate her patient's suffering. As has already been seen in these debatable legal and ethical areas, the solution really involves preventing such a situation occurring in the first place, in this example by the use of adequate analgesia for the patient a short time before pressure area care is attended to.

## Practising procedures on dying patients

Accusations are sometimes made by nurses that procedures are carried out on moribund patients by junior staff long after there is any usefulness in so doing. The supposition is that junior staff are gaining practice.

For example, a patient had been brought to the accident and emergency department already in a very serious condition. Attempts were made to resuscitate him without success. As a final resort, the senior medical staff present allowed two medical students to attempt intubation in the last few minutes of the patient's life.

Legally, the medical staff can claim that this was a final attempt to save the patient's life and therefore necessary. This might in fact have been the case, although the nurses present interpreted it differently as the infringement of the patient's dignity and ease in his last few minutes. There is little that nurses can do in this situation except discuss it with senior nursing staff. On objective reflection after the incident, if it is still felt that the patient had been treated unethically, the matter should be discussed with the senior medical staff.

## 11.4   BREAKING PATIENTS' CONFIDENCES

Two nurses were on their way home from the hospital where they worked. While waiting at the bus stop, they talked about the day's work and in the course of this discussion they mentioned the name of a patient they were looking after and also her diagnosis of carcinoma of the breast. There were at least eight other people standing close to them in the bus queue. One of these knew the woman mentioned and later told this woman's husband what she had heard.

This clear example of a breach of confidence has legal and ethical repercussions.

## Legal basis of confidentiality

The nurse has a clear duty not to disclose any information that she has about a patient, his affairs or his family without his consent. The maintenance of an individual's privacy is an important concept in law.

However, this is an area of the law where there is no direct provision for breach of confidentiality. The law on trespass provides compensation for wrongful interference with liberty, but only in the physical sense (see page 27). Defamation, either as libel or slander, may also be seen as a breach of the individual's privacy, but in practice the defence that the subject matter disclosed is true fails to prevent disclosure of confidential information. Also, the material has to be 'defamatory', that is, of such a nature that the person concerned is lowered in the eyes of 'right thinking' people. The majority of information shared by professional people about their patients is therefore immune from redress in the civil courts in England and Wales and N. Ireland. In Scotland the law on confidentiality appears to be better defined; a person who stands in a confidential relation to another and commits a breach of confidence which results in injury to the latter, may be liable for damages.

The use of an injunction is one possible legal protection. With this, the disclosure of information is forbidden by order of a court of law. However, the award of an injunction is not available as of right, but at the court's discretion, and the court will hame to look at precedents and at the particular merits of each case. The penalty for breach of an injunction is not the award of compensation, but a criminal penalty for contempt of court.

Failure to abide by the professional duty of non-disclosure may have legal repercussions of a somewhat different nature. For example, the two nurses overheard at the bus stop may be subject to disciplinary action, initially at a local level, but if the nurses were repeatedly involved in this type of situation, action by the UKCC could also become necessary. In severe cases, dismissal might also result.

As already mentioned, the nurse must disclose information in a court of law if required to do so (see page 16).

## Verbal information

Clause 9 of the UKCC Code of Professional Conduct states that the nurse must respect confidential information obtained in the course of professional practice and refrain from disclosing such information without the consent of the patient except where disclosure is required by law or is necessary in the public interest. The dilemma facing the nurse is what information she can or should share.

Much of this sharing may take place verbally. A patient frequently confides in the nurse. Clearly if the patient makes a suicide threat or threatens to harm somebody, the information must be passed to the other people concerned with the patient's care. The nurse should try to gain the consent of the patient prior to doing this, but if this consent is refused, the nurse must make it clear to the patient that the matter is so important that it must be shared. Other justification could be that as the patient had decided to tell the nurse, he actually wanted others to know how he was feeling.

The patient may give the nurse information that could have an important bearing on the care to be given to that patient. For example, a patient confides in the nurse that her marriage has been through some bad patches, although things are not too bad at the moment. If the patient has been admitted to hospital for treatment of her varicose veins, there would appear to be no justification for the nurse to tell her colleagues of this woman's marital problems. On the other hand, if the patient was being treated for some mental disorder in a psychiatric unit, this information may be of some significance in her treatment. Thus the nurse will need to assess the significance of any confidential information she acquires. The mental nurse may find that she is more often expected to share confidences than the nurse in a general ward.

Once the nurse has made the decision to share confidential information that the patient has given her, certain principles should be followed. First, she should be wary of passing on too much information. Secondly, she should be careful to express herself in a way that she would be happy with were the patient present. Thirdly, she should ensure that she knows the people to whom she is passing confidential information. They may be trusted nurse colleagues with whom she has worked over a period of time, but there may be people present who are either not entitled to receive this information or who might abuse the privilege.

# Written material

The patient's records or medical notes are an important source of confidential information. There are a large number of people who may quite properly have access to these written records. Clearly, all these people are bound by obligations of confidentiality. The fact remains, however, that the more people who have confidential information, the more likely is a leak.

Additionally, other unauthorised employees may look at patients' records. For example, a porter taking a patient to a department for special tests will take the patient's notes. Although having no right to look at these, he may be tempted to glance. The DHSS suggest that health authorities include in the contract of employment for all their employees provisions prohibiting breaches of confidentiality about personal data and enabling disciplinary or dismissal procedures to be invoked if such breaches occur (see page 83).

It has already been mentioned how open the hospital is to unauthorised visitors. The nursing Kardex is often left unattended at the central desk in the ward, and medical notes may be left lying around before being tidied away after a busy doctor's round. The only practical suggestion to maintain some kind of security of records on the ward is to have them in a place to which there is visible access (it is impractical to lock them away) and advise nurses to be aware of the importance of noticing if any visitors approach these records and to be prepared to accost anyone who starts looking at them.

Confidential health records can be seen by people other than the professionals involved in the patient's care in certain specific circumstances required by law. A court can order information to be released following a request from anyone involved in a legal action, but the court decides what should be released. Medical records can then be given to the applicant or applicant's legal, medical or other professional adviser. In Scotland, access to the records can be offered to an independent medical expert of the patient's choice if the original doctor does not object. If he does object, the court can order their production.

# Automatically processed data

The Data Protection Act (1984) affects what is held on computer and what use is made of it. A data user has to register, this public register being controlled by an independent registrar, and data subjects have certain legal rights. There are eight internationally agreed principles that form part of the Act. They require personal data to be:

- Obtained fairly and lawfully.
- Held only for one or more lawful purposes specified in the data user's register entry.
- Used or disclosed only in accordance with the data user's register entry.
- Adequate, relevant and not excessive for those purposes.
- Accurate and where necessary up to date.
- Not kept longer than necessary for the specified purposes.
- Made available to data subjects on request.
- Properly protected against loss or disclosure.

In most health authorities a large number of employees' personal data are now held on computer and under the Act, the employee can request to see this information and the data user should supply this in an intelligible form within 40 days of the request.

Minimal health data are held at present on computer. On the whole the kind of information held is simple in form, for example a record of women having had or requiring cervical smears. The situation is changing all the time, however. General practitioners are more and more using computers for the storage of medical information, though still retaining written records, as there is at present a limit to the amount of material that can be stored in a computer memory.

People do not have the same right of access to personal health data as to other types of personal data. There are specific exemption clauses under the Act so that although a patient may request personal health information, the doctor may refuse to divulge any or all of this material on the grounds that the information may be harmful to the mental or physical health of the applicant.

An interesting practical sequel to this is as follows. A patient feels that his hospital consultant has not given him full information but has no right of access to his written medical notes. However, his GP successfully gains full information and transfers this to the computer used for patient records. The patient can then request the information under the Data Protection Act and if the GP does not consider it harmful to his patient's health, he can now legally allow him access to the information.

## The public interest

A number of situations have been described where confidential information has been made available to others in verbal, written or automatically processed form. However, although in all the examples given ethical as well as legal decisions have had to be made, by far and away the most difficult situation involving the sharing of confidential information is that concerning the public interest.

The UKCC has received a large amount of correspondence on this particular aspect of the Code of Professional Conduct. Three examples are quoted below:

'A sister in a psychiatric day hospital found a patient possessed large quantities of controlled drugs that he could not have obtained legally.'

'Accident and Emergency Department nursing staff found that the unconscious patient they were treating had a gun on his person.'

'A community midwife saw substantial quantities of stolen hospital property when visiting the wife of a hospital employee.'

The UKCC published an advisory paper to elaborate on Clause 9 of the Code. In this it was emphasised that it must always be the individual practitioner's decision on whether to disclose confidential information or not and this decision cannot be passed to anyone else, neither can she be required by a superior to disclose or withhold information against her will. However, in order to assist her in making a decision she can always take the opportunity to discuss the matter fully with other practitioners. Whatever her decision, the nurse must be able to justify it, and it is wise to write down the reasons that she used in making the decision.

# 11.5   WHAT TO TELL THE PATIENT

Mr Laker was 42 years old and a well-built and athletic man. Out of the blue, he had what appeared to be a 'stroke'. He was admitted to hospital and various investigations were carried out. The resulting diagnosis was of a malignant cerebral tumour and it was likely that, at the most, Mr Laker would only live five months. The doctor gave Mrs Laker this information. She instructed the doctor not to tell her husband as she felt he would not be able to cope with it.

The decision was made to proceed with radiotherapy as a palliative measure. Mr Laker was told that further treatment was needed for his 'stroke', and he gave his consent without asking any further questions.

This short case study raises a number of legal and ethical issues in the debate on what to tell patients.

# Legal duties

In gaining consent for treatment, the doctor has a legal duty not to mislead the patient. The importance of informed consent was discussed in full in Part III. The patient must be given enough information in order to reach a decision, and this normally involves the doctor pointing out any negative outcomes as well as positive benefits. This still leaves the doctor with room to manoeuvre if he feels that giving too many details would lead to the patient becoming unnecessarily anxious or depressed. For example, when dealing with the very emotive subject of cancer, the doctor may make the decision not to use that particular word, as he feels that the patient may lose heart and refuse treatment which could be of very great value to the patient. A number of malignant diseases are now amenable to treatment, or can at least be controlled for a limited time.

Thus, the doctor could, in the above example, justify not telling Mr Laker that he had a malignant cerebral tumour as he has no legal duty to tell the patient the whole truth. It would, however, be legally unacceptable if he told him that any treatment suggested for his 'stroke' would cure him.

# Ethical problems

The question of what is the truth is of major concern to doctors and nurses, particularly where malignant disease is involved. Calling an ulcerating malignant growth an 'ulcer' is certainly part of the truth, as is telling the patient that he has a 'blockage' when his bowel is obstructed by a large cancer.

At present, the doctor is entitled to decide what to tell the patient, and the nurse should bear in mind that truth does come in many forms. An increasing number of doctors now believe that in keeping their patients well informed, they are better able to co-operate in their treatment and care. However, the fact remains that where the prognosis is poor, not all patients want to know the full truth. Thus, what the patient is told will vary because of these very personal considerations. It is worth noting in the case study that Mr Laker did not ask any further questions, perhaps suggesting that he did not want to know too much.

# The right to know

In the case study, the doctor told the wife of the diagnosis and the wife made the decision that the patient should not be told. This raises a further important legal and ethical query.

Professionally the doctor has a duty to maintain confidentiality between himself and his patient (see section 11.4). To tell the next of kin rather than the patient himself could therefore be regarded as a breach of confidentiality, except that it is usual to assume the patient's consent to this sharing of confidential information. If the patient does not want certain people informed, he must make this clear to the doctor and other staff involved. Ethically it is not straightforward. As pointed out above, not all patients want the full truth, but the doctor should on both legal and ethical grounds approach his patient first. Some patients will give clear pointers—'Don't bother me with all the details, doctor; discuss it with my wife'. Unfortunately the doctor is sometimes left feeling very unsure of how much to tell the patient and how much to tell the next of kin. The nurse may be able to give assistance in this predicament. As the nurse is with the patient for longer periods, she may pick up indicators from the patient of what he wants to know and what his feelings are about possible diagnoses.

A further problem faced by the staff caring for a patient with a poor prognosis is when that patient specifically says he does not want to know. There may be important reasons why that patient should know if he is unlikely to live many more months. For example, the patient may be planning to start a business and invest all his savings in this. It would obviously take some time before the business became productive, and the patient's death would put his wife and two young children in a very difficult financial situation.

Does a patient, as well as having a right to know the 'truth', also have a right not to know? The ethical answer is probably yes, but both doctors and nurses caring for such a patient will feel bound to try to persuade the patient at least to discuss the problems of starting a business when his health is uncertain.

Occasionally, another problem arises when a patient asks to see his medical notes. A short 'No' in answer may result in the patient saying, 'Why not, they are my notes, aren't they?' The answer is that legally the health authority is the owner of any medical records, although this does not give them the right to make decisions as to who has the information contained in them. This is controlled by the doctor and at present there is still a majority feeling by the medical profession that patients should not have access to their medical records. The nurse may similarly make a decision as to which nursing records the patient has access to and the present move of encouraging patient participation in planning care includes allowing patients to read their nursing notes. (For implications of the right of access to computer-held information, see page 241.)

## What has the patient been told?

This is an area that very much involves the nurse. As the doctor has the duty of informing the patient of his diagnosis, the nursing staff may find themselves in the awkward position of not knowing what the patient has been told if communications between doctors and nurses are poor. The nurse finds herself having to redirect the patient's questions in order to discover what he knows.

Where such decisions are discussed between different members of staff, it is not unusual to find that a record of what information has been given to the patient has been made in his medical or nursing notes (see page 123). Such a method of dealing with this practical problem seems very sensible and should be widely recommended.

## 11.6   THE NURSE OUTSIDE HER PLACE OF WORK

Miss Hutchinson, a qualified nurse, was out walking on her day off. She witnessed a road accident and went to give assistance. One person appeared to be badly injured and she gave what help she could until the ambulance arrived. This person was left with some permanent disability and later sued the off-duty nurse for having caused the damage.

## Legal considerations

The standard of care expected of a nurse is greater than that of an ordinary person (see page 28). Even off duty, the nurse is expected to show greater care if she becomes involved in someone's treatment. Thus, the first aid that Miss Hutchinson rendered would be evaluated in a different way from the first aid carried out by someone without a nurse training. For example, if an ordinary citizen moved an injured person and permanent damage to the spinal cord resulted, that citizen would probably not be liable in negligence. However, in similar circumstances, the off-duty nurse should use her knowledge of the dangers of moving the injured person and could be negligent if she does not apply this knowledge.

In most circumstances, the reality of the situation is taken into account. At the site of an accident, the off-duty nurse acts in an emergency situation. She can only weigh up priorities and deal with the problems without the resources to which she is used. She is not expected to act in any exceptional way, only to demonstrate the skill of an 'ordinary' nurse.

Some difficulties may arise in the courts in deciding what it is reasonable to expect. Nurse training has changed considerably over the last twenty years and first aid is now given only a small number of hours in the training programme. The nurse could to some extent argue that the present day registered nurse's liability is only slightly more than the ordinary citizen's and considerably less than the qualified first aider's. As always, each case has to be assessed individually.

## Ethical aspects

From the above discussion, the nurse may feel that the safest action to take legally would be to walk in the opposite direction of any accident! While this is probably true, no nurse with any conscience could act in this way. It is worth stating that it is rarely necessary for the off-duty nurse to state her profession.

## REFERENCES

Culver, C. M. and Gert, B. (1982). *Philosophy in Medicine*, Oxford University Press, Oxford.
Department of Health and Social Security (1977). *The Extending Role of the Clinical Nurse—Legal Implications and Training Requirements*, HC 77 22, DHSS, London.
Faulder, C. (1985). *Whose Body Is It?*, Virago, London.
Körner, E. (1984). The Protection and Maintenance of Confidentiality of Patient and Employer Data: A Report from the Confidentiality Working Group, HMSO, London.
National Consumer Council (1983). *Patients' Rights; a Guide for NHS Patients and Doctors*, HMSO, London.
Skegg, P. D. G. (1984). *Law, Ethics and Medicine*, Clarendon Press, Oxford.
Tate, B. L. (1977). *The Nurse's Dilemma—Ethical Considerations in Nursing Practice*, ICN, Geneva.
United Kingdom Central Council (1987). *Confidentiality*, A UKCC Advisory Paper, UKCC, London.

# Appendix I Law and the Psychiatric Nurse

The following parts of this book are of specific relevance to the psychiatric nurse, but should be read in conjunction with the rest of the text.

Chapter 2, p. 24 Criminal law defences; lack of capacity to form the necessary intention—'not guilty by reason of insanity'.
Chapter 3, p. 43 Psychiatric training and the EEC.
Chapter 4, p. 71 Violent patients; common situations, prevention, financial recompense.
Chapter 5, p. 121 Failure of supervision and negligence, e.g. suicide risk.
Chapter 5, p. 126 Injuries to patients; force used for self-defence.
Chapter 5, p. 134 Detention of patients—overview.
Chapter 6, p. 144 Mental Health Act: patients' rights; nurse's role. See contents for chapter subsections.
Chapter 8, p. 195 Drug addicts.
Chapter 11, p. 233 Administration of treatments to unwilling patients: (i) confused; (ii) suicidal.
Chapter 11, p. 238 Breaking confidentiality; justifications, the public interest.

# Appendix II Law and the Nurse in the Community

The following parts of this book are of specific relevance to the nurse in the community, but should be read in conjunction with the rest of the text.

Chapter 1, p. 12 Juvenile courts—involvement of the Health Visitor.
Chapter 1, p. 15 Giving evidence in court.
Chapter 4, p. 74 Violent incidents; avoiding risks in homes and on streets.
Chapter 5, p. 108 Consent to treatment and children; responsibilities of parents, parents' refusal to give consent.
Chapter 5, p. 113 Negligence and staffing levels; reporting concern, management responsibility.
Chapter 5, p. 118 Accidents in the community and possible negligence; physical harm, mis-statements.
Chapter 5, p. 126 Male nurses, female patients; vulnerability to accusations of assault.
Chapter 5, p. 128 Documentation of patient's refusal to receive care.
Chapter 5, p. 130 Witnessing a will.
Chapter 7, p. 187 Section 7.4. Occupier's liability to visitor or trespasser.
Chapter 8, p. 193 Controlled drugs; possession and storage.
Chapter 11, p. 230 Extending role of the nurse.
Chapter 11, p. 238 Breaking confidentiality; sharing information with colleagues, the public interest.
Chapter 11, p. 246 The nurse outside her place of work.

# Index

safe system of working 67
safety representatives 66
schedules (Misuse of Drugs Act)
192
search, police 19
seclusion 176
self defence 25
self discharge 135
sentences 25
setting nursing goals 125
Sex Discrimination Act (1975) 54
Sheriff's Court 10
shop stewards 62
shopping for patients 133
sickness benefit 75
and dismissal 94
slander 28
social workers 175
solicitors 14, 20
staff reports 79
standard of care 28
statements 15, 20
statutory controls of nursing 39
Instruments, Rules or Orders 7
maternity pay 76
sick pay 75
sterilisation 211–3
strike action 64
student conduct committee 51
subpoena 10
substantive law 8
succession, law of 30
suicide
attempted 236
risk 121
summary offence 23
summons 9
superannuation 76
supervision
failure of 121
orders 109
Supply of Goods and Services Act (1982)
140

suspension 87

telephone enquiries 185
termination of employment 92
torts 25
Trade Unions 30, 61–5
transplants 225–9
coordinators 228
donors 225, 228
grounds for removal of organs 226
trespass 27
trespassers 186
tribunals 13

Union with Scotland Act 5
United Kingdom Central Council 40
Code of Professional Conduct 205
membership 42
utilitarian code 204

ventilators 219
verbal consent 103
vicarious liability 26, 112
violence 71–5
visitors 183–6
voting rights 171

warnings 85
Warnock Report 222
warrant 10, 18
White Paper 6
Whitley Councils 62
wills 30, 130–2
written consent 103
wrong
operations 119
treatments 120

X-rays 197

young people, legal classification 24